WATERSKI GIRL WONDER

A Journey of Perseverance

WATERSKI GIRL WONDER

A Journey of Perseverance

SHELLIE BLUM

Waterski Girl Wonder: A Journey of Perseverance

Please feel free to visit online www.ShellieBlum.com or www.Waterski GirlWonder.com for bonus pictures and videos of some of my World Record feats.

ISBN: 978-0-9963669-0-8

TABLE OF CONTENTS

CHAPTER 1

A Tough Beginning

The first memory of my life was getting the air knocked out of me by being forced to dive off a high dive, not jump! Perhaps this was a foreshadowing or metaphor for my future. In this memory I am four-and-a-half years old and standing out on the end of a fifteen-foot high dive at a military base in Belton, Missouri. My oldest brother, Brad, floats below me, calling up to me: "You better dive, or else!" My other brother, Brent, is coming up the ladder, and he's saying the same thing.

Because our family usually lived on military bases, we always had access to swimming pools, and even our off-base houses during the early years had pools. And we were always stationed around water: my dad, Tom Blum, was a captain in the Marines and flew fighter jets off aircraft carriers, a real-life *Top Gun* guy. That's one reason my mom had literally taught me to swim before I could walk or talk. Another reason was that my oldest brother, Brad, fell off a pier at Laguna Beach back when the family was stationed at El Toro in Santa Ana,

California, when he was just five years old. When they pulled him out, he was blue and not breathing, though he was resuscitated. From that point forward, everyone of us had to learn to swim as soon as possible.

So even though I was just a little kid, I had no problem jumping off the high dive. I had done it many times before, but what my brothers were asking me to do was dive. My little brain was telling me even Evel Knievel was probably scared the first time he had to jump, right? My knobby knees were knocking together, but I don't know which I was more scared of: the dive, or what my brothers had planned for me if I *didn't* dive.

My mom, Carol Blum, has told me that back then the adults used to make the kids get out of the water and take swim breaks. On this particular break it was evidently my turn to put on a show. What better show than a tiny little kid going off a high dive, right? Although I knew I'd be okay, it's hard even now for me to imagine the scene. I was always small, and probably a young-looking 4-year-old. My mom is 4'10", and as an adult I topped out at 5'2"—although the University of Missouri basketball team listed me at 5'4" (yeah, right!).

So there I stood on the edge, toes over the ledge, my head swiveling back and forth between my brothers, and everyone on the sides of the pool watching and waiting. Brad said one more time, "Dive, or else you know what's gonna happen!" and so I dove. *Splat.* I landed on my stomach. I tried for my first gasp of air, but the wind had been knocked out of me. There was no air, just a gasp and groan combined. Then the groaning turned to moaning and then I was rolling around in the water until I could get my bearings to dog paddle to the side of the pool. Like I said—it was kind of a metaphor for much of what would follow in the years to come.

I was born on Mother's Day, May 10, 1964, at Camp Lejeune Marine Corps base in Jacksonville, North Carolina, and it has been said, there was "something" in the water. This was my mom's fourth childbirth, so you would think my coming into the world would be routine. It was anything but. The nurses told my mom she wasn't going to deliver for another few hours and left her alone. She begged them not to leave but they did. When the nurses finally returned, I had already made my entrance into the world. Maybe it was the shock of seeing me there, dangling precariously between her legs at the end of the table, but they didn't do the normal routines of checking me over, so it wasn't until later that the doctors realized that I had no roof to my mouth, a condition known as a cleft palate. Fortunately, I didn't have the hair lip or outside physical deformity that often goes along with it, but it was clear from very early on that at a very young age I would have to learn to deal with pain. Starting out life with just my mom to guide me might have been another foreshadowing of my life's trials and tribulations, with a theme song from Helen Reddy: "You and Me Against the World."

I had my first corrective surgery when I was about six months old. Obviously, after the surgery, I was in a lot of pain—so much that whenever my mom left my crib side at the hospital, I wailed inconsolably. One time I used my little hands to tear at the stitches, and the nurses found me with a bloody mouth and all the surgery work destroyed. They waited until I was about 18 months old to try another corrective surgery, but this time they put me in a baby straight jacket so I couldn't tear at the stitches. I'm told that nevertheless I gnawed as best I could on the side of my crib. There wasn't enough skin available from the back of my throat and the sides of my mouth to cover the whole roof of my mouth, so I was left with a little hole at the top of my mouth. This made learning to talk difficult and affected my speech. I think the whole experience, although the painful part happened when I was too young to remember it, toughened me up. Well, that and growing up with an older sister and two older brothers.

As I grew older, though, I learned to use the little hole to my advantage. My brothers and sister asked me to perform tricks for their friends. "Shellie, show 'em!" they'd encourage me. I would take a gulp of Kool-Aid, preferably red, and push it through the hole at the roof of my mouth. It would stream out my nostrils like a faucet.

"Cool, huh?"

"Wow, can she do other things?" the friends would ask.

"Yeah, if we smoosh up peas or carrots, she can do those too!"

And the friends would beg to see it. Then one of the siblings, most likely Tamara, would say, "It'll cost ya." Sometimes the friends paid and sometimes they didn't, but I was always ready to perform.

Even when I got older I found ways to use the little hole for tricks. I sometimes used it to bet guys I could out-guzzle them. I learned exactly how much was the perfect amount so that in one giant gulp I could swallow a glass of draft beer in just a couple of seconds. No one ever beat me. One time in college that ability won backstage passes that got me and one of my girlfriends into a Rick Springfield concert in Columbia, Missouri. At a bar, we had met the guy who followed Rick Springfield around with a camera videoing him, and my girlfriend bet him that I could beat him. He and I faced off, each of us with our hands wrapped around a glass of draft beer. She said, "On your mark, get set, go," and in one fluid motion I had raised the glass to my mouth, gulped the beer in two or three seconds, and slammed the glass down on the table. The challenger wasn't even a third of the way done. He stopped mid-swallow and looked at me smiling with my hand on the empty glass. We were invited to the after party, and got to be Rick Springfield groupies for the night.

All four of my mom's kids were born in different states, but always on or near military bases. My brothers, Brad and Brent, are the same age for six days out of the year—from December 16 to December 22. My sister, Tamara, is one year younger than they are. My mom was really popping them out, but then after Tamara a three-year lull until me. I've been told I was a mistake. As I learned to do from an early age, though, I turned that negative into a positive. In third grade, our class was instructed to write about ourselves. I wrote that "I just knew I would be the best mistake my mom had ever made." The teacher called my mom to tell her about it. It was neither the first nor the last time a teacher would call because she just had to say, "You are never going to believe what Shellie did today …"

Brad was born in California, Brent in Kansas, and Tamara in Missouri. Most of my early memories are from Missouri, but I do remember playing football with my brothers in a grass lot at the end of our block in Los Alamitos, California. Not the watered-down version of flag football but real tackle football. The boys would be fighting over who was who: "I'm Bubba Smith!" or "I'm Roman Gabriel" or the one everyone fought over "I'm Joe Namath." Our house had a pool and a pool table, so all the kids in the neighborhood liked to hang out there. We had huge Marco Polo games.

This is also the time my brothers started bringing boys to the house who were nearer their age and betting them money I could out-wrestle them. I must've been about five. I can remember the exchange of coins, probably quarters and dimes, if I could make them say, "I give!" My patented move was that when they least expected it I would ram my head into their stomachs, knocking us both to the ground then pinning them on the ground with my knees bent and my crotch up against their chins. This inevitably forced them to try and pull their legs up to catch my head and to try and pull me backwards. I knew this would be their next move, and was always ready for it, so that I would catch both their feet and pull them down towards the ground like a pretzel. My next move: "Say you give! Do you give?" They always did.

Our family moved a lot. After all, my dad was a military man, a Marine pilot. He also became a captain for TWA in record time. I am proud of my father, but I don't remember that much about him. I have a framed picture of him taken by the UPI that says "Marine Capt. Tom Blum appears to be challenging the world's weight lifting record by holding up the helicopter that picked Commander Allan Shepard from his epic sub-orbital space flight. Blum is actually checking the mechanism that is used for recovering U.S. space capsules from the water, while Capt. E. O. Marquette holds the aircraft in a hover position. The two Marine pilots from New River, North Carolina, performed the maneuver during a stopover at Grosse Isle Naval Air Station 8/5/62 while on a cross country flight." This might have been a bigger UPI story had it not been the same day Marilyn Monroe died.

When my mom and dad weren't fighting, things were good, but I remember being afraid of my dad when he was drunk. I try to remember the good times. Now that I am older, my mom has told me some of the horror stories about his abuse, but because I was the youngest, my brothers and sister did their best to protect me from it when it was happening. He accomplished a lot in his short life and evidently tested out as genius on the IQ scale, but everyone knows there is a fine line between genius and crazy.

His family was from Missouri. After he left the military and TWA, we moved to his favorite vacationing spot in Lake of the Ozarks, Missouri. There he bought a bar called Lefty's Living Room. Isn't that just what an alcoholic needs to do, own a bar? My mom and dad had divorced earlier, then re-married each other again. If that is not proof of a tumultuous relationship I don't know what is. My dad probably considered himself a man's man—he owned a bunch of guns and rifles and liked to hunt and fish. Our first house on Horseshoe Bend, at "The Lake" as everyone always called it, was beautiful. We had a sidewalk down to a dock, we had a ski boat, we had a cabin cruiser, we had a jon boat or flat bottomed fishing boat, and we had a paddle boat. And we had our dad, who liked to drink too much and get into fights with anyone who he thought had challenged him. He loved to brag that he had never lost a fight in that town and he never would. When my dad was in our lives we always saw the brighter side of the coin. We always had the best of everything. But at what price? We would find out later.

One time after my dad had been drinking he was yelling from the second floor balcony of our house for me to go back down to the boat to get his fishing pole. I hurried down, scurried back up to him, and handed it to him. Then he asked me to go back down and get his fishing tackle, so I hurried back down and started back up. When I was about halfway up the sidewalk, he yelled at me to go back down and get the boat keys. I finally figure out that he was messing with me, and stopped mid-way up the sidewalk and defiantly put my hands on my hips. I stared up at him. He yelled down to me, "Shellie Ann, go get my f**king boat keys!" I yelled back up at him, now with my defiant clenched fists on my hips, "You get your own fr**king boat kwueeze!" At that very moment there was a strike of lightning with a simultaneously clap of thunder right above his head. And he said to me, pointing to the sky, "You see what happens if you disobey me?"

He went back inside chuckling about it at first. If that had been the end of it, it might have been a funny family story, but then he started an argument with my mom about where I had learned that kind of language. It was obvious where I had learned those words, because at that time my Mom wouldn't have said, "Shit if she had a mouth full." The argument escalated into a screaming match about me needing speech therapy for my cleft palate. "There's no f**king way one of my kids needs help like that," he shouted. "It's gotta be your f**king fault she was born like that!" All the while I was crouched at the bottom of the stairs listening to the fight, holding the boat keys in my tiny fist.

In first grade, I was busy making a name for myself by beating up any boy who would dare to challenge me. When a new boy came to our school, the other kids told him, "If you can beat up Shellie Blum you can beat up any body at our school." The fight with the new kid would usually start with him making fun of how I talked or pulling one of the pony tails that I sported every day. My play ground fights were many and I spent a lot of time in the principal's office trying to make him understand that "I nevah started that fight." The principal at my grade school, Eddie Jordan, called my mom one snowy winter day and explained that my first-grade teacher had sent me to the office for punishment because while we were made to stay inside during recess because of the snow, I was trying to teach the other kids how to play poker. Eddie Jordan got a kick out of this, being a former card dealer in Vegas. Little did my first-grade teacher know that being sent to Eddie Jordan's office was no punishment at all. He and I spent the rest of the afternoon playing my favorite game of five-card draw, aces, deuces, one-eyed jacks, and kings with the axe, wild.

My second-grade teacher was a little younger and hip than my first-grade teacher and may have seen my potential. She called my mom around Christmas time to explain that she had been asking if any of students knew any Christmas carols, like "Silent Night" or "Joy to the World." I was not shy, so my hand shot right up. When she called on me I told her I knew "Joy to the World," and she asked me to sing it for the class. She motioned me up to the front of the class, so I got up from my desk and walked up there. She said, "Whenever you're ready."

I took a deep breath and belted out the pop song from the radio. "Jeremiah was a bull frog…dun nut dun…was a good friend of mine…dun nut dun…I never understood a single word he said, but I helped him drinking his wine, yes he always had some mighty fine wine. Singing Joy to the World. All the boys and girls now. Joy to the fishes in the deep blue sea. Joy to you and me."

The teacher let me sing the whole song. She didn't stop me, and said I did a good job. I think she was impressed because even though I was falling behind in my studies and sleeping a lot in class, I could remember all the words to any song after hearing it just a few times. I was the only one on the bus who knew all the words to "American Pie," and my sister counted on me to keep it going when we got the kids to sing it with us on the bus.

This might have been about the time my second-grade teacher told my mom that they might have to "hold me back a grade". As I said, I had been sleeping a lot in class and wasn't keeping up with the other kids. My mom and dad were probably fighting more than usual and I wasn't sleeping at night. My teacher said that she would be willing to work with me, but only if I would put in the time. My mom brought me downstairs at the Lake House and we had a one-on-one talk. She said, "Honey, Mrs. Dorendorf wants to hold you back. Or you can stay after school and she will tutor you."

My mind was racing. This felt monumental. "Hold me back" was just the nice way to say, "You flunked!" I begged my mom, Pwease don't let 'em hold me back. I will do whatever I have to do." I started crying. "Pwease, pwease, mom!"

"Okay this is your decision, but remember it will be a lot of work," my mom said. "And you have to see the speech teacher, too."

"Okay, okay I will do anything just don't let them hold me back!" From that point forward I would stay after school, and everyone in the family had to find excuses for my mom to pick us up after school so my dad wouldn't know I was being tutored. He would have gone ballistic. He did when he finally found out, but by that time it was too late; I had already been "passed on condition." That meant that if I continued to do good work in second grade they wouldn't hold me back. I passed on to third grade, and getting good grades was never a problem for me again.

While my mom and dad were getting divorced, my mom and all of us kids lived in a singlewide mobile home. My brothers and sister probably hated the time we lived in that singlewide mobile home at that trailer park, but I loved it. I made a great friend there—after I pinned him with my patented wrestling move and made him say "I give"—and we became the best of friends. We were the same age and our birthdays were one week apart. His name is Donnie Taylor Rambo. We did all kinds of crazy things, like the time we accidentally set an outhouse on fire and it burned the electric wires so that the whole park lost electricity. My mom and everyone was scurrying for water buckets, and as we were running my mom yelled at me, "Shellie Ann, did you start that fire?"

"Uhhhh, no," I said, but my mom gave me The Look. So I had to say yes. That is the last time I tried to lie to my mom. I got my first real guilt trip, and Donnie got an ass whooping from his step-dad Jim Rambo. Jim Rambo could lay on a bed of nails and have a big cinder block laid on his chest and then someone with a sledge hammer would break the block on his chest. He also wrestled bears. This was a great guy for my mom to have in her corner. I think this may be part of the reason my dad didn't try too much to bother my mom while we lived there.

One day, Donnie's dad decided he was going to teach his son how to box. We were bare-fisted and I was blocking most of Donnie's punches and not throwing any until Donnie hit my Snoopy watch with the flying Woodstock second hand that my dad had given me. The watch broke and a fit of anger surged over me. I finally let my first and only punch fly. It hit Donnie square on the nose and his nose started to bleed. He ran off crying, and I went home. Later that day I was sitting in the tire swing Donnie and I had made in the tree right next to our singlewide. The next thing I knew I woke up lying on the ground next to a bat. Donnie had come back, snuck up behind me, and hit me in the chin with the bat. He'd knocked me out cold, and I ended up with three stitches in my chin. That was okay, though, because sometime later I accidentally dropped a barbell on his foot and broke it. I got stitches, he got a cast.

Donnie told me that after he started crying from the bloody nose, his dad gave him another ass whooping and told him he better go back and fight me to make it right. He told him no girl is supposed to beat a boy. Donnie didn't mean to hurt me that bad. And I really didn't mean to drop the barbell on his foot. He was my best bud during those days and we played in the woods for hours.

One morning my dad, drunk, came to the trailer park in his brand new Ford Thunderbird and started a fight with my mom. He yelled, "My f**king car is worth more than this whole shitty trailer you live in. Come on baby, come back to me." My mom was trying to stand her ground. Later that night, he came back. I was lying on the couch that folded out into a bed, pretending to be asleep. It was dark. I could barely make out the images and figures, but I kept my eyes a slit open to see what was happening.

I could hear my mom's voice. She was sitting calmly on a kitchen chair while my dad's voice got bigger and meaner. Then suddenly he got behind her and yanked the chair out from under her. She fell to the floor. She got back up, put the chair right, sat back down, crossed her legs and in a very calm voice said, "Oh, big bad Tom Blum is gonna show everyone how tough he is." I couldn't believe how calm she seemed outwardly, but inwardly I knew she was scared—scared to death. How did I know this? I could see the hot cherry on the end of her cigarette shaking like a leaf. But she did talk him into leaving, and that made me very happy because I was scared, too. And I wasn't used to being scared—of anything.

CHAPTER 2

In My Element...Water

After my big high dive, the next life event to knock the wind out of me happened January 9, 1974. My mom and dad had gotten back together and we were living in a new house in Arrowhead Estates, closer to Osage Beach where my dad's bar was. My dad had talked my mom into going with him for a job interview in Kansas City, Missouri. When a winter storm made it inadvisable to drive all the way back home to the Lake, they decided to stay an extra day in their motel room. My dad had a cousin in nearby Blue Springs who was in the process of separating from her husband, who was threatening to take her kids. I guess my dad was bored just hanging at the motel, so he decided to make the short drive to his cousin's house and see if he couldn't help straighten things out.

At the time, my dad was supposed to be "on the wagon," but naturally he fell off. It was probably because he had been drinking that day that my mom didn't go with him to his cousin's house. It's just as well, as it turned out. Shortly after he got there, my dad got into an argument with the soon-to-be-ex-husband. The argument escalated into a physical altercation, and before long the man was fighting for his life against my larger, stronger, and alcohol-fueled dad. The man ran upstairs into his bedroom closet and locked the door. My dad charged up after him, and the man shouted from behind the door, "Don't come in here, Tom, I have a shotgun. I'll shoot! I swear I will! Don't come in!" My dad hated to be told what to do, so he kicked the door in. The blast in the chest from a 30-ought-6 shotgun dropped him flat. He died instantly.

This was supposed to have been just a little weekend trip, but when my parents didn't come back when I expected them, I started to worry. When the neighbors called and said we needed to go to their house, I *knew* something was wrong. After all, we'd stayed by ourselves plenty of times before. I was 9, Tamara was 12, and Brent and Brad had just turned 14 and 15. We dutifully went over to the neighbors, where I found their mom stirring something in a pot on the stove and was whispering to her oldest son, who was 18.

There was something about the way she was stirring that pot that told me something wasn't just wrong, something was *really really* wrong. It was just a sense I had, and it's weird because none of my other siblings had picked up on it yet. So I went into the younger kid's room and knelt down by the toy chest on the floor, clasped my hands together and placed them on my forehead and said over and over and over again, "Please, God, don't let it be my mom. Please, God, don't let it be my mom. Please, God, don't let it be my mom." I did this for what seemed like forever until it had turned into a kind of transcendental chant. I think I was even swaying forward and backward a bit. During my chanting prayer the phone rang and I could hear Tamara talking, but I couldn't make out what was being said.

Then Tamara rushed into the room, grabbed my shoulders, and looked me in the eyes. "Dad's dead. He's gone." I started shaking and crying uncontrollably, and doing that weird hiccupy thing kids do when they can't catch their breath, and that turned into hyperventilating.

Then my sister slapped me in the face. We had things we had to deal with, and I needed to focus! Like, how were we going to get to our mom? How were we going to get to the funeral? My dad's body wouldn't be brought back to the lake to be buried; there would be a military funeral at Fort Leavenworth, Kansas. But at the moment our mom was still 200 miles away in Kansas City, our car was in Blue Springs, and we were in Osage Beach. There was a blizzard of snow on the ground and some of the main roads were shut down.

After a bunch of phone calls, we had our solution: my mom's "go to" guy, the grizzly bearded mountain man, Jim Rambo. He had a Jeep with chains on it, and he "weren't skeered of no roads being closed." He would get us there. So all four of us kids crammed into the back of his Jeep and he drove through a blizzard to get us to my dad's funeral. It was cold, very cold, and Jim Rambo's heater didn't work so we huddled even closer.

Meanwhile, my little mind was working over what everyone would say about the whole episode. Maybe I was worried it would bring shame on us, or our dad's reputation. This is what all the kids at school would be talking about. Our dad had already built up quite the reputation of being the bad-ass of our little town. He had been thrown in jail a couple of times for shooting off his guns at local establishments—in a way, literally shooting up the town, like his screen idol John Wayne in all those Westerns he loved so much. So at least at that moment I felt as though we were the gang left over after the Big Tough Guy gets outgunned. "Did you hear the Blums' dad got shot? He got in a fight with some guy and lost."

Of course, maybe my thoughts were all jumbled just because of the ride. I was crushed into a cold Jeep with a mangle of my siblings' arms and legs, all of us teeth chattering from the cold and from the fear that comes from slipping and sliding all over the place. I felt guilty, sad, and confused, which may be why I started a new chant: "I'm going to make my daddy's name famous. I'm going to make my daddy's name famous. I'm going to make my daddy's name famous." Somehow it helped keep my mind off the freezing cold.

Finally, we got to wherever it was we were heading to view the body. From the doorway I could see my dad's casket towards the front of the room. I think my mom wanted to protect me from seeing my dad dead, but my grandmother told her it was the right thing to do.

"They should all see him like this, Carol, so they know it's real—that he's dead—to bring closure and not be afraid of him anymore."

My brothers and sister had all made their way up to him ahead of us. My mom took my hand and we started walking towards the casket. I was so very short I couldn't really see him, she asked me, "Do you want me to lift you up so you can see him better." I looked back at her with frightened eyes and shook my head no. I wanted to do it myself.

I put my hands on the side of the casket and pulled myself up onto my tippy-toes. I got a quick last glance of his face, and remember thinking, "Oh, shit, if he knew how weird they combed his hair he would f**king kick their asses!"

That part of my life, life with the Tough Guy, was over. I no longer had to be afraid for my mom because of my dad, and I no longer had to fear him myself. The three-volley gun salute at the ceremony at the Fort Leavenworth cemetery was uneventful. As the guns fired off their rounds, I thought *gunfire was the last noise dad heard before he died.* Then just after the last gun blast of the salute, a clump of snow slid off a branch and fell on his coffin with a thump, like a final good-bye. Someone handed my oldest brother, Brad, the flag that had been draped on my dad's coffin; it was of course now folded in a triangle.

As it turned out, my dad's cousin's soon-to-be-ex- husband may have saved my dad from an even more painful, slow, and agonizing end. The autopsy report revealed that his liver and kidneys were so badly damaged from all his years of drinking and partying that he wouldn't have lasted much longer any way. It seemed fitting somehow for him to go out in a blaze of glory, and I wonder now if in the back of his mind he knew and had been thinking just that. I wouldn't put it past him.

After that, though, it was just the five of us—my mom and us four kids. It didn't take long for my mom to figure out that my dad had left us with quite a bit of debt. Yes, we owned the bar, but it was mortgaged to the max, and he had already borrowed against it several times. That was how he afforded all those cool toys.

My mom never really had a job of her own, though she did help my dad out sometimes. But when he was alive, he was the man of the house, and he insisted that he would make the money and that my mom wasn't allowed to have a "real" job. After he was gone, though, she had to make her own way. It wasn't long before the bills piled up so high that we lost the house and stayed in a motel room until we moved into a one- room cottage behind the bar we owned. My mom started bartending. She was collecting food stamps and getting food from the county, and I remember my brothers and sister being ashamed of it. I didn't care if the peanut butter and cheese came in big silver cans or solid gold boxes: I was eating it and it was good.

Eventually my mom started making good enough money bartending that we were able to move out of the cottage behind the bar to a nice two-story house down the road in Harbor Heights Estates. That house had a tree that was about a free throw's distance away from the sidewalk to the house, so my brothers put up a basketball goal on the tree, and that became my new baby sitter. I would dribble the ball up and down the sidewalk, stop directly in front of the tree and shoot a shot just about the same distance as a free throw. I did this for hours on end. I was 10 going on 11, and I had already decided I loved being physical—and competitive.

My high dive as a little kid was just the beginning of my precocious affinity for water. By the time I was six I had discovered water-skiing, and I never looked back. My brothers first taught me to ski on trick skis that they had outfitted with rudders; I learned to slalom soon after. When they took me out into the channel instead of our cove, other boats would follow along to watch me. I was 6 years old, but again, because of my height, I probably looked 4 or 5 years old. It didn't matter. People were starting to say I was a natural.

Sometime around third grade, the new super-cool physical education teacher, Judy Elliott, had noticed me and my competitive drive. My favorite game at the time was scooter racing—you know, those small wooden platforms in gym class with a little wheel under each corner? I was unbeatable on those scooters. And I think Coach Elliott was equally impressed with me having set the school's record for the most knee-seat drops on the trampoline when I had never seen a trampoline, let alone used one. Most of the kids were afraid of the trampoline, but not me. I volunteered to jump right up there.

Once those of us who were brave enough to try the trampoline learned the basics of bouncing, Coach Elliott taught us how to do knee-seat drops. That quickly turned into a competition to see who could do the most in a row, and although I know I could have kept going, she stopped me when I had done over 200. That took a lot more stamina than the thing we did in gym class with the huge painted parachute, in which we all stood in a circle and held onto the edge of the chute. We waved the parachute up and down, with "Beautiful Balloon" playing in the background. It was beautiful, graceful, and took a certain amount of timing and skill, but it wasn't exactly a competitive sport. Still, I loved the pageantry of it, and I loved the groovy new young PE teacher, who had blonde hair just like me. I figured if I could find a way to combine athletic competition with performing, I'd be in heaven, but at the time I was pretty sure there was no way to make a living doing anything *fun*.

At the end of my fifth grade year, just before summer was about to start, Coach Elliott asked me out of the blue, "Shellie do you know how to ski?"

"What, like water-ski?"

"Yep."

"Can you ski on one ski?" she asked.

"Of course." I mean, couldn't everyone?

Coach Elliott explained that she, her husband, and another couple were putting together a water-ski show, and she wondered if I wanted a job riding in the boats as the spotter, the one who passes on to the boat driver all the hand signals from the skiers for things like *faster* or *slower* or *take me to the dock*. I had never heard of a water-ski show, but I knew what a show meant, and I was all for it. Especially because, as it turned out, I would even get paid to do it. My eleven year old brain was thinking, "*Holy crap! I get to ride in a boat all day and get paid, too? Where do I sign up?*"

When I told the Coach that I was worried that I might have trouble getting there because my mom worked all the time, she assured me that she would find me a ride. It was my first real job, and it was in professional water-skiing show. That made me think that maybe soon I could actually be in a water-skiing show, not just in the boat. Could there be any more of a fun way to make a living? I didn't think so.

The first show was a success, and it became a regular thing. I started hounding the best girl skier I knew. She was in her early 20s and I wanted her to teach me to barefoot ski. I had been watching the guys do it and just knew I could, too, but it took a while to wear her down. Finally, one day she gave in. "Okay, Shellie, if you are really, really serious about learning to barefoot, meet me here tomorrow early about 9 o'clock," she said. Then she flashed a wicked grin. "Oh, and wear two pairs of shorts, one on top of the other. "

I was so excited I didn't ask why. I would later learn the two shorts were to try and prevent water from shooting up places that it shouldn't! The next day I showed up early.

"Ok, so how this is gonna work is you are gonna come up out of the water on one ski," she said. "I just want you to practice planting your foot in the water. Take your back foot out of the binder and put your heel in the water, see?"

"I think I can do that," I said. I mean, *duh*, right?

We drove over to a cove where the water was always smoother; it was protected on three sides, not like the show circle, which was wide open. I got in the water wearing my two pair of shorts, and got up deep water on the one ski. She got the boat up to about 28 miles an hour and she made an OK sign, and so I pulled my back foot out of the binding and put my heel in the water just as she had showed me. Then I saw her give a thumbs up sign, which was her way of saying, "Good job, just keep it up!" But in my eager 12-year-old mind I thought she meant step off, and so I did. I pulled my other foot out of the binding and stepped it back down onto the water!

I could tell by her body language that she was pretty excited. She was yelling from the boat, whooping and waving her free arm from the steering wheel. I couldn't hear what she was saying, but I knew she was amazed, and so was I. It felt weird to look down and see only my bare feet skimming across the surface of the water. In the evolution of learning to barefoot water ski people later learned to barefoot ski utilizing easier techniques, like standing up from a sitting position from a kneeboard, or by hanging onto a "boom" or stiff metal bar sticking out attached to the side of the boat. The "boom" had not been invented yet. So, it was pretty amazing that I learned to barefoot water ski from a slalom step off *longline* in back of the boat—on my first try!

I barefooted until she had to cut the engine because there was no more room, then I climbed back into the boat and we zoomed back to the ski show circle. She couldn't wait to tell someone, and it just so happened the only person there was our ski show director. When she told him what had happened, he couldn't believe it, so we all three went back over to the smooth cove and I did it again.

Shortly after that they put me in the show, doing a solo barefoot act. The announcers started calling me, "The 12-year- old Girl Wonder." I don't know for sure, but I am pretty sure, I was the only 12-year-old girl barefooting professionally in a ski show in 1976.

The first year the water-skiing show had a Bicentennial theme; even the boats were red, white, and blue. I did a small little one-tier pyramid dressed up as Becky Thatcher, and I stood on the shoulders of blonde twin boys who were dressed as Tom Sawyer and Huckleberry Finn. I also got pretty good on a kneeboard. Before my act, I would tote the big board up and stand with it on the stage so everyone could see that the kneeboard and I were about the same height. Then I'd slide down a 60-foot ramp onto the water to start my routine of spins and turns, which climaxed with me going over the 6-foot jump ramp on my knees. Ouch!

I did a solo barefoot act and rode in the boats to watch for the skiers' signals. And I always performed in the finale act which had me climbing to the top of the human pyramid, three tiers high. Then I would pull out from my hiding place in the back of my bathing suit, just as we came in front of the audience, the American flag. My arm shot up with extra force as I proudly displayed the Old Red, White and Blue unfurled and flowing in the wind. I even parked cars before the show and put bumper stickers on them. For all that, I made $25 a week and I was so happy! I gave all my checks to my mom to help out with household bills.

All that summer, the first of many, I worked at the Lake of the Ozarks Water-ski Show. There was nothing I loved better in the world.

CHAPTER 3

Boys Rule...Girls Drool?

In sixth and seventh grade things changed a little bit for me. For one thing, I developed a crush on an older man. Gary Prewitt was in seventh grade, I was in sixth. He was a whole year older, and had already moved down the road to the "big school." His family owned and sold mobile homes, and one of his neighbors just happened to be my best friend, Mamie Nicholson.

I'd met Mamie when I was in first grade. When we'd lived in Los Alamitos, California, I'd had a best friend, AnneMarie Alvarez, who had pretty dark brown hair and eyes—the opposite of me. We'd been inseparable, so when we later moved to Missouri I missed her a lot. Then one day in my new school I spotted a kid who looked just like AnneMarie. I walked right up to her and said that we were going to be best friends, and she looked at me as though I were nuts. We argued about it almost every day, and get into fights, but the way it worked was that if I could make her laugh before the school's end, that meant she had to be my best friend again.

"You're gonna be my best friend," I'd say.

"No I'm not," she'd say, rolling her eyes. So I would pretend to fall down the stairs and make her laugh, or she would challenge me to say something bad to the play ground attendant, Mrs. Pope. She was old and didn't think it was funny at all when I walked up to her with all the kids watching and wondering what I would say. One day I asked her, "Mrs. Pope, can I go to the poop box?" Of course, she instead sent me to the Principal's office. But it worked. Mamie and I were best friends, and there was nothing she could do about it. It got to the point that the teachers had to separate us because I helped Mamie with everything. I would sometimes even do her homework.

Anyway, Mamie lived right near Gary Prewitt. She acted as translator for our pre-adolescent version of courtship: Gary gave Mamie a message for me. "Tell Shellie I can ride a wheelie on my bike for three seconds." That was code for he liked me.

So I gave Mamie a message for Gary. "Tell Gary I can ride a wheelie on my bike for a block." I wasn't really sure what that was code for, but it was the truth. And it worked, because after that Gary spent a lot of time and effort trying to win me over. I'm not sure why. Maybe he liked the fact that in sixth grade, I was still willing to fight any boy in our school. In any case, he was my first "boy friend," and he and another boy, Alan Mead, were my on-again off-again boyfriends all throughout high school. High school was grades 9 through 12, but shared the "big school," School of the Osage, with the Jr. High, grades 7 and 8. I loved going there because it was a short walk away from what everyone called "The Strip," a bunch of touristy shops and bars that led up to Bagnell Dam—and Bagnell Dam was what made Lake of the Ozarks, one of the largest man-made lakes in the world.

Coach Judy Elliott was my P.E. teacher in sixth grade, though, and I was afraid that once I went off to the "big school" she might forget about me and not ask me back for the next summer to water-ski. But right before the end of school, my prayers were answered.

"Shellie, we'll be doing the ski show again this summer. Would you like to work for us again?"

"Oh my God, yes!"

Once again I would have my dream job. And once again I had to figure out a reliable way of getting back and forth to work. I couldn't just keep bumming rides from everyone. I decided I should ride my mini bike through the woods.

There were two water-ski shows a day. We had to be at the ski show at noon to set up and do pre-performance jobs for the show at 1:30. The ski show lasted about 2 hours, and then we cleaned up afterwards, and by 4:00 p.m. the skiers who could drive went home or out for a bite to eat. Then everyone had to be back at the show by 7:00 p.m. for the same routine. The night ski show started at 8:30 and ended around 10:30. That meant that after clean up we might get home around 11:00 p.m., which is pretty late for a 13-year-old to be riding a mini-bike through the woods. But I did it. My little hillbilly redneck mind had me duct taping a flashlight to the handlebars of my little Honda MR 50 dirt bike.

Because I didn't drive yet, most days I would stay at the ski site between shows and practice or play around on the jet skis, or gave water-ski lessons, or—my favorite—take one of the big Rally Sports or Glastron-Carlson boats, up the channel to "The Clown." The Clown was a floating restaurant on the water near the Grand Glaize Bridge. And just below the popular nightclub, The Top Sider. It always caused quite a stir when people saw this tiny girl driving up in a big beautiful sparkly boat with not one but two 175 hp Evinrude engines on the back. Tourists were probably expecting me to crash the dock or something, by then driving a boat felt as natural as walking to me. I would pull up to the dock, split the throttles, and turn the boat on a dime to back in or maneuver any way I needed to. I just loved the twin engines because you could do so much with them. In later years we started using Ski Nautiques. They were great, but I miss the old days and the Rally Sports and the Glastron-Carlsons. Now those were ski boats!

To make a little extra money for the owners, and for me, I gave ski lessons before the first show and in between the day and night shows. I really enjoyed it, and was always very enthusiastic for the students, and tried to make each lesson a never-to-forget lifetime experience.

Mostly, I got the young kids who were just learning to ski, but every once in awhile I would get a barefoot lesson with someone older. That was a challenge. There I was at 13 or 14 trying to convince a 20- or 30-something-year-old guy that "yes," I was going to drive that big boat and "yes," I was going to teach him how to barefoot. At first it would be awkward, but it never took long to convince people that I knew my stuff, and it was going to be a good experience. I was at the top of the list for requested instructors, and when my ski students came back for more, they always asked for me.

So in seventh grade I thought I was pretty damn tough. In school that year, I got to pick an instrument to play in band. The instructor let it be known that the band was in serious need of trombone players; so to please him I picked the trombone. No one told me it wasn't a feminine instrument; I was just trying to make my band teacher happy. And I ended up loving it, because we got to walk in the front of the marching band so that we didn't goose the musicians ahead of us with our slides. A lot of people ended up dropping out of band, but I played all the way through to my senior year. I couldn't even imagine quitting. Not only did I play trombone in the band, pep band, and jazz band, but I sang in chorus and an-all girl sextet that did well in all the competitions we entered. I loved performing, and although this all took place on dry land, it was still exciting for me.

But that year I learned that maybe I wasn't as tough as I thought. We were all at a football game. My brothers were playing on the field, my sister was cheerleading on the sidelines, and my mom was sitting in the bleachers. Suddenly, a crowd of people started gathering around a scuffle on the side of one of the end zones—and I was smack in the middle of it. My sister heard my name being shouted and ran up to us. She was tired of trying to stop my many fights so this time started shouting her own words of encouragement. "Get 'em, Shellie, get 'em! Don't let him beat you! Come on, Shellie, get him!"

I started to get the upper hand and used my "patented" move on him, pinning his feet up over his head, and made him say, "I give!"

To myself, I thought, "Whew, that was a close one. I almost lost that fight." And while I was getting up and the circle of onlookers was dispersing, he got up and unexpectedly kicked me in the stomach. It knocked the air out of me, and when I doubled over I realized for the first time that during the fight my shirt had been torn open, shredding what was left of my pubescent dignity. *That* was the blow that made me quit the fight. My sister cuddled me up and took me to my mom in the bleachers, where she could see that I was visibly shaken and near tears. It was my last youthful fight with a boy. I thought it would be my last real fight with a man ever, but I would turn out to be wrong about that.

By its second summer, the Lake of the Ozarks Water- ski show was really becoming a tourist attraction. We were competing with attractions like "Lee Mace's Ozark Opry," "Denny Hilton's Country Shindig," and "HillBilly Town" (a mini-amusement park with Go-Karts, Sky Slides, Bumper Cars, a Tilt-A-Whirl, and an arcade). All of these places were competing for customers in the region. Summers were the time everyone made his or her money, and then the whole area kind of hibernated during the winters. During the summer, Fridays and Saturdays were our big nights; people drove from all over the Midwest to come see what the Lake of the Ozarks had to offer. They would stay in places like The Lodge of the Four Seasons on Horseshoe Bend or Arrowhead Lodge, a little way up from Bagnell Dam and my school. Another great spot on the other end of the Lake was Tan-Tar-a Resort. There were plenty of places to stay in any of the other little hotels or motels along the road in between the Bagnell Dam and the Grand Glaize Bridge.

At the time, Bagnell Dam and the Grand Glaize Bridge were the only two spots you could get across the Lake of the Ozarks, which has over 1,100 miles of shoreline—more than Lake Michigan. So when one of our shows was done and the people were let out and driving home, you knew it: traffic could backup for miles. We had to hope our show was good enough to keep the people talking about it and coming back since they had to put up with that kind of traffic. I guess it was, because the people came back year after year. I am sure some of the returning audience may have picked up on that for the first three years of the show, I was the 12 year old Girl Wonder. Hmm? That's curious!

Before the ski show started the girls and guys had different pre-show jobs. The guy announcer always parked cars with one girl skier. The girl announcer would sell tickets from the booth. The other girl skiers would be sent to the Pro Shop, which sold T-shirts, souvenirs, and water-ski equipment, to the Snack Bar, or to do dock set up. Dock set-up was the best place to be, because after you set up for the ski show you could practice. I hated being in the snack bar; people can be so rude.

"I asked for a hotdog with ketchup, not mustard and just ketchup. I can't eat this!" someone might say, as though I'd handed over a pile of dog excrement and not just an overpriced convenience food.

"I'm sorry, Ma'am, yes, you wanted just ketchup," I'd say with a forced smile. "Here, let me get you another." And in my mind I'd imagine wiping the hot dog off with a dirty rag, layering it with ketchup, and slapping it back on the same bun, all the while thinking damn, you don't have to be so mean about it. *Why didn't you eat before you came here. And lady, if you only knew, in about 20 minutes you are going to be clapping for me.* A lot of customers didn't notice that most of the workers pre-show were also the performers.

The guy skiers' pre-show duties were nothing compared with what we girls had to do. Their toughest assignment was that they rode the "breakwater" dock out from the shoreline to its position in the back of the water-ski show circle. The breakwater dock protected the show circle from the channel water, which was almost always rougher than the water deeper in any cove, and our water-ski-show cove was more like a wide-open enclave to the rougher channel water. Some boats parked in the slips and we would shuttle them into our docks and they would be actual paying customers, but most of the boats passing by just stopped and tried to dock and watch the show for free. The breakwater dock was 200 feet long and had two 70 horsepower engines on either end. The guys would sit on the engines or use the handle to guide the big dock out to the mouth of our ski show circle. It was a lazy job, but it was the pain in the butt pre-show and after show job for the guys because it took so long.

The only other pre-show job for the guys was wiping down the boats and gassing them up, after which they got to practice their skiing. That made me jealous—especially on those days and nights when I was stuck in the snack bar with a perfect view to be watching them. During the halftime break in our two-hour ski show, only girls had to work in the snack bar; the guys never worked in the snack bar. For the after-show duties, the girls stored away costumes and equipment and swept the stadium. If the guys finished parking the boats, putting away equipment, or bringing in the breakwater early, they would help sweep up all the trash left behind. But no guy ever, ever had to clean up the bathrooms—the worst of all the girls-only jobs.

I was starting to see the inequalities in how the pre-show, halftime, and after-show work was divvied up between the girls and guys, but in the beginning I loved my job so much I didn't care. As I got older, it really started getting on my nerves. Between what I saw at the shows and at school, I slowly—but not deliberately—started becoming a "Norma Rae" or feminist, though, at that point in time in my life, I didn't know what either label meant.

My brothers' and sister's reputation as rebels had always made things challenging for me in school. (My oldest brother, Brad, had jumped off a big paddle wheel boat on a dare during his Senior year class trip in New Orleans; and from that time forward there were no more Senior class trips.) So early in my eighth-grade year I was sitting in my Home Economics class and noticed that the top button on my cool sleeveless vest was unsnapped. I pushed in on it with my thumb and at the same time unconsciously stuck my tongue out. The teacher screamed out at me, "I know all about your brothers and sister, so don't think you're gonna come in this class and pull a stunt like that with me!" I was in shock. Was she talking to me? Did she think I was sticking my tongue out at her? How weird was that?

That was the same teacher who would give me a 1,000-word theme every time I "took the Lord's name in vain." I had a habit of using the word God in decidedly non-religious contexts. It got to a point where I spent any free time I had writing 1,000-word themes ahead of time, because I knew it was just a matter of time before Miss Bechtelheimer caught me "swearing" again. I tried to outsmart her and say things like, "Mamie, you are never gonna believe what Alan said, Oh God! bless America!" I'd dart my eyes over to Miss Bechtelheimer to see if she was going to give me a 1,000-word them. Sometimes I got away with it.

One time I didn't. Mamie and I were standing in line to leave art class, which Miss Bechtelheimer also taught, when I slipped up and said, "God!" Miss Bechtelheimer was standing right next to me. She leaned in even closer and looked right into my eyes and said, "That will be a 1,000-word theme."

I'd had it. I said, "God."

She said, "That will be *another* 1,000 words."

Again I said, "God."

She got so close our noses were just about touching, and started to say, "That will be another 1,000 words."

But I cut her off and said, super duper fast in perfect staccato rhythm, "God God God God God God God God God God God God God."

She made me go to the principal's office. Mr. McGowan was a little sympathetic, especially because I started saying things like, "I really don't mean to do it—it's just a bad habit, an accident. And isn't there some law about separating church and state?" That cracked him up. He made me write the 1,000 words, but that was the last time I had to write a theme for saying God by accident.

I began to notice how much certain men couldn't bear the idea of women outperforming or outsmarting them. Take the whole foul-shooting fiasco, my Grandfather in Santa Ana, California, was a retired Lieutenant Colonel who served 30 years in the Marine Corps. He was also a bigwig at his local Elks Lodge. He called my mom to ask her if the Osage Beach Elks lodge was holding the Hoop Shoot Contest, and if so he suggested that I enter, since he knew I liked basketball. My mom signed me up. The competition was grouped by age, not gender, but there were never very many girls competing. The contest consisted of shooting as many successful free throws as possible in 60 seconds; the person who sunk the most baskets won. When the starter said, "On your mark, get set, go!" The stopwatch started. I was like a machine, shooting one free throw after another, swoosh, swoosh, swoosh, swoosh, like Forrest Gump playing ping pong.

I won first place at the County level. Then I won at the District level. I was set to go to State level, but when my mom and I got to the State championship in Jefferson City, Missouri, a large man who seemed to be in charge pulled us aside and said, "Your daughter is not going to be able to compete today."

My mom said, "What? Why?"

The large man said, "Because this is for amateurs only, and your daughter is a paid athlete."

"You mean her water-skiing?" My mom was shocked. "That makes no sense."

"This is an amateurs-only competition, Ma'am," he insisted. "Your daughter cannot compete."

We never checked with anyone else. My mom and I just left the gymnasium, while my eyes welled up with tears. We read in the local paper not long after that the large man's son had won the competition.

Every summer the ski show would develop some kind of theme; one summer the theme was movies. And we had an act in which King Kong supposedly got loose and ran through the audience down to the stage and then down onto the dock. Of course, this was just one of the guy skiers dress up in a monkey costume. He would steal one of our boats and chase me, the young blonde to a flivver. A flivver is a tiny fiberglass boat with a 25-horsepower engine on it so it could really fly; we used it to pick up fallen skiers and dropped off skis. I would outrace King Kong in the tiny flivver, while he ended up back on stage yanking down the shorts of the male announcer to ex pose boxer underwear with hearts on them.

To get to the flivver I ran at top speed down the landing ramp and then hopped in the flivver so the chase could ensue. It got a lot of laughs from an appreciative crowd, but one day it ended with a little more excitement than usual. Racing down the ramp I slipped on some moss and at the bottom I hit my shin on the side of the flivver. I saw white bone, then immediate blood. I finished out the act, but then was taken to the hospital for five stitches—my first hospital visit from working at a ski show, but certainly not the last.

Most of the events passed without incident. That was probably the same summer I learned to jump on jump skis over the 6-foot jump ramp. There may have been other 14-year-old girls jumping the ramp in the late 70s, but if so I doubt that they were doing it day in and day out (or night in and night out), in a professional water-ski show.

Water-skiing at night is more difficult because you can't see outside your spotlight, but at least the water is almost always very calm. One ski show act we did was called the Canoe Paddle, and at night it was even more fantastic. A guy would pretend to be whispering to the announcer interrupting him, until finally the announcer would invite him up on the stage to clear things up.

"What's going on, Morris?" he'd say. "Come on up here where we can all hear you."

The guy skier would say something like, "I have a bet with all the other guys that I can ski on just about anything. And they handed me this." He'd hold up a canoe paddle for the audience to see. "And I am going to prove that I can."

The announcer, of course pretending this was all impromptu, would say something to the driver. "Hey, Barry, bring the boat over here. Let's give Morris a chance."

The skier would come up out of the water and circle around in front of the audience with his foot in the handle ("Look, Ma, no hands!" the announcer would say) and as the skier circled back around toward the landing ramp he'd lean way back to produce a huge wall of water around the skier—such a huge wall of water, in fact, that the audience loses complete sight of the skier and starts to wonder if he is even still back there on the canoe paddle.

The original performers of this act were always males much bigger than me. They all used a tiny piece of rope hidden in their hands to help get out of the water with the handle facing up and out of the water. I found a way to turn the paddle around and start in deep water with the paddle end up, eliminating the need for the cheater rope around the handle. But the spectacular part of this act was the beautiful fountain of water you could make by leaning super-far back on the paddle. At night, the spotlight would flash different colors against the huge wall of water that made the fountain even more brilliant. That gave the guy skiers a chance to pop the canoe paddle off their feet at the end of their act so no one could see the rope. But I just reveled in the beauty of it, because at the end of my turn on the paddle, I landed on the ramp and brought the paddle back up on the stage with me.

I am proud of my innovation because from that point on, the Canoe Paddle Act predominately turned into a solo act for a girl—and at that time, solo acts for girls were far and few between. Girls skied in the parade of pennants or flag line. We could ski in doubles in which a guy would do adagio lifts with us, (adagio is when the men lift the girls above their heads for beautiful statuesque positions). We could ski in the ballet line, and of course we were always part of the pyramid. There were some ski shows that had a Star Ballerina spot, but that's about it. Girls could also be part of the comedy act, which usually ended in the girl getting dunked in the water for laughs. Girls played a part in just 4 out of 22 acts. We were considered filler acts, acts that were there to give the guys time to prepare for the more exciting acts like barefooting, ramp jumping, and kite flying. And we were never allowed to drive the boats for an act, although in cases of emergency I was allowed to drive, but only because I knew how to ski them. I am proud to say I even drove for the four- or five-man jump, even at night, which would have been virtually unheard of in the water-skiing world.

There was no denying it: I was an athlete, not just a beauty in a bathing suit. During my freshman year, I would try out for all three sports: volley ball, basketball, and track. I played on the junior varsity volley ball team and was honing my skills as a pretty good setter. Then basketball season rolled around and I was reunited with my grade school P.E. teacher and boss from the ski show, Judy Elliott. Coach Elliott knew my potential playing basketball, and bumped me up to the varsity basketball team. Not only that, she started me. We were never a very good team, but I did my best to go along with all the plays during the games until in the last quarter, when I would just start doing my own thing to try and gain us a win. My scoring average my freshman year was pretty high in the state rankings, at 19.7 points a game. Not bad considering our whole team's total average score was usually between 40 to 50 points. After basketball season came track. Since I'd never ran track before and didn't know what I would be good at, my freshman year I tried everything. I threw the discus, pretty far but not as good as our best. I tried hurdles and was pretty fast, but not as fast as our fastest. I tried sprints, but I already knew my best friend, Mamie, would always be able to smoke me sprinting. I even tried high jumping; the cool thing about that was that the one time I jumped my absolute best, I got third place. I jumped my height, 5'2", at a time when not many girls were doing that yet. I was a pretty decent long jumper, but I always seem to get only a second or third in that, too.

Then one day the coach put me in the mile because the girl who was supposed to run it was sick and had to drop out. I filled in, won the race, and was about four or five seconds away from setting a new school record. From that point on, I ran distance. I ran the last leg of the two-mile relay team (a half- mile), then I ran the open mile, then I ran the open half-mile, and then I ran a leg on the mile relay team (a quarter mile). It was only at the state level that anyone could beat me in the open mile or half-mile. I won the conference and district championships all four years of my track seasons in the open half-mile and mile.

My obsession with sports—especially water-skiing—didn't leave me with a lot of time for my boy friends, and I think they knew it, which made them want to go after me even more. I was starting to get a little more serious about liking boys, but at the same time I was having little secret crushes on girls. In fact, I had two celebrity posters on my wall: the one of Michael Jackson in the famous yellow sweater vest, and one of Olivia Newton John. I hated the way my boyfriends would try to make me hold their hand in the hallways, or even worse try to kiss me at my locker. I was just not into being someone's possession, as a lot of my girlfriends seemed to be. It made me feel weird. But how could I even think about sex when I had not even started my period? For whatever reason, I did not start my period until the summer after my senior year. At the time I worried about it, though now I miss those days. I was a late bloom or, as I like to say now, a late Blum.

During school, my girlfriends were all bragging about having sex and The Big O, and I had no idea what they were talking about. I also had trouble with my teeth, probably because of having been born with a cleft palate. I had to make several visits to ear, nose, and throat (ENT) specialists, along with dentists and orthodontists. I had two healthy front teeth, but for some reason the teeth beside them just weren't coming in or were underdeveloped. In most all of my middle school and high school pictures, I did not smile showing my teeth, because for a few years I *only* had two front teeth, and braces on those. Ugh. Finally an orthodontist made me a special bridge that I could wear to fill in the spaces on the side of my two front teeth.

Thank God for the Missouri Crippled Children's Fund because we could never have afforded any of that or the corrective surgery I had done around my junior year of college on the roof of my mouth. That one was really painful, not like the surgeries when I was so little I didn't even remember them. The doctors likened it to getting my tonsils out but with ten-fold pain. The surgery was supposed to help my nasally voice, and there would be no more peas or carrots coming out of my nose. I would miss that trick, aw.

I wasn't quite sure how to feel about my body or my looks in general. I was a little embarrassed about my teeth issues, which made me a little self-conscious when I imagined how boys looked at me. But I wasn't completely without confidence about the way my body looked. Mothers in the South used to tell their daughters they should cup their hands in front of their chests and pump them together, chanting "I must, I must, I must improve my bust." I didn't do that, but maybe the knowledge that having breasts would be an asset for a girl on skis somehow gave me the hormonal surge I needed to grow breasts just big enough to look decent in my swimsuit. More likely than wishful thinking to control my hormones was the fact that the sport of water-skiing works your pectoral muscles like none other. I spent my early adolescence with horrible teeth and no menstrual periods. So thank goodness I had a little something to show in my breast area. I would not be confused as a little boy waterskier. However, during those earlier summers with no hair down there, I had to put a little piece of cloth in between my bathing suit bottoms and body so my bathing suit wouldn't show that embarrassing "camel toe" effect. Ugh!

I had a lot going for me, but I was still in no danger of getting a "big head." I struggled with myself-esteem or self- image, which may be part of why I developed early on a strong sense of empathy for the underdogs. I have always been very protective of people who get picked on, and who are not part of the in crowd. I was never part of any crowd, but I tried to be on the edges of every crowd. People often told me back then that I should be a lawyer. I think what they really meant was that I should be an arbiter or mediator, or the ultimate form of deciding a fight, a judge. That idea started to appeal to me—being a judge—and that would mean becoming a lawyer first. So I stayed focused on my grades, playing in band, playing sports, and water-skiing in the summers. I figured that maybe if things worked out as I wanted, I would go to college, become a lawyer, and change the world. My innovation to the Canoe Paddle act was just a small step in the right direction.

CHAPTER 4

Appearances Matter

The summer after my freshman year, I continued to improve my water-skiing skills, and was even starting to train new girl skiers. I could take a small-sized friend of mine with average athletic ability, teach her to ski, teach her four filler acts and make her part of the ski team in about two weeks, give or take a few days. I taught a lot of my guy friends how to perform several of the guy skiing acts, too. It was only later when I worked at Cypress Gardens that I realized there was an actual position for this called the "girls' lead," or the boss of the girls. What happened to me at the "Lake" instead was I would bring in my friends, new girl skiers and guy skiers, teach them everything I knew and everything they were capable of learning—and then the guy skiers would then go on to make twice or more as much money as me and be promoted to a position of Assistant Water-ski Show Director.

Another reason why they were promoted over me may have been my refusal to join the "Straight Arrow" club. The Straight Arrow club was a group of skiers who wanted to live a pure life and spread the gospel; some of them even wore baseball caps with an arrow pointing straight up on them. They said theirs was a religious club committed to walking the path of righteousness, and doing as Jesus would do. I went to a couple of their Bible studies and felt completely outnumbered and even somewhat bullied. Some of the more fervent members explained to me that people who didn't believe in the Bible and Jesus were going to Hell, and they told me that I had to pray for Jesus to come into my life.

I would ask them about all the other religions. "You mean all the Jews, Buddhists, Hindus, Muslims…they're just automatically going to Hell? I just refuse to believe that. I don't get that." Then I'd keep going down the list. "And homosexuals? People who drink alcohol? People who smoke?"

I kept thinking, *These people are telling me that my own dad went to Hell.* But I was trying to have an open mind, and I wanted to please my boss. So one night when I was about to go to sleep, I started praying. Suddenly I had this weird feeling that something was in my room. Was it the Holy Spirit? Was it the devil pulling me back? Or was it the workings of the imagination of a teenager's mind after being told at a Bible study that a lot of the people she cared about and loved were going to Hell. Hell, *she* was going to Hell. I was so upset and scared, I called my mom at work, something I never did. She told me we would talk about it the next day, but not to panic. I was not going to Hell. I never did join the Straight Arrow club.

The tensions I felt about the inequalities and lack of fairness all around me, though, continued to grow every summer. Toward the end of the summer of my near-religious conversion, many of the skiers had to leave to go back to school and left us working with somewhat of a skeletal crew. This was always the time of summer when some less-experienced people were encouraged to try positions for which they might not be ready. One night I was trying to make my last step up onto the top of the pyramid. The girl underneath me and to my right side had performed the same position climbing in the pyramid on the left side, but because the boat pulled us counter-clockwise in the show circle most of the momentum and weight pushed towards the right. I had my left foot firmly planted on the shoulder of the girl to my left, and my right hand on the side of the neck of the girl underneath me on the right, but every time I pushed on her neck to make the final step up, she would lean away and wasn't keeping her shoulder firm and in place for me to step up on. We were just about in front of the crowd and I was still not at the top of the pyramid, so I started yelling, "I can't, I can't…it's not gonna work…I'm gonna fall."

One of the guys yelled up to me, "Hurry up, Shellie, just do it. Just do it! Don't be a baby!"

I yelled back down to everyone, "Okay, get ready, I'm going," and I even started to count "Get ready, one…two three!" I pushed one last time on the girl's neck. Again she leaned way to the right so my foot had no shoulder to plant on, so I fell forward and down, taking everyone down with me along the way. I fell into the ropes and felt myself laying on ropes and the front of the middle guy's skis. I was stretched out on my side horizontally, parallel to the water. Suddenly I felt my body start to twist out of the ropes and my left arm jerk out away from my body. All of this was happening, of course, right in front of the audience with the spotlight on us. Everything stopped. Behind the boat were all of us skiers floating in the water, and skis and ropes strewn everywhere. I came up from under the water and holding my left wrist with my right hand, both pulled tight to my chest and just under the water's surface. My left hand was screaming in agony, but I hadn't looked at it.

With the music in the background blaring even louder because there was no roar of the boat engine to compete with, I tread water over to the low-water-level starting dock. I was still holding my left wrist tight to my chest with my right hand, and was turned around so that my back was facing the dock. Someone on the dock grabbed me from underneath my armpits and lifted me up, and I finally saw my left hand. My index finger was pointing back opposite of the way it should with the bone nearly breaking the skin, and my other fingers were bloody with rope burns. I was probably going into shock about then, as I started yelling and screaming at the top of my lungs, "I told you! F**k, I told you I couldn't do it! Look at my f**king hand! Now I can't play volley ball." Whoever picked me up was trying to calm me down and trying to shut me up. I was, after all, still in the spotlight right in front of the audience on the starting dock and Lee Greenwood's "Proud to be an American" was playing in the background on the loud speakers.

They rushed me to the hospital, and the next day I had surgery on my left index finger. My left arm was put in a cast. The doctors told me I was lucky I hadn't lost any fingers, but I didn't feel lucky. All I could think of was this was going to ruin my sophomore season of volley ball. The volley ball coach had me dress out and sit on the bench with the varsity team, but I couldn't play until the middle of the season when they took my cast off. Even then I was not using my hands to set, and I was the setter. I bumped everything, which meant that I cupped my fists together and used the inside of my forearms to move the volley ball around. This protected the fingers on my left hand. But closer to the end of the season my coach pulled me aside. While she was wrapping my fingers with that white cloth tape coaches always use, she told me she would not nominate me for the "All Conference" team if I didn't start using my fingers to set the ball. During this same personal meeting, bordering on intimate at least in my admiring mind, she handed me a little white cardboard note with a handwritten message on it. From that game on I started using my fingers to set the ball and so my coach did indeed nominate me for "All Conference," and I made it.

The little handwritten note said, "To Shellie: If you can't win, make the one ahead of you break the record." I am not embarrassed to say, I ended up having a crush on my volley ball coach. To this day I keep the note she wrote to me taped in a scrapbook with a picture of her taping my left hand fingers before that game. I have that photo because my little buddy Lisa Talleur, a school yearbook photographer, snapped it for me. Lisa was one of those kids that others liked to make fun, but I treated her fairly, didn't stomp on her feelings, and didn't belittle her like some of the others in our class. As thanks, and maybe because she had a little crush on me, Lisa took a lot of photos of me through my high school years. I have always tried to be sympathetic and supportive. I have always known how important it is not to undervalue other people's feelings. I spent too much time having my own undervalued.

Each summer when I went back to my water-skiing, I would try to learn something more. The Lake of the Ozarks started sponsoring a water-ski marathon for Muscular Dystrophy. I really enjoyed skiing in the marathons because it was for a good cause; donors paid for however many miles you skied. The only problem for me was that it always fell on a day I had to work, so I could only ski from early morning until around noon when I had to be at the ski show circle for work. Otherwise, who knows how much I could have brought in for the cause?

I could ski on a chair and saucer, spin around on it and do a handstand on it. I could ski on a jet ski standing forward and backward, do a handstand on it, and go over the jump ramp with it. I could ski on a canoe paddle. I could ski on shoe- skis and go over the ramp with them. I did a slalom act where I had to duck under another person's rope while cutting back and forth across the wakes. I did a one-ski step-off for a barefooting act. But my real joy was jumping the 6- foot jump ramp. First, I learned to jump for distance, but then I learned a helicopter move, which is a 360-degree spin keeping your skis parallel to the water after you jump off the ramp. I was doing helicopters off the ramp at age 18; someone once suggested that in 1982 that may have been a world record first for a woman, but I've always been more interested in doing it than looking up records about it. I landed my first front-flip off the 6-foot jump ramp at age 22, in 1986, which is no doubt a first. I started trying back-flips when I was 20. I never heard of any other girls doing gainers off the 6-foot jump ramp in 1984. The back-flip in the water-ski world is called a "gainer" because you are moving forward while throwing yourself backwards. The gainer became my nemesis, my great white whale, my Moby Dick. It was all I thought about when I was on the Lake.

At school, however, I had something else on my mind. During my junior year, my high school nominated girls other than seniors for

Homecoming Representatives. I very much did *not* want to be a part of this, as I had seen the quarreling, catfights, and bad blood it caused among my older sister's friends. But I kept hearing rumbles that my name was among the nominations for Homecoming Representative. I went to talk to my high school counselor about how I could gracefully bow out of such an "honor," and she wisely suggested I shouldn't refuse because the School Board Members, the PTA members, and other "powers that be" might not look too kindly on that slight when it came time for graduation and scholarships. I knew I would need their support, so did nothing. Besides, I thought I would be safe given what was going on with my ear, which had begun draining.

Following another visit to the ENT doctors, I ended up having my first surgery on my left ear when they removed a benign cyst called a cholesteatoma, and so for about three weeks after I had to wear a white bandage that went all the way around my head with a white plastic protective ear cover cap on my left ear. It looked like a piece of bulky one-sided wrestling headgear. Given how sensitive I already was about my looks, I figured this would save me from having to deal with any possibility of being a Homecoming Representative. I was wrong. I was nominated, and so for homecoming my junior year I had to pick out a dress and act pretty when riding the floats in the parade, and sitting at the game.

My nightmare magnified in the fall of my senior year when I was nominated for Homecoming Queen. Again I wanted to refuse to even be considered, but I still feared the possible repercussions. The nomination put a big wedge between Mamie and me. She had a time-consuming boy friend who played on the sports team. He had even talked her into sharing his locker. Up until that last year, Mamie and I had always shared lockers. It was the players who really voted for the Queen, and rumor had it that Mamie's boy friend had been asking the guys from the team, "Do we want a fag, a dyke, as our Homecoming Queen?"

He had to be talking about me. I didn't think even he would be so slimy, so I figured there was nothing to the story—until Mamie started acting kind of weird towards me. Finally she confronted me on the bleachers during one of our team practices. She asked me point blank, with a very "God I hope not" tone to her voice, "Shellie, are you queer?"

I was in shock. I couldn't believe my best friend was asking me that. Clearly the story about her boy friend was true, and he was spreading the rumor that I was gay. Now, I didn't know how to answer. I hadn't had sex with any of the guys I dated, and I had crushes on some girls—even teachers and coaches. I could have said, "I'm not really sure what I am, but what does it matter? Aren't we friends?" and then maybe try to have a conversation with her about my feelings. Instead, I just flat-out denied it.

Mamie won the Homecoming Queen that year. I was glad she did, but if I thought then that if I had won, maybe the humiliation would have been worth it, because it looked as though unless I really messed up the rest of my senior year I was going to graduate Valedictorian, and that would surely mean I would be up for a bunch of scholarships from my school. I had gone along to get along just as my counselor had advised me, and I was going to have a chance to try out for the University of Missouri Basketball team. Life was good.

I was pretty sure that in the history of the School of the Osage not one of their athletes had been asked to try out for a Big Eight College team, much less make the team. But my mom was dating a former assistant coach of the Wichita State Women's Basketball team, and even though our basketball team was never good enough to play at the state level championships where I might have been scouted by a college team, the former coach knew that I was good. He made a call to Joanne Rutherford, the coach of the University of Missouri, Columbia Lady Tiger's basketball team and said that she might want to give me a look if she needed to fill out her point guard spot. I was invited in for a walk-on tryout. So I drove to the University of Missouri in Columbia, tried out for the team as a walk-on, was interviewed by Coach Rutherford—and made the team. I would be the first person, male or female, in the history of my school to actually be on a Big Eight College Athletic team, the biggest college in Missouri, *and* I was going to be Valedictorian of my class. Graduation was going to be a very big day for me.

As graduation approached, my mom invited her two sisters, one in Sonoma, California, and the other in Denver, Colorado. She also invited all my cousins, or at least those that could make it. No one told me how to prepare for my big day, but I had prepared a speech in my head. I had gone to both my brothers' and my sister's graduation so I kind of knew what to expect.

When graduation day came, I was sitting in the front row of the auditorium—naturally, because my last name started with a B and we were seated alphabetically. My family, some of whom had traveled a long way to be there, were sitting somewhere behind me in the audience. The principal started calling up our names alphabetically. Who knew there could be so many A names? Finally he said, "Shellie Blum, who is also Valedictorian." I got up, walked up, got my diploma and Valedictorian Plaque, and walked off the stage. My sister, Tamara, was scurrying up to try and take a picture of me before I had moved my tassel from one side of my cap to the other, but I don't think she made it in time. She was probably thinking, as I was, that it was "no biggy," and she could catch me when I came up again. She hid out to the side of the stage, and our eyes met. I looked at her quizzically as if I was asking, "Was that it?" I think I even motioned my hands twisting them palms up, like, "*What the f**k?*" In my mind, I was thinking be calm, be patient, the scholarships are coming, but no, nothing. I watched many of my other friends walk up on the stage and pick up scholarships—this one from that group, this one from that part of the school, little scholarship from the PTA. As the ceremony wound down, it started to dawn on both my sister and me that I was not going to be called back up to the stage.

I was not going to get one scholarship. Out of the 15 or more scholarships handed out that day, I didn't get one. And everyone knew that of everyone there, our family needed the money the most. I was fighting back a mix of feelings—panic, anger, shock, despair. I wasn't sure if I should or could be feeling the way that I was feeling, but the next time my sister caught my eye, she had tears in her eyes, and so I knew there was something wrong. That allowed me to have tears in my eyes as well. The ceremony ended with the traditional throwing off the graduation caps into the air. All the caps went up into the air—all but one. Mine.

I saw my sister, who was now standing right up against the edge of the stage, tugging on the principal's pants leg and yelling. "What about my sister? What about Shellie?"

He just ignored her. I stood up, started pushing past all the people with my head held down so I would not have to make eye contact with anyone, until I made my way outside the auditorium, I briskly turned around and simultaneously thrust both fists into the air, my hands turned palms in so that the view at the tips of my middle fingers was the four foot lettering at the top of the gymnasium doors, "SCHOOL OF T HE OSAGE INDIANS" and with both of my middle fingers pointed sky ward and towards the doors, I yelled, "F**k you!" This time I could not hold back the tears. The counselor was wrong. Going along to get along did not work, and I would never fall for that again.

The summer before I went off to college was pretty gratifying. They finally held the Muscular Dystrophy Marathon on the one day our ski show did not perform, which meant that for the first time I would be able to ski for as long as I wanted, not just until I had to knock off for work. I went around to all the businesses to have them sign up for donations.

"How far do you think you will ski?"

I told them the truth: I planned to break the record.

"What's the record?"

"I think it's around 300 miles."

They'd all take a look at me and laugh. "Yeah, right. Okay, put me down for a dollar a mile." One man actually signed at five dollars a mile.

My mom rode in the boat to watch me, but I don't remember who drove the boat or which marina donated the boat for us to use. And I can't remember who paid for the gas, but if any of them are reading this, I would formally like to thank them all again. We started out at about 8 a.m. at Casino Pier, a dock by Bagnell Dam, at the zero-mile marker. The way it worked was that I would ski through the channel to Tan-Tar-a Resort and the 26-mile marker, which made one trip equal to 26 miles. It took an average of one hour for me to make one trip, and then we'd turn around and I would head back to Bagnell Dam.

After my eighth trip back to Bagnell Dam the boat driver signaled that we had to stop and get gas. If we were going to keep going, I had to sit in the water waiting; contestants weren't allowed to get into a boat because that would be considered resting or quitting. I was exhausted, so while I was sitting there in the water waiting, I thought maybe it would be okay if I *didn't* break the record. I was already the last holdout, so I had skied the farthest, but I hadn't yet broken the record. My legs and arms were screaming at me, though, and I was really, really tired. I wanted to quit. While I was thinking about how great it would feel to just climb out of the water and relax, I looked up and saw, sitting patiently on the dock at Casino Pier, a poster child for Muscular Dystrophy. Evidently the little boy had sat there all day in his wheelchair waving to the skiers as they made their way back to the starting dock, meeting and thanking each one who came in. That really tugged at my heart. I thought, "If that little boy can sit there all day in pain and smile, wave to us and encourage us, then I can keep going." So I did.

I made another trip to Tan-Tar-a and back again to the Bagnell Dam dock, and there he was still sitting there in his wheelchair, still smiling, still waving. So I waved back, acknowledging him, and then I started waving circles around my head signaling to my mom I would make another trip. When we got to Tan-Tar-a Resort I wasn't sure I could make the turn around and keep going, but I realized that I had to make another trip back. I had to see my little friend again. I couldn't stop on that end, but it was getting dark and I was sure they wouldn't let me ski in the dark. So I waved my hand over my head in circles at Tan- Tar-a Resort and headed back to the poster child for Muscular Dystrophy.

Because of him, for my little buddy in the wheelchair, I kept going. When I finally stopped it was 8:30 p.m. I had skied non-stop for 12½ hours—312 miles. When I got out of my skis and up onto the dock, I could barely walk, but I hobbled over to him and gave him a big, long, hug. He had stayed there all day for me. We got our picture taken together, the two of us holding onto my trophy for making the most money and my trophy for skiing the farthest and breaking the record. All the goodness that sprang from that day was because of the little smiling boy in a wheelchair. I loved my life.

CHAPTER 5

The Big Jump

The day after the Muscular Dystrophy Marathon, I packed my car for my big move to Columbia, Missouri. Scholarship or not, I was going to college. After all, my sister Tamara had gone to the same college three years ahead of me. What I couldn't figure out in filing the financial aid paperwork, she could show me. I needed to go up early to go through Sorority Rush week, and of course to check in for the basketball team orientation.

The first day of Rush I caused quite a stir. At every Sorority House I visited, I walked up and in the front door barefoot, carrying my high heel shoes. Right away, the people inside would start asking questions about it. It ended up being a great icebreaker, though I hadn't planned it. It was just that after water-skiing for 12½ hours and 312 miles just the day before, my feet and ankles were so badly swollen I couldn't wear my high heels. I told them all about the smiling little boy, and how he'd spurred me on. I made some friends, but I ended up not joining any sorority even though I was asked to pledge.

My sister had spent time ahead of me as a Kappa Delta, but she hadn't stayed with them long; she'd quickly grown tired of all the rules and regulations, and warned me that I would have a rough time of it. Still, I enjoyed the experience of Rush week. Sometimes just for fun my sister and I still sing the Kappa Delta house song.

My freshman year I was very busy, between basketball practices and meetings and trying to get good grades in all my classes. I sat the bench most of the year, but I know my competitiveness helped keep the other players motivated and conditioned, and I certainly helped keep the team's grade point average up—my first semester my GPA was 3.9—so even though I was probably the worst player on the team, I did contribute. I also provided some comic relief. I remember sitting on the very end of the bench with another freshman player, and together we would sneak popcorn from the pep band. Sometimes I would grab one of the players' trombone and belt out an OOM-PAH-PAH or two. The band loved it. (Coach Rutherford was not so thrilled.)

Even though I only played in one game the whole season, about two minutes total, I didn't quit so I garnered my first university-level varsity letter. We were the Big Eight Champions that year. At the end-of-the-year party, the team was trying to decide where to go as a sort of victory vacation, and they finally agreed: the Lake of the Ozarks! Of Course, that turned me into the de facto tourist guide during the whole trip, but I didn't mind. Nobody knew the Lake better than me. Maybe I passed on some of my enthusiasm for the Lake, too: I hear Coach Rutherford now lives there.

At the end of the first school year I went back to the water-skiing show and kept doing my thing. In fact, I kept it up every summer, although I was getting more and more resentful of my underpayment and for my unacknowledged and undervalued position of training new skiers. Thank God, I had my returning ski lessons to bring in some extra money. I seethed as guy skiers who I had *introduced* to show skiing passed over me in pay and position. I understood that it made sense to pay the guys a little bit more: their higher velocity skiing acts, especially the Delta Wing kite flyer, put them in greater danger and risk of injury. But I was right there beside the guys skiers, literally, skiing in the jump acts, and I weighed anywhere from 40 to 90 pounds lighter. I was barefooting every show, and sometimes I would be the only chance for the audience to see barefoot skiing because of the rough water.

On super-rough days during my solo barefoot act we would get a longer rope and I would have to step off my ski inside the boat wake instead of my usual outside-the-wake start, but I always made the straight shot into the landing ramp and went up for my bow, leaving my ski some 250 yards away from the stage and floating in the water as proof I was on my feet. There were several times throughout my skiing career when it was so choppy that I was the only barefooter able to make a successful step-off. Toward the end of my Lake of the Ozarks career there were a few seasons when I never even fell, which is almost unheard of in the ski world. I never mentioned that out loud—I never bragged about it—but I knew that some of the skiers were aware of it, and some of the bosses knew, and that filled me with pride. They couldn't take that away from me. I would ski the summers, and then go back to college.

The summer before my senior year and my college graduation, I was working on backwards slaloming in preparation of doing a back step-off to backwards barefoot. Backwards barefooting and the Delta Wing kite flying were the only two acts I hadn't yet mastered. Jeff Graves, our Delta Wing kite pilot, started training me for the kite. The difficulty was that I was too light for that big of a kite, although I had managed to go up a couple of times with ropes tied on the ends of the wings to help keep me from blowing over. For once my small size was actually holding me back, but I was trying! I worked hard trying to land my front-flip. The falls weren't that painful because I would land on my backside or butt, but when I started trying to learn the back-flip or gainer, those falls *really* hurt.

One day that summer, I was in between shows giving a family their ski lessons. I had taught this same family of four for 11years, as they came back every summer and requested me specifically. I loved that. I might have been stuck in the snack bar at our half-time intermission selling cokes and hotdogs while the guy skiers could be in the

Pro Shop hustling up ski lessons, but I had repeat clients who sought me out, like this family I taught how to ski, slalom, and trick ski. Some I even taught how to barefoot ski. This family, though, wanted to thank me for all my years of teaching and decided to take me out to dinner at The Potted Steer, a rustic well-known restaurant with an excellent reputation and the long waiting list to show for it. This was not McDonalds.

I knew I had to be at work at 7:00 p.m., but I was sure it would be rude to rush the dinner. After all these were paying customers, and my bosses were making money off their ski lessons. Surely, my bosses wouldn't want me to rush out saying something like, "You guys have been really great to me all these years, but I have to leave early before everyone is done with their meal because I can't be late to work." Besides, I was thinking that my pre-show job was dock setup, which really wasn't that big a deal, and meant I had time that I would have used to practice. So I didn't rush the dinner, and I ended up getting to work around 7:20 p.m. When I arrived, the dock was already set up. I thanked the other girl on setup for having done all the work herself and covered for me, and got ready to go to work. It was no biggie, I thought; throughout my 11years skiing, I had set up the dock by myself tons of times, especially during the years when I couldn't drive to work and was stuck at work between ski shows. Those times even without being asked I set up the dock on my own all by myself almost every day.

I asked one of the guys who might have been taking it easy after he gassed up the boats if he would pull me so I could practice some back-flips or gainers. I was determined to get it right. I had always been told to drop my handle at the bottom of the ramp, pop off the top of the ramp, and throw my head backwards. The first time I had tried a back-flip a couple of summers before then, I had landed flat on my back. Now I was making progress, and I slowly had started to make it a little farther around each time I had worked up the courage to try one.

The next stage of learning the gainer was landing upside down. In a few summers I went from landing flat on my back going 36 mph to landing upside down. My helmet knifed through the water, and I would instinctively, involuntarily put my hands up to protect my head, and my hands would become black and blue. By that stage I was actually getting my skis around about three-quarters of the way before the tips would stuff into the water, forcing my whole body to arch backwards like a banana. My upper body would slingshot back down and smack the water hard, mostly on my chest and face, which almost always knocked the air out of me. In my entire skiing career it was the most horrible way to fall.

That night after I was late coming back from dinner with my lessons family, on my first try I fell exactly that way. It was a really bad fall, too, so instead of taking my normal three practice attempts I came in after the first to recover. I had just stretched out on the warm concrete part of the dock to try to collect my bearings, wondering if I should be worried that I was coughing up a little blood, when I heard my boss yelling. He towered over me and screamed down at me, as though I wasn't in enough pain already.

"Shellie, I am so sick of you being late! You are not taking me seriously! We've talked about this before!" he blustered. "Who do you think you are, coming in here 20 minutes late, and then going out to practice gainers? The only thing that matters to you, and the only way I can see to get through to you, is to dock your pay."

I couldn't understand why he thought I would respond to his money threats. I had been there for more than a decade, and my pay had only gone up from 25 dollars a week to 175 dollars a week. And I had given every pay check I ever made to my mom, and only kept the lessons money for myself. (After all, I was managing all of the household bills.) So my "pay" was not a ton of money, yet there he was trying to make me out to be a greedy money-grubbing slouch. Every single guy there, even the newest ones, made more money than I, and a few of the girls did, too. That bothered me, of course, as there was only one other skier who had been there as long as I had—a girl in my sister's class who I loved because she was so witty, funny and pretty—she could always make us all laugh!—that it was no wonder that the ski show director had married her. Good for her, good for them, good for the skiers making better money than me…but didn't this guy know my family could really use the money? That I worked really, really hard for that pittance? I was livid, but I sucked it up, though deep down inside it hurt.

But now he'd gone too far. I was lying prone, stretched out with my hands crossed forming a triangle, palms down on the warm cement, my forehead down on top of my hands, the whole time he was ranting at me. I couldn't believe my ears. I wondered how much longer he would go at me, until finally I slowly raised my head and turned it to look at him, squinting into the sun as he stood over me. I didn't say a word; I just stared him down. I let him see the dribbles of blood on the concrete, and probably I still had some on the sides of my mouth. I slowly got up to my knees, and then stood and started walking past him, still staring at him the whole time, speechless. I had had enough. I went to the girls dressing room, grabbed all my personal belongings from my cubby hole, and started up the hill to my car.

That was not the first time I had tried to walk out on my boss before a show. Another time I had gone through the same motions when I refused to ski in the night ski show during a wicked thunderstorm. That time he had stopped me, and I came back to finish the show after we waited out the storm. But this time was different; this time there was no turning back. He followed me all the way up the hill to my car, and whatever he was saying to me to convince me to come back was just a blur in my mind. It was as though I was in a trance. I got in the car, rolled up my windows, and locked all the car doors. He was banging on my windows saying something, but I just kept looking straight forward. Nothing he could say was going to change my mind. I was leaving, and as I did, I spun my tires, throwing gravel back off of them. In my rear-view mirror I could see him just standing there.

There were still about three weeks left before I needed to head back to college. It was more or less just my mom and me living in our house on Mocking Bird Lane, in a little town called Lakeland, population

98, about two miles on the other side of Bagnell Dam. My oldest brother had been in a horrific car accident when he was 19 and had been in a coma for three months afterward; that left him with head trauma that kept him either in and out of hospitals or, even worse, in and out of jail. My second-oldest brother was beginning to manage some exclusive nightclubs in Dallas and opening some in Japan. And my married sister was wielding her industrial engineering degree at a company in Anaheim, California. Her in-laws lived in the San Fernando Valley, near Los Angeles.

The week I quit, my mom was out in California visiting her boy friend's family in Placerville, so I figured it made sense for me to go to California to visit everyone, including my grandfather and grandmother who lived in Santa Ana. I called up an old ski buddy who was the water-ski show director at Magic Mountain U.S.A. Theme Park, in Los Angeles, to see if I could score some free tickets to the park, and he started asking about my jumping. I told him I never missed on my distance jumps and my helicopters were becoming just as good and consistent. He asked me about my front-flips, and I admitted that while I hadn't made one yet, I was real close, and didn't mind trying them because the falls didn't really hurt. He asked about my gainers, and I told them they were still pretty brutal.

"Well, Shellie," he said. "I can do better than tickets to the park. As it happens, right now I'm hurt pretty bad so I can't ski, and because we are at the end of our season, we're really short-handed. I need a jumper and I need you now. Would you come out here and jump for me, and at least try your front-flips in my show so we have one inverted trick in the act?"

"Sign me up!" I said. I was a little nervous about how working for this boss would be because when he skied at the Lake he was a big-time Straight Arrow club member. And I was 22, and thinking that if I wanted to party a little, he was not going to stop me. But he needed me, and as it turned out it all worked out fine. I stayed free with my sister's in-laws in the Valley, and got paid to go to Magic Mountain and practice my front-flips four times a day in the show. It wasn't long before I was making them consistently. It was 1986.

That's where I was when I got "the call." I was out on the dock practicing doubles with some guy. He had his hand up under my butt with his arm stretched up above his head, and I was sitting on his hand in the air in a seat lift, when the ski show director came out to tell me I had a phone call. I was a little jolted by that news because our family has always gone with a "no news, is good news" type of attitude. Immediately I started imagining the worst, and my boss caught the look on my face and could see that I was a little shaken by the idea that someone was calling me. He grinned. "Don't worry, it's a good call."

"Who is it?" I asked.

"It's a surprise."

It was. I walked into the office and picked up the phone, still more than a little nervous. I used my customary work-setting greeting. "Hello, how can I help you?" My habits of working at the Lake in the Snack Bar and Pro Shop had followed me to my new place of employment.

"Hello. My name is Mark Voisard, and I'm the ski show director at Cypress Gardens," said the voice on the phone. "Is this Shellie Bloom?"

I pulled the phone away from my ear and looked at it, and then looked at my ski show director from Magic Mountain to see if I was I being punked. I remember wondering, *Where's the candid camera?*

"Uh huh," I said, too stunned to be eloquent. I didn't think this was the time to correct the mispronunciation of my last name.

"We hear you are pretty consistent with your jumping, and you can do helicopters and front-flips," he said. "We're starting up a new show down here called 'Ski Fever.' There's a featured spot for a girl jumper and, well, since you're the only girl doing that, we thought we would give you a call and see if you wanted to ski for our new show."

I couldn't believe my ears. I looked over at my boss again, and he was nodding his head up and down really fast as if to say, *yes it's true, it's real, they want you.* I stammered into the phone, "Well, I had planned to go one more semester of school. I'm just four credit hours away from getting a second degree, in psychology. I already have my B.A. in political science."

He didn't miss a beat. "Well I can't blame ya for that. Do you think *after* that you would be interesting in coming to Florida to ski?"

I really didn't know what to say. What I did say was, "I'm really not sure. My plans have been to go to law school, and I've already taken the LSATs. But maybe after December I could work something out, and ski for you from December until the next school year started?" I wondered if I was screwing up a really big break.

"Great!" he said. "Maybe if you come down here and the other girls see you jump, they'll get the fever, too."

"That would be great," I said. "But you gotta promise me one thing—I gotta be able to jump."

"Don't worry, Shellie," he laughed. "That's why we're calling you."

I told him I had to think about it some, and said we should talk in a while after he had all the details ironed out. He agreed to call me in a week. I hung up and pumped both fists, exclaiming "Yes!"

I didn't *really* have to think about it—I knew I wanted to ski some more before going to law school. I had burned myself out getting two degrees with general honors in about 4½ years, so it was a no-brainer for me to take a hiatus before law school to ski. Secretly I was thinking. Who knows where this will lead? Maybe since I was the only girl doing freestyle jumping, I could get some endorsements or sponsorships that would help defray the costs of college and law school. After all, I could always go back to school; I wouldn't always be able to do this type of skiing.

All I have to do was go back home, live at the house in Lakeland, and drive back and forth to Columbia for one last semester. I would save money not living in a dorm, which I stopped doing after my sophomore year, or renting an apartment, which I had done after that. I would drive back and forth from Lake of the Ozarks to Columbia then to the capitol of Missouri, Jefferson City, on Tuesday and Thursdays, so I could finish my last course, which was an honors internship as an aide to the office of the Governor, Kit Bond. Then I would get my two degrees, with honors, and then I would water-ski. But I wouldn't be just water-skiing…I would be water-skiing at Cypress Gardens. No matter how good any other ski show in the country or world thought they were, everyone knew there was no higher pinnacle for show water-skiing than at Cypress Gardens, the water-ski Capital of the World.

I focused on finishing up school. I had given up basketball after my freshman year. I wasn't really good enough, or tall enough, and there was no future in it for me—the WNBA didn't even exist yet. Although my grades were never again as high as they had been when I was on the team, I was still taking honors psychology twice a week, which required me to design and run an experiment, then write a paper about the results. My hypothesis was that people recognize and distinguish among people of their own ethnic group easier than they do among other groups, so I had a string of volunteers look at photos of people of European descent and photos of people of Asian descent. The volunteers were also of either European or Asian descent.

The whole grade was contingent on that final paper describing the experiment and its outcome, but evidently, the professor did not think my paper was honors-grade material. Most likely he was right, though he could have been a little less abrasive about it. He marked up the paper with that famous red ink, adding comments like "horrible communication skills" and "amazed you made it out of high school." I was shocked. The paper was bad, but not *that* bad. I was starting to believe what I had heard one time and that it was true—BS & PhD stood for a bunch of "BullShit, Piled, High, and Deep." Not that it mattered. What mattered was that this particular PhD professor was going to flunk me.

I scheduled a meeting with him. I had recently had another ear surgery to remove another cholesteatoma from my left ear, so once again I was adorned with the lovely white headband with the bulging white plastic bubble covering my ear. I'm sure my professor didn't know what to think, but I was determined to dazzle him with my so-called horrible communication skills. I explained about my cleft palate, my ear problems, and my late development in learning how to talk, my slow development in writing, and how I was sure this was why I had trouble communicating. I meant communicating on paper, but I apparently was doing a pretty fair job out loud: before the meeting was over, the professor knew my whole life story and may have even shed a tear or two. My grade went from an F to a C. *Success.*

I didn't go to my midterm college graduation—my last graduation had left me with a bad memory, and I couldn't care less about the pomp and circumstance. Besides, I couldn't afford a cap and gown. I told them to mail my diplomas to Cypress Gardens.

They were expecting me to be there before January 1, 1987, and had agreed to pay for my travel expenses to move down there. I would start out conditionally at $7.35 an hour, though I had asked for $9, but if I held up my end of the bargain and could perform the jumps that I said I could—namely the Helicopter and Front-flip—then at my 90- day probation period review, I would be eligible for a $1.15 raise. That was the deal.

Work at the Water Ski Capital of the World? I probably would have done it for free.

CHAPTER 6

The Water Ski Capital of the World

My moving expenses were not going to be high. I figured I would only take whatever would fit in my little brown Datsun B-210 hatchback. The night before I was planning to get up early to start driving to Florida, I went up into my room and started pulling down all my awards, ripping them off the walls. I took my bowling trophies (I had a 168 average during grades 6 to 8), my water-skiing trophies (I was especially proud of the two big ones from the Muscular Dystrophy Marathon), and all my track medals went into the trash. I came across my Lady Tigers Big Eight Championship plaque, and my valedictorian plaque; it was hard, but these too, went in the trash. Sorting through my clothes, though, I ran across my high school letter jacket, and I just couldn't throw it away. I pulled it close to my chest, smelled it, and put it on. I remembered one other thing I couldn't part with, a scrapbook my mom and sister had started and kept updated for me. I reached under my bed pulled the book out and ran my hand over the cover. My scrapbook would make the journey to Florida too.

It seems incredible when I think back to this but even at the young age of 22 I was not a big fan of material things, plus I had no one to store these sentimental trinkets. The most important thing I would carry with me to start my new life in Florida was my memories.

It was December 28, 1986, and it was cold and snowy outside. I took the trash outside and dumped it into the big metal can we use for burning, put some lighter fluid to it, lit a match, and watched a big part of my past go up in flames on that beautiful clear crisp night. The next morning I woke up early, climbed into my overstuffed car, and I started driving.

When I pulled up at the main parking entrance of Cypress Gardens on December 30, I was amazed to see that the parking lot was a giant circle that wound around and had two levels. Later it occurred to me that it might have been one of Florida's famous sinkholes turned into a parking facility. The first person I saw walking to his car was Jeff Graves, the Delta Wing kite pilot from the Lake, and I rolled down my window and yelled out "Jeff Graves! I didn't know they let losers like you around here!"

I startled him, and he had to do a double take, but when he realized who it was he came jogging up to my car. I knew I could abuse Jeff like this because he and I had stayed pretty close at the Lake. Jeff never joined the Straight Arrow club. He was a throwback hippie of sorts and had always had a free spirit. He leaned into my car window.

"Oh my god, girl, what are you doing here?"

I told him about skiing at Magic Mountain and the surprise phone call. "And what are you doing here?" He told me about a place called River Ranch, which he said was "a kite flyer's paradise, with people coming from all over the world—and just up the road." He pointed toward I-4. He also told me he was doing some grip work for some television and movie productions.

"But…what are you doing here?" I asked, waving my hand to indicate Cypress Gardens.

"Here? Oh. I've gotten to know some of the flyers and they let me in so I can work out in the weight room," he said.

I was thinking, *Workout room? Weight room? These water-skiers have their own gym?* I asked if he'd walk me in, but he shrugged and apologized, saying he was in a bit of a hurry. He did volunteer to walk me to the security hut after I parked, and as we were heading there and I was taking in the smells, sounds, and scenery, I was growing more and more nervous, but in an excited kind of way. It was all new: a new job, a new place to live, new people. But most importantly, it was The Water-ski Capital of the World. I had never been to Florida, much less Cypress Gardens, so I was seeing paradise up close and personal for the first time. It was a bit overwhelming, but I had Jeff by my side, so it was all good.

The security guard told me where to find Mark Voisard at the ski show circle, so I just started walking in the direction he pointed. Then I encountered the usual arrows you find in almost any tourist attraction that lead you to different parts of the park and followed them to the water, and the big ski show circle with two big stadiums, one to the left and one to the right. I went toward the right only because it was closer, and started seeing skiers, or at least people I thought were skiers since they were people in bathing suits with physically fit awesome bodies. I asked if anyone knew where I could find Mark Voisard.

One girl offered to show me. "I'm Jeanie Baier," she said. "Come with me."

"Thanks. I'm Shellie, a new skier."

Jeanie jolted her head back towards me as we are walking and said, "Oh! You're the jumper—how awesome!"

I was a little surprised, and wondered if everyone knew I was coming. Weird. We walked down a long hallway under the large stadium where the audience sits on bleachers. On the walls are giant photos of girl and guy skiers with captions: SKI ONE 1978, SKI ONE 1979, SKI ONE 1980. Others say MOST IMPROVED 1978, MOST IMPROVED 1979, and I realized I was in their version of the Hall of Fame. I was in awe, and imagined that some day maybe my picture might be up there, too. We stopped in front of a door with a sign that announced, BUSINESS ONLY PLEASE KEEP OUT. Jeanie knocked, and someone yelled, "Come in!"

Sitting in a chair behind a desk eating ice cream out of a cup was a man in a Wisconsin baseball cap. "Who are you?" he asked.

"I'm Shellie Blum."

The guy's eyes widened a bit and he waved Jeanie away with a kind of flicking motion with his hand.

"Mark Voisard," he said. He stared at me a bit. "I thought you would be bigger."

I put both my hands out to my sides down low with my palms facing him. "Nope, this is all of me."

"So, you're Shellie Bloom, the girl jumper? Okay, well, we need to—"

I cut him off mid-sentence. "Blum. It's Blum, not Bloom."

He shrugged. "Yeah, okay, whatever. Anyway, we need to have you sign some paperwork to officially start your employment. You'll get your uniforms and workout clothes, and you'll need to see the girls' lead about your costumes and bathing suits. She'll weigh you in. 'Bout how much do you weigh, anyway?"

I was a little taken aback by the question, but I told him, "I don't know, about 115 pounds? I've been watching my weight, though, so it might be less. I am pretty sure you like your girl skiers light and tight, am I right?" I wanted him to know that I knew what and why he was asking me, and that this wasn't my first rodeo, so to speak. I had been around guy skiers all my life and I knew they liked small but strong girls, because they were easier to lift for the adagio acts and to carry in pyramids. But I wasn't too concerned about my weight; I came to Cypress Gardens to jump.

Later in the day, I met the girls' lead. I immediately liked her. She was very matter-of-fact and businesslike, and by the end of our orientation time together, I was sure she was different from the rest of the girls. I thought of her as one tough chick, and someone who would be in my corner if I needed her. I weighed in at 111½, and she was sure to write in that extra half pound.

The next day I punched in early. I was told we would go out on the front dock and do a morning stretch out, which was the everyday routine, but there was one thing that would be different that day. It was December 31, 1986, and Lynn Novakofski's birthday. Nova, as the skiers affectionately called him, had been the Water-ski Show Director for years and had recently been promoted to Director of Athletics. He was in charge of all the athletes there. Ice skaters, swimmers, divers, trampolinests, jugglers, gymnasts—if you performed at Cypress Gardens, he was your boss.

When I came around the corner of the hallway, there he was, standing tall and regal, and in fifth ballet position. He stood at the end of the stage explaining to everyone that we were going to go on a little jog as a present to him on his birthday. Everyone groaned except me. I was excited. A little jog, a run! We were going on a run! I loved to run. After listening to him talk for a few minutes, I realized that I had seen him before. He had been at our show once in Missouri. He had come for a visit; he must have seen me ski when I was about 17 or 18. I was sure of it. It made me wonder if that was how they had known about me. Did Lynn Novakofski make all this happen for me? Did Nova want me to jump for him? That had to be it.

I vowed then that I would show Lynn Novakofski that he hadn't made a mistake taking a chance on me. I would show everyone I could jump. But first I would show everyone at that moment that I could run, even though I didn't know the course or path. I just stayed close to the guys running in the front of the pack. In the end, when we had finished running about a mile and were heading back to the stadium, I made sure I was right in the front and tied with the guys coming in first. I might have been able to pass them at the end, but decided I would settle with a tie. After all, Nova did not say the run was a race.

Jeanie Baier was right there in the run too. Sometime later, she had confided in me that she liked to run, and in high school, no one could beat her. She was fast! She told me her father was a Pastor, and was very strict. I thought, "Oh, No"! Another religious conversion attempt was coming, but it never did. Jeanie just lived by example. Around Thanksgiving, she surprised me with a home cooked meal. Near Christmas, she knew I was by myself and called to invite me to go Christmas Caroling, we did! Jeanie was the perfect combination of strength and grace. In any photo I have ever seen of her, she stands out. She quickly became my idol, and if there was anyone I tried to emulate in good deeds and water ski ballet form, it was her.

After the run, we all sat back down on the stage. Mark Voisard and Lynn Novakofski were explaining how the new ski show called Ski Fever was going to be planned out. I noticed the stage we were sitting on was foamy, with some kind of gymnastic pad under it. It wasn't hard like the stage in Missouri but had some give to it, so maybe we were going to tumble on it. I wasn't the best gymnast but I knew a few tricks. My mind was drifting off a bit back to Missouri, and how this place seemed so different, while I watched Nova in his ballet pose and listened to Mark explain how each skier would be announced, then run across the stage and perhaps do a gymnastics move in the middle. I could see the look of terror on some of the skiers' faces. Some of the "girl" skiers weren't girls but grown women, probably married and with kids, so I figured maybe they would just wave to the audience from the middle of the stage.

But I was remembering my first year skiing. Our ski show had used the exact same concept, where each skier was introduced and then he or she would run across the stage and wave. At the very end, the announcer would say, "And last, but certainly not least, we have our 12-year-old girl wonder, Shellie Blum!" I would run onto the stage and, in the middle, do as big a round-off as I could—a round-off is like a cartwheel, but you land with your feet together at the end—and right as my feet landed together I would spring back up into the air and twist my body so that I landed the opposite direction. That way I could scurry off the stage waving to the audience the whole way. I added the extra twist because, being only 12 and insecure about my looks, I wanted off the stage as fast as possible.

Watching Nova in his regal pose reminded me of how I'd felt around Wayne Shank, one of the co-owners of the ski show in Missouri. Wayne was the silent partner of the whole enterprise, so I was surprised when one night he came up to me while I was working in the snack bar before it started getting busy, and he just started talking to me. Not chit-chat, either, but a real, in-depth conversation. I was shocked. I will always remember that conversation like it happened yesterday. I just listened in amazement as he opened up to me in ways a grown man just doesn't usually converse with kids. His words remain emblazoned in my memory from that night, and they made up for all the ugly times when some tourist would abuse me about not putting mustard on her hotdog.

Before I could step out from behind the snack bar counter and go out and amaze the audience with my jet skiing over the jump ramp, skiing in the flagline, performing in the criss-cross slalom act, knee boarding over the jump ramp, performing in the ballet line, doing a solo-jump act, skiing on a canoe paddle, sometimes performing in the clown act, doing doubles lifts with a guy, dazzle the crowd in a solo-barefooting act, ramp jumping with the guys in the jump act and climbing to the top of the human pyramid, before I would perform that evening, Wayne Shank said something that meant the world to me then, and still does to this day. "Shellie, you know I've watched you from the sidelines all these years. I feel bad I didn't do more for you," he said, pausing. "I wish... I wish I had done more for you."

My mind was whirling as he continued. "See, you and I"—another pause—"you and I, we're cut from the same cloth, aren't we?" He flashed me a big old grin, nodding his head yes to his own question. Then he started tearing up, and so I started tearing up, then he walked away. Later that same night after the show, our ski show director—Wayne Shank's son—called a skier's meeting. He announced to all of us that his dad had lung cancer.

Wayne Shank died a few years after that. I didn't go to his funeral, but I parked across the street from the church, sat in my car by myself, and said my own "Goodbye." Nova now reminded me of Wayne Shank, and I was feeling all dreamy and nostalgic when I heard my name.

"Shellie, this is when you will jump." Mark's voice and the word "jump" snapped me back to reality. The concept of the new Ski Fever show was to upgrade the whole pace of the show into a fever pitch. In years past, there were fast parts of the ski show and then the slower acts involving the ballet line and the girls skiing. The idea of this new show was that from beginning to end, it would be action-packed. Definitely my kind of show, but I think it put off some of the older skiers, who wanted to stick with the traditional show format.

Because there were the two big stadiums, one to the left as you were facing the show circle (the South Stadium) and one to the right (the North Stadium), the two show styles would be competing with each other for the audience. Every aspect of show water-skiing would thereafter be a sort of competition between the two stadiums and their two skiing teams: the North Stadium was the Blue Team, and the South Stadium was the Red Team. It would be North against South all over again, every day, though without the bloodshed.

When we arrived at work each day, the first thing we did was go to the end of the hallway just outside the office where there was a podium with the work schedule written out. That way we would find out what team we were on that day, and our number would directly correlate to which specific acts we were to ski. There might be some bartering throughout the day and switching of numbers—if both skiers could ski the act and agreed to it. The A-team skied for all the star acts that came from the North Blue team stadium. And the B-team skied for…well, let's just say that the South did lose the Civil War. I tried to convey to the powers that be there might be a better way to describe our teams so as to not demoralize people routinely put on the B-team, but no one was interested in my point of view so I let it go. I was on the B-team, and I and the rest of the B-teamers often joked that we should print up T-shirts but we never did. I didn't care. I was proud to be on the B-team because it allowed me to jump.

The show format was fairly simple. After the ballet line performed and we had landed and taken our bows, the two announcers would start arguing back and forth between the stadiums. The argument would escalate until it ended in a jump challenge. Our announcer in the South Stadium would say, "The Red Team challenges the Blue Team to a jump contest. And we don't just have boys who jump. We also have a *girl*." By this time, I would have already put on protective wetsuit bottoms over my ballet costume and slipped down to the edge of the stage to dunk my water-ski jump bindings in the water; they are absolutely impossible to get on if they are dry. I would have donned my protective helmet—reddish pink, of course—over my pony tail, and racing to get my ski gloves on, which help with gripping the ski rope. I had to hurry to do all that before the announcer pointed at me and said, "And there she goes!"

I would ski off the stage onto the water. The boat would pull me around and I would perform a distance jump, a helicopter, or a front-flip, depending on the skill level of the guy skier on the Blue Team from North Stadium. If it was Mark Vosaird, my ski show boss, I had to lessen my ability and only do a helicopter off the red ramp on the South side of the show circle, so that he could come back and beat me with a front-flip. Most of the time, the scheduling was set up so that the Blue Stadium skier could do a back-flip—a gainer. In that case, I could perform the more spectacular of my jumps, the front-flip. Every once in awhile, there would be a slip up in communication or a last-minute change and I wouldn't realize that the Blue Team skier couldn't do a back-flip. I always wanted to do the harder and more spectacular front- flip, and sometimes without realizing it I ended up forcing the competition jump act into a tie. When that happened, the North Stadium announcer just adjusted the script and adlibbed something. "Well our jumper performed his front-flip farther."

After the Blue Team jumper landed, he would circle right back by the dock of the Red Team and a girl from the Red Team would jump on his back and act like she was mad at him for beating our team. This was the clown act, modified—but not so modified that it still didn't end with the Blue Team guy dumping the Red Team girl in the water for laughs.

Sometimes, I got the number that corresponded to the clown act, which meant that after I landed my front-flip in the jump competition act, I would ski onto the North Stadium dock and be quick-released from the boat so that I could ski right up onto the North Stadium back dock and jump out of my skis, holding onto the handle so that my rope would drag behind me through the hallway until it was safely out of the water and anyone's way. The quick-release is a mechanism on the boat pylon that enables the shotgun rider to quick-release the tow rope from the boat. For example, if one girl in the ballet line falls while performing a trick with the handle on her foot, all the skiers in the line have to be quick-released or the fallen ballet girl will be dragged by her foot. Believe me, this is very scary, and if you are not released soon enough you can really tweak your knee and do some real damage.

Another reason to be quick-released was when the guy skiers were doing adagio lifts similar to what you would see in doubles ice-skating, but on the water. The harness on the guy skier's upper body allow him to have both hands free to lift the girls. If the guy skier falls he has no way to release himself from the boat, so the shotgun rider must be alert and do it for him using the quick-release. And freestyle aerial jumps should always be on quick-release, too. In those, you're traveling anywhere from 35 to 40 mph over a 6-foot jump ramp. You're twisting and turning around your rope and rope handle, so that there is always the potential for you to get caught up in the rope mid-air, or to land awkwardly and get tangled in the rope. You always want the most experienced shotgun rider on your quick-release, someone you trust and preferably a rider who knows how the trick you are performing or practicing is supposed to go and recognize instantly when there's a problem.

When I was scheduled with the number for the clown act, after I jumped I would land on the dock at the North Stadium and be quick-released. I then had to run all the way to the South Stadium dock, about 250 or 300 yards away, and I would barely make it in time to jump on the back of the Blue Team skier to finish out the clown act by being dumped in the water by the skier who had just beat me in the competition. Whew!

That was all put to a stop one day. Nova was coming down to see how things were progressing with the new Ski Fever show and I ran smack into him in the hallway, dragging my jump rope behind me after being-quick released on the back dock. He realized that I was performing back-to-back acts and exclaimed, "What is this, the Shellie Blum show?" From that day forward, my friend Betty Bonifay stepped in to help me. After that, if I drew the clown act number, Betty volunteered to do it for me so I could still jump. I will never forget her generosity. That was Betty, always putting others before herself and doing what was best for the show.

The only other way a girl skier got both her first and last name mentioned was if she was given the star ballerina number, or if she was in the adagio acts. But even in the adagio acts, she had to share the spotlight with the guy skier who was lifting her. Imagine nine or ten girls every day vying for the one spot in the show where they could shine and really show off their skiing ability. Now try at the same time not to think "cat fight"—it's nearly impossible. But I will say that except for that, I loved my fellow "World Famous Aquamaids," as we were called. There was a lot of camaraderie.

I worked hard on my Star Ballerina swivel skiing but it was never acknowledged. During the whole time I worked at Cypress Gardens I was never allowed to do the Star swivel act. Wait! That's not true, I was allowed to do the Star Swivel act but just one time. On my one special day there was a hurricane coming and there were literally 3 to 4 foot swells from the wind. In the first show, the girl who skied the Star Swivel Act fell. In the second show another Star Swiveler's attempt was unsuccessful, by the third water ski show of the day, no one wanted to do the act, my hand shot up and I said enthusiastically, "I'll do it!" It wasn't the prettiest of Star Swivel acts, but I didn't fall. The fourth show of the day, the ski show was cancelled. The only time I remember Cypress Gardens closing down due to the hurricane weather. I admit I was never the most graceful of Swivel skiers, but like I always did with my skiing, I pushed the limits.

At the time most girls were working on 360 degree turns called "overheads", which meant you pulled the rope over your head and spun 360 degrees under it kind of like a pirouette in ballet, or maybe equivalent to the ice skating jumping terminology, the "axle". If you were really good, you could do a "720" which would be two turns with one pull of the rope, or the ice skating term, the "double axle". There were a few girls, at that time in 1988, that were doing a "1080" which would have been three rotations from one pull of the rope, or the ice skating term "triple axle". But what I was doing is what I called "never ending turns", which meant with one pull of my rope I could muscle as many turns as I wanted. I lost track after about 7 or 8 rotations. A few people knew and saw me do this, but to this day, I have never gotten credit for it.

I was not the Nancy Kerrigan type of graceful Star Swivel water skier, but more of a Tonya Harding who to my knowledge was the first female to push for the "quad" jump in ice skating but minus me trying to bash anyone's knees over it. Because I had my jumping, I didn't feel the need to compete for and fight to do the Star Swivel Act.

I was what I called in Show Water Skiing an "A to B Water Skier" meaning it was more important to me not to fall, to make it from point A to point B, namely the stage for my bow. I doubt Fred and Ethel sitting in the stands from Sioux City, Iowa would realize that my style and grace seemed a bit lacking. Ethel would not turn to Fred and say, "Oh my God Fred, did you see that! That Star Swivel girl didn't point her toe all the way through her turn!" She might however say, "Oh no! Fred, she fell, she's not supposed to be sitting in the water like that waiting for the boat, Aww! That's so sad, poor thing." Yep, I was definitely an A to B water skier.

Not long after they put a stop to me doing the jump act competition and the clown act back-to-back (which for one thing would have meant a girl getting her first and last name mentioned more than once in the show), the media department sent a memo to the ski department. The media department, which had its own bosses and controlled its own destiny, had decided that they wanted to use me in a media blitz. During front dock morning stretch, Mark came out holding a piece of paper.

"The media department is gonna film you all day," he said, dropping the paper into my lap where I was sitting with the soles of my feet pressed together, bouncing my knees up and down.

I read the memo.

> As discussed, we are planning our 1987 Northeast media tour. This year's will be conducted a bit earlier based on recent research, which indicates vacation planning up North is generally done 2–4 months in advance. We have slated Apr. 27–May 1and May 4–8 as our travel dates. We appreciate your consent for us to use Shellie from water-ski as we feel she would provide us with a unique athletic angle to pitch to sports editors and sportscasters.

> She will also be promoting the new ski show! Please be aware we will be scheduling video and photo sessions with her in the next several days. We will also be taping her in the ski show in general. Thanks in advance for your department's cooperation. I'm confident we'll see terrific results. Cc: B. Smith, S. DeWoody, L. Novakofski and M. Voisard, Louise Murtaugh.

It took a moment for the enormity of what I had just read to sink in. "What?"

"Yeah, I guess they are gonna send you all over to talk about the new Ski Fever show—you know to try and bring more people into the park?" he said. "In between all the shows today they're gonna bring a film crew down here to video you skiing. I guess you'll bring the video with you on the talk shows."

I was in shock. Film crew? Talk shows? Media blitz? As Mark was walking away I yelled after him. "What about Ballet practice?"

"Skip it. Stay here and play football with us," he said.

How cool was that? My boss was going to let me skip ballet practice and play football instead. Usually after morning workout and before the first ski show, we girls had to drive to a dance studio for ballet practice. It wasn't that I didn't like ballet practice; it was just that I felt like we were all suffering delusions of grandeur to think we could be anywhere in the class of real ballerinas. It made me feel like a poser, similar to the weird feeling I had when after the ski show we were involved in a "meet and greet." I didn't mind the chatting and answering questions, but when people would asked for an autograph I felt funny about it. I mean, I was just a water-skier.

It was the same in the ballet studio. I'd be prancing across the floor trying to perform grand jetes and catch sight of myself in the mirror, and I just couldn't take myself too seriously. Some of the girls were very serious and I was happy for them, but somehow the more serious I tried to be the more my reflection would make me just stop and burst out laughing. That would always elicit the frustrated "clap, clap" from the instructor, Annie Campbell—bless her heart for putting up with me. But all in all, I learned a lot from Annie and her dance studio. The most important part, and I did take this seriously, was the perfect synchronization of our arm ballet movements. I would never have to grand jete on the water, but I did want our ballet line to be best in the world.

Believe me, there is nothing like the sight of seven or eight or even nine girls coming at you all on one ski, all of them performing perfectly synchronized choreographed ballet arm movements in complete harmony. We were the best in the world! That was thanks to Nova's, our very own Lynn Novakofski's influence. He didn't stand at fifth-position attention all the time for nothing.

So for that one day, I got to play flag football with the guys. It was great fun. I even remember throwing a touchdown pass to Punky. Then the filming crew came down to the ski stadium. I had no idea what they wanted me to do. Finally one of the camera guys asked, "Well, can you do tricks on the skis?"

"Yes. Of course, I can. Do you guys want me to trick ski?"

They all said yes, so I went inside to find some trick skis, which have no rudder on the bottom so they can slide around on the water easier. But I couldn't find a matching pair. That made me a little nervous, as I wasn't very good on trick skis, and though I could perform on a single trick ski that would have increased the likelihood of me falling. Actually, I hadn't skied on trick skis at all in several years. I didn't mind falling, but I didn't want to start out that way. I figured as the day progressed I would get into my harder, more spectacular skiing. So I reluctantly dragged out the two unmatched trick skis, hoping my camera debut was not going to be a catastrophe. As it turned out, by the end of the ski session I was even having a little bit of fun, twisting and turning and even twisting over the boat wake—a move known as a "wake 180 out" or, if you're coming back into the wake, a "wake 180 in." The boat brought me back to the dock, and I skied right onto the landing ramp without even so much as getting my hair wet.

"Shellie, we want to see that barefooting stuff," said the cameraman. "We hear you can do that. Will you do that for us?"

I told him sure, and said I would do a running start, deep-water take-off, and ski around the show circle. I pointed to the end of the landing ramp dock where I had just finished trick skiing to show where I'd start, then circled my arm around the whole cove or show circle to explain how I would make the big loop and land back where I started. This was a difficult act for anyone who had done it several times, but I hadn't yet tried it at Cypress Gardens! During that same type of act in Missouri our show circle had gone counterclockwise, but the boat at Cypress Gardens would be pulling me clockwise. That might seem like a small enough difference, but when your body is used to the centrifugal forces pushing it one way, you get use to it. Going the opposite way, I knew I would have to adapt—on the fly.

The boat took off, I ran down the ramp, and jumped into the water, landing flat on my back and wrapping my feet over the towrope. I waited for the boat speed to pick up, then took my feet off the rope, placed the heels of my feet in the water and slowly started to stand up on my bare feet. The different boat direction did almost make me fall as the centrifugal force unexpectedly threw me outside the wake, but I managed to catch my balance and settle into my ride around the lake, even letting go with one hand at one point to fix my hair as naturally as if I had been on skis. I barefooted around the lake and landed back where I started. *Whew! I made it. I had not fallen.*

We went again and did the same thing but from a different camera angle. The first camera angle had been from inside the boat; the second one was from the shore. I made both trips around the lake without falling, although the second trip around was harder because I hadn't rested in between, and now I was fighting the boat wakes from my first path around. Especially toward the end of the filming you can see me starting to grimace when I see my previous boat wakes coming right at me, but once I made it through I relaxed, smiled, and waved for the camera.

After that the camera crew asked me to jump, which was what they really came to see. So I put on my protective jump wetsuit, which has extra padding in the butt and chest areas, both protection but also to keep you floating as easily as would a regular Coast Guard–approved safety jacket. I put on my jump helmet but I didn't wear any gloves that day; I thought the photos and filming would be better and more feminine without them. I took off from the dock sitting down, and immediately waved back at the camera. I did a long-distance jump over the ramp, and when they pulled me back around and I did a helicopter off the same ramp and then, after going around again, a front-flip. The helicopter and front-flip were history being filmed: the first such jumps caught on official film of a female water-ski jumper.

The media department took all my water-skiing footage from that day and spliced it up, matching it to an up-beat, up- tempo song written especially for the Ski Fever show. The result was a cool little video almost three minutes long that I got to take with me for the "media blitz." I got to do a number of talk shows, and I almost made it on the David Letterman show, but I'm pretty sure I was bumped for some "real" celebrity, not just some chick who water-skied. I got to ride in a limo in New York City, where I took pictures of people trying to look in through the tinted glass at me. I did a couple of radio talk shows—the video wasn't much use there—and I remember looking up in wonder at the ABC building and Radio City Music Hall. It felt like a dream. I did the best I could in the interviews, and I had hoped I didn't come off as sounding too hokey. I just kept trying to remember that I was there as a pitchman, or rather as a pitch*woman*, and that I was there to sell the new ski show at the new and improved Cypress Gardens. I really did want everyone to think they had to come to Florida to see what we had to offer. And the Ski Fever show *was* good: we had record attendance the years I worked at Cypress Gardens.

When I returned to Cypress Gardens after the media tour, though, the atmosphere and attitude around the ski department was cooler toward me. It wasn't so much that everyone gave me the cold shoulder, but some of the skiers were a little put off by the attention that a "rookie" was garnering. I couldn't express to them that although I was new to Cypress Gardens, I was not a rookie performer. I knew that if I had tried to explain it that way, it might only make things worse, so I just stayed at my end of the girls' locker room with my fellow B-teamers. We cranked up my jam box on "Don't Worry, Be Happy." We were.

Soon after my return, the girls were all excited because we were getting new bathing suits. I was the last one to get her suit, and when the girls' lead handed it to me I noticed that it seemed kind of big. The label said size 12. I could make do with a size 10, but I was comfortable in a size 8, though if I had to I could squeeeeeeeeze into a size 6. Had they just run out of suits? Was the girls' lead trying to make me feel bad? Did she want me to think I was a big girl?

I never did know what happened, but Gayle Millis offered to swap out her size 10. Gayle was tall for a show skier, and it was hard for her to keep her weight down. She was a solid skier, but never quite made the A-team. We became close friends very fast, and she confided a lot in me about her dieting and exercising to try and keep her weight down. She got teased about her weight, and it really crushed her. Sometimes she just wouldn't eat, and other times I would catch her binging. One thing she had confided was that her dad had molested her when she was a child, and I am sure this added to all her insecurities.

Gayle and I hung out together after work. We'd go to the bar across the street from the parking lot of Cypress Gardens called the Ski One Lounge. One night as we sat at the bar, Gayle started crying. I tried to talk with her, but all I could get out of her between sobs and sniffling was that she heard people were talking about her weight and were saying that she and I seemed too close for comfort and that maybe we were gay.

I shrugged. "You know how I feel about you, and I know how you feel about me, and that's all that matters. Let them play their little games all they want, we'll just keep 'em guessing, won't we?" I joked. "Come on—we've got some major flirting to do. Look over there!" I pointed in the direction of some cute guys by the pool table. This seemed to cheer her up, if only for the moment.

The next day, at the morning stretch out, Gayle made sure she sat really far away from me. *That's okay*, I thought, *she has to do what makes her comfortable*. I sat there feeling a little sad, doing my soles-together knee bounce, when Nova comes walking up onto the stage. He leaned over and kind of whispered in certain skiers' ears, including mine: "Do you have a passport?" I said no. He said, "Well, then, you better get one, because you are going to Jordan to ski for King Hussein."

In several of the years past, Cypress Gardens had sent a small crew over to perform ski shows for King Hussein. How lucky for us—King Hussein was a big fan of show water-skiing and an avid water-skier himself. Before we left for Jordan, Mark pulled me aside in the hallway and told me that along with performing ski shows, there was going to be a ski race in honor of King Hussein's birthday. The race was something new and Mark wondered if I wanted to be on one of the teams. He explained that each team would have three people on it—one to drive, one to watch, and one to ski—and that all three could rotate in and out as needed when the skier got tired. The race would go from the water-ski resort at the tip of the Gulf of Aqaba in the Red Sea to a little island outside of Egypt and back. Nobody knew how long it would take, because this was something new.

"Count me in!" I said. "Do you think it would be okay if I skied the whole race by myself?"

He laughed at me and was sure I was joking. Then he gave me a funny look. "It's supposed to be over 50 miles, you know. It's a race but it's like a marathon to Egypt and back!" He walked away chuckling to himself. I was chuckling to myself, too.

The flight to Jordan seemed to take forever. We flew from Orlando to New York, from New York to London, then from London to Amman, the capital of Jordan. I knew nothing about what to expect. At the time I barely knew the difference between King Hussein of Jordan and Saddam Hussein of Iraq, but everyone kept telling me, "Don't worry, we're skiing for the good guy."

When we finally landed in Amman, I couldn't help but think that I had just stepped into the movie *Lawrence of Arabia*. We took a bus to the beach resort of Aqaba, right at the tip of the Gulf of Aqaba.

As you looked out from the beach resort dock you could see parts of Israel, Egypt, and Saudi Arabia. We met the owner of the Aqua Marina Hotel, Simon Khoury, and I started to understand his connection to Cypress Gardens: throughout the history of Cypress Gardens, many celebrities as well as dignitaries have visited or laid claim to skiing there, including King Hussein, and his son the successor, King Abdullah II. Cypress Gardens opened on January 2, 1936, as a botanical garden planted by Dick Pope Sr. and his wife Julie. Many movies have been filmed there, including a string of Esther Williams classics. Elvis Presley and Johnny Carson both skied at Cypress Gardens. The Water-ski Capital of the World's heritage, and infamy, runs deep. Anyway, Simon Khoury, the hotel owner and host of His Majesty King Hussein's Birthday and International Water- Ski Festival in Aqaba, Jordan, on November 14–16, 1987, skied at Cypress Gardens at one time. I cannot pinpoint when, whether it was in the 1940s, 1950s, 1960s, or 1970s, that Simon Khoury skied at Cypress Gardens, "back in the day." And it meant a lot to him.

The race meant a lot to all of us, so it's painful to talk about. After the water-ski race marathon to Egypt and back, a reporter interviewed me, and even now when I think of it I remember how fuming mad I felt after the race, and boy, I was fuming mad! What follows is the article he wrote for Water-ski International magazine:

> *Water-ski International* was at the 15th annual water-ski festival in Aqaba, Jordan, this year to help King Hussein celebrate his 52nd birthday. And we left him with a present, too, a shattered windshield in his Barefoot Nautique—one of about 35 small and large boats he owns.
>
> Editor Chris Boiling joined a team of show skiers from Florida's Cypress Gardens in a nine-boat ski race to Pharaoh Island in Sinai and back to Aqaba, a distance of about 40 kilometers. They had gone about a third of the way when disaster struck. "The Red Sea had turned quite choppy by this stage," said Chris. "We took off from one wave and nosedived into the next. We were swamped with water and broken glass. There was nothing else we could do but haul in the skier, John Fendt, and return to the starting point at the Aquamarina Hotel, where the King was waiting to applaud the winners. The driver, Neil Albright, had cuts over his face; it was a good job he was wearing sunglasses, because he even had glass down his wetsuit. The observer, Kim Zimmerman,

had glass splinters and cuts in her leg. I'd escaped quite lightly with just a few small cuts on my neck and left hand. But our problems weren't over then. On the way back we strayed into Israeli waters and were chased by a gunboat whose crew politely told us where to go."

"The other two American teams fared much better, taking first and second places. First were Joel Baker, Robert (Punky) Forgiana and Craig Lesser. Behind them were an all-girl team of Shellie Blum, Cheryl Orloff and Carmen Padilla. Twenty -three-year-old Shellie skied the whole way without falling once. She is a truly remarkable skier. In the Cypress Gardens show she does the ballet on swivel skis, barefoots, takes part in the pyramid (now up to five tiers), and is one of the Rampmasters. She can already do helicopters and forward flips and is working on a gainer/backward somersault. She is probably the best if not the only female freestyle skier in the world, and certainly one of the most versatile. Third home—and first of the six Jordanian teams to complete the course—was Prince Abdullah. Prince Mir'ed Ra'ad was sixth. Three teams dropped out altogether."

You might wonder why when the reporter/editor interviewed me after the race, I was fuming mad. Here is what the article didn't say. When the "all-girl team" landed at the dock, Simon Khoury yelled to my boat driver, "No, no you have not finished the race—you have to go out and around that buoy out there!" and he pointed to a buoy about 50 yards away from the dock. I was sitting in the water at the edge of the dock from which I had taken off for the race, thinking, *How can this be?* I had just skied non-stop for almost 2 hours in the Red Sea and now that man was yelling that I had to get back up and ski around a buoy 50 yards away? It didn't make sense. We had completed a big circle to Egypt and back. When we left the dock in the first place we had gone past the buoy he was pointing to; then I skied to Egypt and came back, past another buoy on the other side of the starting dock. We made one giant circle, so why did we have to go back out and around the buoy we had already passed at the start? At the time, I was just tired and confused, but knew for sure I would do what he told us because I wanted to finish the race.

In the beginning of the race, the water wasn't so rough near the hotel, but once we got out into the Red Sea, it was really, really, really choppy. I was maneuvering the giant swells on my jumpers. The Red Sea swells were so huge—9 to 10 feet high in some places—that I sometimes lost complete sight of the boat that was pulling me! They probably wondered sometimes if I was even still back there, but they could tell I was since the rope was still taut. For my own part, I would be staring at the rope coming through the middle or top of a swell and in an instant I would try to figure out the best way up the swell and then back down. It was a little like a cross between surfing and skiing snow moguls: sometimes I would bust through or pop off the top of the swell and then either land off the top onto another wave, or end up at the bottom of another swell. Or I would have to find a way to work my way up the swell and then ski down the other side of a giant wave. It was terrifying.

Once I reached that stage of the race, I knew I would have to ski the whole way by myself, because even though Cherie Orloff, my observer, and Carmen Padilla, my boat driver, were excellent top-notch water-skiers, I knew there would be no way they could handle these 9-to-10 foot swells. I was hanging on by sheer survival instinct.

At times I really feared for my life—not just because of the waves but because there were several huge gunboats following us for quite some time. They had their guns pointed at us and were yelling and shouting in their foreign language to me. I couldn't figure out if they were flirting with me or threatening to kill me, but I damn sure knew I was going to do everything in my power not to fall. I just kept skiing, and every once in a while, when the rough water would allow me to let go with one hand, I would flash a peace sign up to the gun boats chasing or following us. I'll never know which it was.

As we got closer to the end and back to the starting dock, the Red Sea was not so rough. I looked over to my left and saw the all American-guy team. I thought, "How could that be? They started before us?" And why had they stopped? It looked like one of them had fallen, and they were switching skiers. I said to myself, "Just get me back to the dock, Carmen." She did, which is where I was sitting when Simon told us we had to go back out and around that damn buoy.

My boat had been running non-stop for around 2 hours. When Carmen tried to restart it, though, it had had enough. It wouldn't start, and now the boat was floating over our rope. The boat wouldn't start, and the rope was caught up on the prop, and I was sitting in the water being told I had not finished the race. I started yelling.

"Come on! This is bullshit! Please, please, Carmen! Start the damn thing!"

My crewmates finally untangled the rope, then they got the boat started. I got back up and went around the extra buoy after sitting in the water—done with the race, as far as I was concerned—for over 10 minutes. The all-American guy team supposedly beat the all-American girl team by 1 minute and 39 seconds. To add insult to injury, later when King Hussein was handing out the trophies on the dock, he smiled and grabbed the biggest trophy from the table and handed it to the guy skiers. When he started to grab the second-biggest trophy from the table, Simon stepped in. He handed the King the smallest trophy from the table, and the King then handed that tiny trophy to me. I bowed my head. As I took the trophy, I said, "I am so sorry for my language while I was sitting in the water at the dock."

The King smiled, and replied in a very thick accent. "Don't worry, my dear. I have said much, much worse."

I next moved on to Queen Noor, who was taking off her sunglasses for a more personal greeting with me. I shook her hand, bowed my head, and said the same thing, "I am so sorry for my language while sitting in the water at the dock."

She was born in Washington, DC, so her accent was no problem. "It's okay. Congratulations for skiing the whole way by yourself. That's just so amazing!"

I have never been so proud and angry at the same time. How could I start after the first place team, finish before them, and end up in second place? Later that evening, we were at the resort bar listening to the band play cover songs like Madonna's "La Isla Bonita," and

I noticed that my ankles and feet were swelling. My legs were really sore, and I worried that I might not be able to perform for the King's Birthday the next day. I had a rum and coke, and naturally my soreness started to feel better. I kept drinking to self-medicate, but not so much that I would be hung over. Fortunately, I performed my helicopters and front-flips in the ski shows the next day for the King and Queen, and I never fell once.

The rest of the trip we were given time to sightsee, and everyone was excited about seeing one of the "New Seven Wonders of the World," Petra. Everyone went but me: I stayed back and taught five guys I had befriended from the resort how to jump. They knew how upset I was about the race, so they went out especially for me and had a small trophy painted to say, in Arabic, that it was for second place. The trophy the King had handed me didn't even have any writing on it. They also gave me another little trophy just for me that said this:

To: Shellie Blum, "Rampmaster"
Thanks, Coach
From: Jordanian Rampmasters "To Be"

While I was with my Jordanian buddies in the town, I noticed that there were few women on the streets, and the few who were there wore traditional hijabs. They were not allowed to walk even with the men, they had to walk behind. Somehow the few that were outside started making their way towards us. One woman came up to me and started touching my shoulder, so did her friend, another touched my forearm, then one other woman joined in. I asked Madji, one of my new friends who could actually speak English, "Why are they doing this?"

He said, "They want to touch you because they know you touched the King. Also, because they know you're the girl that skied all the way to Pharoah's Island by yourself, the water touching the shores of Mount Sinai" Then I asked, "What is Mount Sinai?" Madji said back to me with a tone of disbelief, "That's the mountain that your Bible says Moses brought down the Ten Commandments, it's also near where he parted the Red Sea." Madji laughed and said with an even thicker, more deliberate, Arabic accent then his normal voice, "You didn't know you were skiing in Holy water!"

I came away from the whole Jordanian experience thinking how differently, and yet in a profound way, how much the same women get treated all over the world. The impact of knowing how lucky I was compared to the second-class treatment of some of the other women in different parts of the world would sadden me and stay with me forever. But, I would carry some pride and honor in knowing that in that small moment of time and space, I may have impacted their lives to show them that women, too, can be bold and do brave things.

That being said, I will always remember the race to Egypt and back as similar to Aesop's fable, The Tortoise and The Hare, only the Tortoise was female, therefore wasn't allowed to win.

When we got back to Cypress Gardens, it wasn't long before I bumped into Nova. He congratulated me on my skiing. "I heard you did pretty good over there." Nova never said much, so this was actually a pretty big compliment for him.

"Thank you. I guess I did." I was waiting for him to say something about my cursing in front of the King and Queen. I was all prepared to explain myself—that I had no idea the King and Queen were on the dock that day—but he didn't mention it. I was glad of that.

What he did say surprised me. "What's next? What are you going to do for an encore?"

I didn't miss a beat. "I'm gonna learn my back-flip, so I'll have three freestyle tricks to qualify and be the first girl to challenge the men on the 'Coors Light Freestyle Water-ski Pro Tour.'"

"If you can do that, you might be able to get some sponsors and endorsements," he said.

"Hmmm, I think you're right. But for right now, I'll be lucky to find someone to drive for me and ride pin for me."

Nova smiled. "Yeah, good luck with that." He started to walk away. His smile meant good luck finding the driving and rider, not so much learning my back-flip or the gainer. I think he knew I would master that.

When I went into the hallway, I saw all the girls in front of the mirrors practicing their ballet arm movements. I heard the girls' lead ask, "Where's Shellie?"

"She said she was going to practice jumping," said Gayle.

The girls' lead response was snide. "Well, I guess we have to let her do that."

I went into the locker room and sat with my jump wetsuit on, staring into the mirror, concentrating hard. I put a tape cassette into my jam box, and cued up Madonna's "Over and Over." The lyrics of that song helped psych me up. While I listened and concentrated, I put on my ski gloves and helmet, almost like I was preparing for battle. I poked my head into the guy's locker room and yelled, "Hey? Is there anyone in there who can pull me jumping?"

There had been hustling and bustling noises a moment before, but it went dead quiet. I heard someone say "shhhh" to the others.

"Come on!" I yelled. "I know you are in there. Just someone come pull me. And I need a pin rider, too. Please?" I don't know who said what to whom in there, but finally Dave Dotter and Joel Baker came out.

Joel said, "I'll drive."

Dave said, "I'll ride."

Dave Dotter was one of the few guys who could perform the gainer, so I was glad to hear he would be riding for me. Joel Baker was one of those guys who refused to believe I could jump with him, but in the end I think I had won him over, and it didn't hurt that I would do his jump number in the four-man jump act for him on days that his back was sore from doing the bottom middle of our four-tier pyramid.

Joel was one of our big guys. The big guys didn't normally specialize in freestyle jumping; in fact, they usually didn't care if they jumped at all. And if your back is sore, the crushing landings in jumping can really hurt your back. Joel was there to lift the girls. We had a couple guys who I'm guessing weighed between 200 and 220. I remember one day when the Florida Seminoles Football team was visiting Cypress Gardens, and in between ski shows, the quarterbacks from the team were throwing a football to a couple of our guy skiers who were wearing their double harnesses so that their hands were free to try and catch the ball as they skied by the stage on the water. They kept missing the catch, bungling the ball. I remembered my dad saying to my brothers when he coached them for Pop Warner Football when we were young. If he said it once, he said it a hundred times. He was pounding it into my brother's head, "If you can touch it, you can catch it!" I was pacing on the stage and jealous, I wanted to try to catch it, but had never worn a double harness, so I talked Joel into carrying me on his shoulders.

As we came by the stage one of the quarterbacks threw the ball, it was a little behind me so I had to lean really far back on Joel's shoulders so much so that he rocked back, the front of his skis pulled off the water and I was sure we were going to fall backwards but we didn't fall. I snatched the ball out of the air for the first successful land to water catch! The rest of the team standing on the stage and sitting in the stadium, jumped up, clapped, whooped and hollered with cheers for the first successful catch. And unless he wasn't there because he was practicing for baseball, Football Hall of Famer, Deion Sanders was one of those football players yelling and cheering for Joel and me. Like I said, Joel was one of our big guys.

This was probably around the same time the girls had started training me to do the middle of the bottom tier of girls in the pyramid. Here's how it was structured: Picture four of the strongest men on the bottom of the pyramid—the absolute biggest and strongest in the middle of the four guys on the bottom. The next tier is three girls, the strongest or biggest girl being in the middle on that tier, then you have two light girls on the third tier, standing on top of the three girls just below, and then you have the final girl, the smallest girl, on the fourth tier, the top. The lightest girl who climbs to the top rides on the shoulders of the girl on the bottom for a little, so that middle-bottom girl has to be pretty strong.

In Missouri, I always climbed to the top of our three-tier pyramid, so I went from the top of the pyramid to the bottom middle at Cypress Gardens. This change would offend most ski girls, but I didn't mind; whatever position they would put me in, I would do it to the best of my ability. I concentrated especially hard on pulling my legs together so that the two middle guys below me didn't have to struggle to keep the pyramid together. Several guys told me that when I did the middle of the pyramid I made it easier for them, and that made me proud. Every day before each ski show—and we usually did four a day—I did 100 stomach crunches, telling myself over and over, "Strong back, strong skier." Many skiers have back problems. I never did.

Anyway, Joel and Dave were the ones who volunteered to help me work on my gainers. I told Joel to pull me 36 mph, the speed at which the guys did their gainers in the jump act. I cut both wakes before the ramp and at the bottom of the ramp, dropped the handle, and at the top of the ramp I used both hands and my head and throw myself backwards. I flew through the air and then landed SMACK on my back. The boat circled back to me and Dave said, "That looked like it hurt. Maybe you should go in?"

"Two more," I said.

Carmen, who was practicing doubles on the front dock, ran into the hallway to yell to anyone listening, "You guys, come on! Shellie is trying gainers!"

All the guys hiding out in the locker room came hurrying and scurrying out to the front dock to watch. The girls practicing ballet arm movements in the hallway showed interest and followed. On my next gainer try, I cut across both wakes, dropped the handle, and threw my head back. That time I get a little more rotation and landed upside down, head first. SMACK.

I heard the skiers on the dock saying, "Ow!" "Ooooh!" and "God, that one must have hurt!" The boat circled back around and once again Dave asked if I was okay and if I was ready to quit.

"Nah, those kind don't hurt too bad," I said. "One more, then I'll go in." I got back up on my skis and tried one more. I cut across both wakes, dropped the handle, popped off the top of the ramp, and threw my head backwards. That time I got three-quarters of the way around, so my 6-foot jump skis stuffed their tips in the water and bowed my body backward like a banana. My chest and face slingshot back down into the water. SMACK.

I started rolling around in the water with that familiar moaning and groaning, the air knocked out of me. Joel sped the boat back to me. Dave said, "Shellie? Shellie? Are you All right?"

I moaned back to him, "Oh, God that hurt." I started to cough up a little blood, but that was a good sign: it meant I had regained my breath and was starting to recoup.

Dave said, "Oh shit, she's hurt. What are we gonna do? I think she's hurt real bad!"

From the water, I tried to calm Dave down. "It's okay, it's nothing. This has happened to me before, in Missouri," I said. "I just broke a few blood vessels in my chest. It'll go away—just give me a second." After a few more moments of rolling around in the water, I started to feel better. Dave and Joel helped me back into the boat and we putt-putted back to the starting dock. Dave had always been rooting for me; he was an A-teamer renegade. And I am pretty sure I won Joel over that day.

Every day after that I would go out and try three gainers. I learned how to fall in ways that didn't hurt quite as bad. After I threw my head back and would get about three-quarters of the way around, I would spot the water and instead of letting my skis stuff straight in I would twist to the right so that I would SMACK the water on my left side. It was still a hard fall, but it didn't knock the air out of me, and I didn't cough up any blood. I was just left with a huge bruise up and down the left side of my body.

A week or so later, when I was sitting in the girls dressing room playing Madonna's song "Over and Over" trying to get psyched up for my next round of three gainer attempts, I added something new to my psych-up routine. I bowed my head, shut my eyes, and with my hands cupped in prayer position said, "Dear God, I've never really tried to talk to you before. Well, there was that one time when I was a teenager, but we won't count that, because I've never really decided if you were around. But I've come up against something I can't overcome. I'm beginning to think a back-flip is impossible for a girl to make. I'm constantly arguing with the guys and try to explain the trick is harder for girls because of our lower center of gravity, but they think it's a cop-out. Maybe it is. I'm not so much afraid of failure, but I don't think my body can keep taking the beatings. If I don't at least get around to my skis today, I might have to start accepting the fact that girls weren't made for doing gainers and quit trying them. Or maybe you could help out. Well, ski ya later. Amen…or awomen. No offense, just a little humor."

I finished my prayer, and began suiting up for battle, donning my usual armor of wetsuit, helmet, and gloves. I had a new driver this day, Hank Amos. He was the newest guy skier and he was hot! Plus, he was a freestyle jumper. Both Dave Dotter and Hank Amos had water-skied on the Freestyle Pro Tour, and both could do a mobius—the next level freestyle trick a skier learned after the gainer. It was a full twisting back-flip, which means that you wrap the rope around your waist so that as you start the back-flip you can at the same time twist out of the wrapped rope performing a full twisting back-flip, or a mobius. So I had two of the best skiers in the world driving and riding in my boat for me this day.

My buddy Bob Forgiana—Bob was Punky's dad—wanted to tryout his new camera, so he rode in the boat too. Bob had taken me under his wing early on; he thought my long-distance jumping had potential to compete on the World Tour. He may have been right. The one time I entered a contest at Cypress Gardens, they measured me at 117 feet. It wasn't a sanctioned competition so wouldn't have been official, but it was the one time in my life I was measured for jumping. The world record for women in long distance jumping at the time was held by Deena Brush-Mapple at 156 feet. Maybe I could have been competitive in women's long distance jumping on the Water-ski Pro Tour, but I wanted to concentrate on the uniqueness of my freestyle jumping.

I had made my prayer, had my crew of three guys in the boat, and was set to make my three attempts at gainers, thinking if I don't at least get one ski under me, I might have to give up. Dave, Hank, and Bob had convinced me to stop dropping the rope at the bottom of the ramp. I thought they were crazy. I had always been told to drop the handle. They told me I was ready, and that I would never be able to land a back-flip if I didn't start holding onto the handle.

My first try was a complete bust. I cut across both wakes, got to the bottom of the ramp, and freaked out when I tried to hold onto the handle. It totally messed up my timing and I just went over the ramp and dropped the rope at the top. I didn't throw my head back at all. Nothing. I just landed straight up and down on the water without the rope in my hand.

The guys brought the boat back around, laughing. "Come on Shellie. You *have* to hold onto the handle. Don't be such a baby. Just do it!"

Familiar words to me. Come hell or high water, with that next gainer try, I would hold onto the rope. I cut across both wakes, held onto the rope at the bottom of the ramp, popped off the top of the ramp, and threw my head back. I didn't let go of the rope. When I saw the water coming at me about three-quarters of the way around I still had one hand on the handle and I could pull on it. This extra pull allowed me to get one ski down on the water. The other ski stuffed its tip, making me do a split, so when the boat pulled around, I was in some pain, but I was very excited.

"Did you see it, did you see it? I got one ski under me? I mean, ouch! But I got one ski under me! I can do this!" I told Hank, "Hit it." That means "go, boat!" in the ski world. The boat pulled me out of the water and I skied around for the setup. I cut both wakes, popped off the top of the ramp, let go with my left hand and held onto to the handle with my right. I threw my head back and made it all the way around—a full rotation!—and landed on both feet. I didn't quite get my left hand back onto the handle, so I lost my grip with my right hand and just kind of casually fell off to the right side. But it was an easy fall and for the first time since trying gainers, I fell with no pain. The boat circled me and I was screaming, "Again! Again! I am gonna make this one."

The guys are excited, too. Dave said, "See? I told you holding onto the handle would help. Whoever told you not to?"

"My boss in Missouri, and Scotty," I said. "Doesn't matter now, though. Again, again. Hit it!" I circled around for the setup. I cut both wakes, popped off the top of the ramp, threw my head back, and made the full rotation backwards. I came around with both feet under me, grabbed on tight to the handle with my free left hand, and skied away. I was screaming at the top of my lungs, jumping around on my skis. I looked up to the sky to thank God, then signaled the boat to take me in by patting the top of my helmet.

Unbelievably I made my first gainer when Bob Forgiana was riding in the boat filming me. When we made it inside under the stadium to the office podium, he filmed me some more, doing a short interview. "How do you feel about that... that new trick you just did? Let's hear it!"

I was trying to remain calm and seem humble but it was hard to contain my enthusiasm, so I simply said, "Good!"

Bob grinned. "Good? Do you feel good about it?"

I said back, as calmly as I could, "Yeah, I feel good."

Then I was interrupted by Dave and Hank yelling in the background. One of them screamed, "YEAH!"

So I cut back in. "Took me a long time to learn it, and a lot of bad falls." Bob asked if I felt that I had learned it, and I answered, "I think so. I think at least now I know it can be done, so I won't give up trying."

"But you did learn something today though, by making it."

"Oh, yeah." What an exciting moment in my life. Like it was destined to be, with Bob Forgiana catching my first history-making back-flip/gainer, then interviewing me afterwards. My prayer earlier that day in the locker room had been answered in a big way!

I walked slowly to the girls' locker room, sore, but very happy. Then suddenly Mark came charging out around the office door.

"What in the hell do you think you're doing?"

"I am walking to the girls' dressing room."

He shouts at me angrily. "Someone told me you are trying gainers!"

"Yeah, that's right," I said. "So what?"

By then Mark was basically yelling at me. "So what?" There was a pause like he was struggling for another thought. Then he screamed at me, "So what if you get hurt? I don't want to hear about or see you trying back-flips in MY show circle ever again!"

A crowd of skiers had gathered for the showdown. "Wait a minute," I said back loudly. "Let me understand this. You *schedule* back-flip practice for guys who don't even want to learn...who are scared shitless to learn...and who probably won't earn a penny more in pay if they *do* learn it. But you forbid me to learn? Now, why is that, Mark. Is it because it's the one trick *you* can't do—and maybe you're too old to do? Or are you too scared to try?"

He yelled back at me. "Why is the back-flip so important to you?"

I was about to cry, but I didn't dare. I tried to be tough instead. "Because unlike you, Mark, I refuse to be stagnant. I have dreams, and goals. I want to be the first girl to challenge the men on the freestyle Pro Tour! I have to have three tricks to qualify. I have to be consistent. You hired me as a jumper—let me jump!"

Mark got up in my face and said, "I'm warning you, Blum. If I hear of or see you doing gainers in my show circle, there will be hell to pay!" He turned around and started to walk down the hallway.

I called after him. "Speaking of pay ...oh yeah! It's been long past my 90-day probation. Where's my evaluation and that dollar-fifteen raise you promised me? I've stood by and watched all your favorite kiss-asses get *their* raises while I...I I've held up my end of our deal. I wonder who I need to talk to to get you to be fair."

Mark swung around, steaming mad. "You want fair? You want an evaluation? Tomorrow, after you punch in, you report directly to my office. I'll give you your evaluation," he said. "But today—you...leave...here... NOW!" He jabbed his finger at the door to punctuate every word.

I stomped off towards the girls' locker room. I threw my makeup, cassette tapes, and suits into my locker and slammed the door. I grabbed my purse and started to walk out, but Gayle pulled me aside.

"Shellie, I've been skiing here for 6 years. You can't fight them. Don't rock the boat."

"Gayle, I'm already in the boat, and I know it's gonna rock!" she grabbed my arm with a real look of concern, but I shrugged it off. "I'm okay. I'll see you tomorrow."

The next day I walked into the hallway and punched the time clock. I walked to the office, where I found Mark sitting behind his desk and the girls' lead sitting in a chair beside the desk. Mark motioned for me to sit in the chair opposite him. He then turned a piece of paper around on his desk and slid it towards me, asking me? "Shellie, have you ever heard of Norma Rae? I answered with a look that conveyed my thought, "*Duh*", but I said "Yes." Then he said, "Well, you wanted your evaluation, here it is. We all put it together. Read it, and sign it."

I grabbed the paper and started reading, I heard Mark and Lynn's voices in my head as I read the review. "Shellie has a good knowledge of her position, but has a hard time putting it into action. Shellie is always willing to take responsibility, but has a hard time conforming to our way of doing things. Shellie has to be reminded to be professional regarding her job. Shellie is a temperamental performer, and only gives her best when she feels like it. She needs to practice the female aspects of her job before jumping and barefooting (i.e. Swivel & doubles.) Shellie seems to have a problem conforming to our program, and is always trying to stir up the other employees into thinking the way she does. Shellie does not possess the prettiness, style and grace that is needed to fit in with the other female skiers. At times she finds it necessary to fight the system and tries to arouse others to her way of thinking. Shellie needs to adjust her priorities to meet "our" needs. I am suggesting a three-day suspension without pay for her outburst yesterday."

I was near tears, but would not let them fall. I angrily looked to the girls' lead. "Are you going to let him do this to me?" She said nothing and looked down. I looked at Mark and back at the girls' lead, shaking my head, no. After an awkward pause, I said to both of them, "This is a bunch of bullshit. I'm not signing anything. I see there is a space for employee comments. You're going to get a rebuttal."

I got up from the chair, giving them both one last look of disgust. When I walked out, I left the door open and walked straight to the Public Relations Department. There I sat down at an empty typewriter and inserted a blank piece of paper. I shut my eyes and took a deep breath. I opened my eyes, I let out my breath, and started typing, though as I did my eyes were welling up with tears.

I have never felt so unjustly reviewed in all my skiing career. Water-skiing professionally for 13 years, I can speak with experience. The above review is a vicious attack on my being. On a scale from 1-10, 10 unsatisfactory, my average score of 6.5 makes it appear as though I am incompetent as a skier and performer. It was written and assumed that I ski my best only when I want to ski my best. I can assure anyone that my performances are one hundred percent effort. There was no mention of my new skills and improvement, no mention of my dedication to ballet lessons, no regard to the publicity Cypress Gardens has received in being the employer of the only female freestyle waters ski ramp jumper in the world.

Instead, I feel, I have been punished by my male supervisor for my achievements as a female pioneering in a males-only sport. His attack on my femininity is totally unwarranted, and is only his opinion. I feel my female supervisors are aware of my abilities as a female performer, but are unable to voice their true opinions for they are threatened and intimidated by repercussions they would incur should they support me and disagree with their male supervisors. Furthermore, I have been misled as to my role in this job. I was originally hired as a female show jumper. However, I am never scheduled to jump, and must ask as a favor from my male peers to jump; even then, I am turned down.

Words describing me as "temperamental" in the review can only be used by those who understand and perpetrate the action.

The review has made it clear that I must "conform." If this means limiting my skills and ability to buffer my supervisor's ego at the expense of a more spectacular performance, I must question this conformity and my male supervisor's motives.

To put it simply, I have been labeled by my male supervisors and regardless of my practice and effort to be the model employee, I am involved in a vicious circle with no resolution, but only the satisfaction of letting my injustice be known.

After a confrontation with my supervisor I was very hurt and upset. With the okay from my female supervisor I was allowed to go home. In returning to work the next day I was laid off for three days without pay for disciplinary reasons. This too is unfair. I was unable to perform after the confrontation, I was sick to my stomach, and crying.

I took the evaluation and my rebuttal to the Director of Athletics, Lynn Novakofski. Nova saw me coming and opened his door, saying, "Hold on, we're going to the President's office."

"How did you know—"

"Bad news travels fast." We walked down the hallway to another door that said President Bill Smith. Inside, the man referenced by the sign, the president of the company, pointed to another man in a chair to the right of Bill Smith's desk. I recognized him as the Director of Entertainment, Stephen Dewoody. So there I was with the Director of Athletics, the Director of Entertainment, and the President of the Company.

The president spoke first. "We hear you're having problems with Mark."

I handed my rebuttal to Lynn Novakofski. "Read this. I'm not the only one that has a problem with Mark, but I may be the only one who stands up to him," I said. "I don't understand how he can keep me from doing back-flips. It seems a little like discrimination. And why is it that the girls are paid so much less than the guys? Maybe I should be asking an attorney these questions."

The president cut in. "Now, let's discuss this. No one needs to do anything hasty. I'm sure we can work this out."

"Lynn, you know me," I said. "Does this evaluation seem fair to you?"

"There has definitely been some miscommunication between the two of you," Nova said. "Maybe some time apart would help. The ski show director from Marine World Africa in Vallejo, California, called me recently. He said he needed a jumper. Maybe you could go ski out there for a while, let things cool down between you and Mark? Afterwards, there's a skeleton crew going to Scandinavia for a two-month tour. You can be the featured jumper over there. Two months in Vallejo, two months in Scandinavia—not a bad deal for someone who is supposed to be suspended three days without pay."

Nova tore up the suspension notice. "Take the three days to get ready for Marine World." He said. "They'll be expecting you. Think of it as a working vacation."

"Will my job stay secure for when I come back, with no chance of a pay cut?"

The Director of Entertainment spoke his only words of the entire meeting. "Of course."

"And I will be allowed to practice and perform back-flips?"

"Yes, we will talk to Mark while you're gone," said Nova. "Get your gear together. Leave here today, and arrangements will be made for you to be in California in three days."

I stood and shook all of their hands, saving Lynn's for last. Then I said to him, "Thank you. I'd like to have what we've discussed here today in writing. Please." He nodded.

As I walked out, I played an imaginary conversation in my mind about what was being said after I left. The president would say, "What's really going on here?" Lynn would say, "She kind of has us over a barrel. There is some merit to her complaints." The Director of Entertainment would say, "He's right. I've checked into Mark's file. There have been other written complaints." The president would say, "Can we do something about Mark?" Someone would say, not really—he knows some things and could really do some damage. Hopefully, sending this Norma Rae away for a while will do the trick." Then the president would say, "You all better hope so!"

It probably went nothing like that, but a girl can dream can't she?

CHAPTER 7

Back-Flips with the Devil

Skiing at the Marine World Africa USA theme park was a blast, and far different from the atmosphere at Cypress Gardens. I lived with my aunt and uncle in Sonoma, California, about a 40-minute drive from Vallejo, where the park is located. At Marine World Africa USA the skiers weren't resentful or dismissive about my jumping. Instead, they embraced it. I skied with Brett Wing, a kind of hybrid skier who was very well respected in both the competition ski world and the show skiing world. In competition skiing, you have long-distance jumping, slalom skiing, and trick skiing—that's the big trio—and there is also a barefoot competition tour. In show skiing, you have the water pageantry and performance routines at theme parks or the occasional small traveling water show.

Competition skiers practiced and went on their respective Pro Tours to try and win competitions for cash prizes. The cash prizes really didn't amount to much, but the sponsorships, or endorsements enhanced your reputation and your bank account. Of course, the more the competitors' reputations grew, the more product manufacturers profited, so it was a great arrangement. Marketers know that people covet the products their idols use. They want to use the same jump skis as Sammy Duvall, world champion long-distance jumper wear the same bathing suits and sunglasses as Camille Duvall, world champion slalom skier... drive the same boats as Deena Brush-Mapple, women's world champion long-distance jumper... and perform on the same skis as Cory Pickos, world champion trick skier. There were plenty of world-class competitors out there. There were barefoot competitors like world champion Ron Scarpa, also, the world champion brother-sister team of Rick and Lori Powell, and you'd have to throw in my best buddy, Jennifer Calleri, world champion barefooter many times over, all of whom competed in their own competitions and Pro Tour stops. There were freestyle water-ski jumpers competing at the Water-ski Pro Tour stops, along with the three-event skiers. And along with sponsorships, endorsements, and tour winnings, they could make additional money running or teaching at a school.

Most skiers who competed in freestyle jumping came from a show skiing background, as I had. I knew that if I wanted to make a name for myself, it would probably be on the World Water-ski Pro Tour. The Pro Tour competition often started in Orlando because of the weather. One year when Orlando was to be the first stop of the season, I wrote to the directors of the Pro Tour and asked if I could ski an exhibition in between the three-event skiing, maybe just before men's freestyle competition. I received the okay, so I got a chance to go over the ramp and perform one of my tricks. At the time, my helicopter and my front-flip were solid, but I was still trying to make my gainer consistent. Skip Gilkerson, who was in charge of that part of the Pro Tour, came up to me before the jump. He said with a scratchy deep voice, "You can go over the ramp, just one time, right before men's freestyle, and you better not fall. One try, got it?" I nodded and started walking down to the end of Lake Ivanhoe, where he pointed out the starting dock.

I was loaded down with my helmet, jump rope, wet suit, gloves, and six-foot jump skis, struggling a bit, when a golf cart pulled up alongside of me. "Hey. You look like you could use a lift," she said. I almost dropped my stuff I was so surprised: *omigod, that's Deena Brush-Mapple, the women's long-distance record holder.* Trying not to sound star-stuck, I said, "Yeah, please that would be great. Just down there to the starting dock." I didn't really need to tell her where to take me; she had been there many times. I will never forget that day, and the kindness that World Champion showed me. I think it was her way of saying she respected what I was trying to do. She knew what I was trying to do because the word was spreading that there was a woman planning to challenge the men in freestyle. I think Deena Brush-Mapple giving me a ride in a golf cart to the starting dock was her way of saying, "You go, girl!"

I still wasn't sure if I would do a helicopter or a front- flip. I had never skied at Lake Ivanhoe, never skied over that ramp, and had never met the boat driver who was going to pull me. When Deena Brush-Mapple and I pulled up to the starting dock, I got another shock. My boat driver was to be none other than Ricky McCormick. McCormick, another world champion, Water-ski Hall of Famer, and top-notch name in the competition ski world, got his skiing start at the Lake of the Ozarks! Now, my mind was made up: I would do the front-flip.

I asked Ricky to pull me at 35 mph. He pulled me off the dock and we headed toward the Lake Ivanhoe ramp. I went over it and executed a perfect front-flip. I was ecstatic. McCormick pulled me back to shore, and I landed at the water's edge where all the people were sitting, arriving just in time to hear the announcer say, "How about that, ladies and gentlemen? Let's give Sheila Bloom a round of applause!" They did, and I didn't care a bit that the announcer had said my name all wrong: I had just made history. I made my front-flip. I could see Deena Brush-Mapple smiling from a short distance away where she stood by the golf cart.

After my blowup with Mark, I'd been told that after spending a few months in Vallejo at Marine World Africa USA, I'd join the skeleton crew going to Scandinavia as the featured jumper for a two-month tour. The Scandinavian tour was hectic; this was the Cypress Gardens crew skiing all over Norway, Denmark, and Sweden, like a traveling circus. We would drive all night and day, set up a whole ski show site, ski a show or two, and then move onto the next town.

The jump ramp, because it was portable, was smaller than normal, so we only had a three-man jump act. The finale act of every jump act is the four-man or three-man front-flip. The front-flip is actually harder to be consistent on than the back-flip or gainer, because the landing on the front-flip is blind, meaning that as you rotate around you cannot spot your landing. Any gymnast or diver will most likely tell you they would rather do a back-flip than a front-flip for just that reason. When it came time for the jump act finale, if one of the skiers fell, we would try it again. On the second try, if everyone made it, great—we would all ski in for our bows. But if someone fell, we left them in the water for the pick-up boat.

In Gotenburg, Sweden, the water was particularly rough and there was lots of wind. The swells weren't as high as they'd been on the Red Sea, but it was really rough water. The two guys I was skiing with in the jump act decided that they would turn the finale jump into a smorgasbord: one guy would do his most consistent jump at the time, a helicopter; the second would do his favorite jump at the time, a gainer; and I was stuck doing the front-flip, which was actually the jump we were *all* supposed to do on the finale jump. When we tried the first smorgasbord finale, one of the guys fell, so we got up to try again. On the second finale jump, because of the roughness I stayed curled up in my front-flip tuck even longer than usual and managed to stick the landing, busting through the bottom of the wave we landed in, but both of the other skiers had fallen.

Lynn Novakofski was furious: the two guys got a beat-down scolding on the bus. Everyone heard how mad he was, first because they had changed the act without telling anyone—especially the announcer, who was announcing a three-man front-flip finale—and second, because of how bad it made them look that I was the only skier who made it in for the bow. This made for some extra tension during the tour.

Most everyone else but me on the tour was paired off, with spouses, partners, girlfriends, or boyfriends. Maybe because I felt a little alone, I started writing every day in a journal. We were given money each day for our food, but I saved most of mine. Every night most of the skiers would take their per diem money and go to the bars and drink. Because I didn't join them, some of them seemed to think I was being snobbish or trying to act superior somehow. It was really just that I took very seriously what was said in the brochure we handed out to the crowds in the towns before performances. Not the part that said, "Come see the oldest barefooter, Banana George!" No, what I took seriously was the part that said, "Come see the only female freestyle water ski ramp jumper in the world!"

Sure, going out drinking would have been fun, but it would also make my day job all that much harder. I took that seriously. I did not want people to come to these shows and be disappointed. I always imagined some old couple sitting in the crowd and seeing me fall in the jump act. I could too easily picture the man elbowing his wife and laughing. "Well, what did you expect, she's only a girl." The thought of that made me cringe—so much so, in fact, that I never fell in Scandinavia. Not once.

When I got back to Cypress Gardens from Vallejo and the Scandinavian tour, it was a weekend. The bosses were almost always off on the weekends. And the new skiers had their two days…well, whenever. It was near the end of February 1989, and I was getting excited about the Coors Light Water-ski Pro Tour. Our first tour stop for the year would start at Lake Ivanhoe in Orlando, Florida, on April 16. My debut would be three days into the tour, on April 19, so I had about a month and half to get ready, and I was prepared to throw everything I had into preparing the three tricks I needed to nail to qualify to compete and challenge the men of the Freestyle Pro Tour: my helicopter, my front-flip, and my back-flip. The front-flip and helicopter were no problem; I felt as though I could probably do those in my sleep. The back-flip or gainer was still a challenge, though, so I intended to make the most of every chance I could get between ski shows at Cypress Gardens to practice, and maybe even try to sneak in a few attempts during the shows. During my last blow up with Mark, he made it clear that I wasn't allowed to do gainers, but supposedly the higher ups made it okay for me. But I couldn't be sure.

It would be a major coup for the organization, though. I would be the first woman to challenge the men in freestyle jumping. Water-ski Hall of Famer Barbara Heddon Clack, the first woman to jump over 100 feet, had written a nice letter of recommendation to the Women's Sports Foundation, as had Bob Forgiana and Lynn Novakofski, and the foundation honored me with a $1200 dollar grant to help defray the costs of travel and expenses to challenge the men's-only freestyle jumping competition on the Pro Tour. The water-ski company JOBE Skis donated a pair of jumpers to me. So I was getting some help, and even had a female sports attorney agent from Orlando sending query letters out to potential water-ski sponsors. I was hopeful that I could make a little money somehow and be able to pay back or donate the $1200 dollar grant. It was an exciting time.

I figured if I try some gainers, when the four-person jump act was weak and we were short a gainer jumper, I might get my chance. I was right. On many weekends, when the normally strong crew was off, some of the retirees would come out to play. One Sunday we had a couple of "old timers" (as the younger, newer skiers affectionately called anyone over, say, 25). One of the old timers was very proficient at the gainer, and at our third show of the day, one of the guys asked if I would ski his jump number, and naturally, I accepted. I never once refused a chance to perform in the jump act. The Ski Fever show had long since gone back to the traditional pace of ski shows, and so now my only chance to jump was if one of the guys asked me to sub in or—something I rarely dared do—I asked a guy if I could please do his jump number. That was hard, because it was a little like saying to the men, "Hey, I know I am as good as you, if not better, so would you sit this one out instead of me?" I could never ask a gainer jumper if I could take his number, because that would mean that the jump act would be less spectacular since I didn't do the gainer consistently *yet*.

The jump act normally went like this: it would start with a four "man" ride over, which is self-explanatory—it's a straight jump. From here on out I will describe the act saying "jumper" instead of "man" so no one gets confused that I, in fact, would be jumping with the men. That first jump would be followed by a two-jumper helicopter with a split, which is when two of the jumpers would do helicopters over the ramp, and two other skiers would ski past the ramp and then cut under the helicopter jumpers.

Next there would be a two-jumper front-flip or helicopter with a criss-cross, in which two jumpers would do either front-flips or helicopters going over the ramp and the other skiers would criss-cross underneath them. The fourth jump would be the four-way helicopter in which all four jumpers would do a helicopter off the ramp. That is actually more impressive than it may sound, since most jump ramps are just 14 feet wide and most jump skis are about 6 feet long: picture 24 feet of hard fiberglass skis spinning over a 14-foot space without thwacking into each other (not a pretty sight). The fifth jump would be the double gainer (two jumpers doing back-flips, not one jumper spinning twice!). Sometimes if there were not enough jumpers who could do gainers the show would substitute something else spectacular, like a single jumper performing the mobius, the back-flip with a full twist.

And then would come the finale jump. This was almost always a four-jumper front-flip. I hate to reveal a trade secret, but in that jump, the closest skier to the crowd would do a fake fall after landing the front-flip. That would really get the crowd going: they'd be yelling for the skier to recover—and, naturally, he always would. Actually, I should say, I always would, because most of the time I was in that spot.

But not on that one Sunday. We were all suited up and waiting to start the jump act when one of the old-timer skiers started freaking out on the back dock. I'd never seen him before, but I knew he had to be a good jumper because he was one of the gainer guys. But obviously he had never seen me, either. He had seen all four pairs of jump skis lined up and the boat getting ready to pull around to pick us up, and he started to panic, thinking that the act was clearly missing one jumper.

"Where's the other guy? Where's the fourth jumper. He better hurry! Someone run and get him!"

I was standing right there all suited up, wearing everything but my helmet, staring at him, thinking, "He's got to be kidding. Can't he see me standing right here?"

But he was not kidding. Finally, one of the other jumpers said, "Shellie is our fourth jumper. She jumps with us."

The old-timer looked me up and down doubtfully and said, "What spot do you jump?"

The spots are numbered one, two, three, and four. The one and four spots are on the outside, and the two and three spots are in the middle. I usually jumped the number one spot, which meant I would be closest to the crowd and would do a lot of the skiing underneath jumps and ropes. There were a couple of reasons this spot was best for me. One reason was that the jumper closest to the boat gets the most slack in the rope, which didn't affect me as much because I weighed a hundred pounds less than some of the guys. Another reason was that I was a foot shorter than some of those guys, so it was easier for me to cut under—especially on the double-jump with a criss-cross, where one jumper would have to pull up on the rope and duck under another jumper's rope. I could get really low and under that rope. But for some reason, this old-timer skier, wanted the number one spot, so I was moved to the number two spot.

We took off from the dock and it went pretty smoothly until we got to the four-way helicopter. This jump had me the most nervous, because I knew that if the old-timer didn't cut out far enough off the side of the ramp, our skis would lock up. Someone as small as me would not win that battle. We had our ropes wrapped around us, ready for the jump, when I noticed the old-timer swinging outside the wake—waaaaay outside the wake, as if to separate himself from the rest of us—as we turned the corner to head toward the jump ramp. Even though I was pretty sure he was thinking that since I was just a girl, I would crash into him if he didn't give me a mile of space, when I saw how far out he was cutting I wanted to warn him about something I knew he hadn't thought about. I started to yell to him, but he just scowled and turned away as if to say, "I know what I'm doing! You're the newbie here, and worse, you're just a girl!" He stuck his nose up in the air at the sound of my voice, and I don't think he ever knew what hit him. Wham! He hit the new floating dock I had been trying to warn him about.

The four-jumper act suddenly turned into a three-jumper act. The old timer had broken his leg. A pick-up boat rider told me later that the old-timer had cursed me all the way into shore—as if I'd moved the dock there just to trip him up! In any case, that left us with just three jumpers for the rest of the jump act. On the finale three jumper front flip, one of the other jumpers fell on our first try, and on the second attempt, both skiers fell, so that I came in, *the girl*, on my own to take a solo bow. I'm sure this made the old timer's blood boil.

The last ski show of the day. We were down to a three jumper act. One was me. The second was Joel Baker, a good jumper but couldn't do a gainer, and the third was a fairly new jumper, Ty Engeseth, who was still working to perfect all three of his jumps.

Before the last show, we had to decide who should do the gainer. After all, our old-timer gainer guy was off in the ER being fitted for a cast. Ty Engeseth was more consistent than I was on gainers, and I had never tried one in the show, but Ty wasn't sure he was feeling up to the gainer; he said his back was hurting from doing so many pyramids. Joel Baker was a very solid no-fall kind of jumper, but he had never learned the gainer. I really wanted to do the gainer, and Mark wasn't there, so I thought it might be my only chance. But I also didn't want to spoil the show somehow. Reluctantly we left it that Ty Engeseth should try a single gainer during the jump act.

I don't know what got into me. No, that's not true. I know perfectly well: *I love freestyle ski jumping!* During the jump act, Ty started his cut toward the ramp for the single gainer, and at the very last possible second I decided to go with him. We both popped off the top of the ramp, we both threw our heads backwards, and we both landed our back-flips perfectly. He must have been in shock that I was right there beside him, but no more so than I was. We looked at each other, gave each other a high five, down low, and I started screaming. As we circled around for the three-person front-flip finale jump, I was whooping for joy. But it got even better. When we all three landed our front-flips, the other two jumpers hit their butts really hard on the water, sending a flume of spray up from their skis. And there I was, the one closest to the audience, landing perfectly, with no spray, having just done one of my best front-flips ever. Then I pulled one ski off the water and put it behind my back to perform my fake fall—from which I magically was able to recover, as always.

How do I know this? Because once again, fate played a role: the mom of one of my best friends, Jennifer Calleri, happened to be filming that day, and she had the complete video of my first-ever attempt and landing of a back-flip in the ski show—another world record first.

The next day, when Mark returned from his weekend off, we hadn't yet tangled since my return, but he must have known that I was back in town. There on the morning schedule I had been given an actual jump number, meaning that I was scheduled in one of the jump acts. But there was also a handwritten notation in between the 12:00 o'clock and 2:00 o'clock ski shows that said, "Jump practice MANDATORY." This made some of the guys mad, and maybe even mad at me, because to them jump practice was like a punishment. But I was happy. This meant I could practice without the added frustration of having to rustle up a driver and rider to help me. It was also a sign that the powers that be had in fact spoken with Mark while I was gone, and that I would be scheduled to jump and be allowed to practice my back-flip.

Mark had scheduled the jump practice for after the noon show. Since most of the skiers left to go to lunch then, it probably upset some of them even more since now they'd have to practice before they could go. I went about my normal routine of cleaning up the skis from the beach, and putting away equipment. I wanted the guys to get their turns in before me because I didn't want them to hold me responsible for keeping them from going to lunch. When I finished cleaning up, I grabbed my jump skis, helmet, and gloves and laid them on the starting dock last in the line of skis, away from the other guys' jump equipment. I was fine with going last, and still just happy to have a driver and rider to practice.

Punky went out first and did some long-distance jumping. When you long-distance jump, it's okay to have a bungier rope because it actually gives you an extra little whip and speed into the ramp. Usually the distance jumpers go one after another so they don't have to swap out the rope. While Punky was out there I sat patiently and casually on the low stadium wall at the end of the row, chatting with the guy next to me at the end of the line. Then Mark came walking around the corner, spotted me at the end of the line of jumpers, and barked, "Get your gear on, Blum, you're next!" I was taken aback, wondering, "Why me? Why next?" But I guess I also wanted to comply and of course I wanted to impress him. I have always wanted to impress my bosses. So I started scurrying around to get into my wetsuit, helmet, and gloves on, and to move my jump skis to the front of the line.

When I was ready to go, though, I noticed that the bungy rope from Punky's long-distance jumping is still on the boat pylon. I was sure I didn't want that rope, because I wasn't going to be jumping for distance but to start practicing my three qualifying tricks to challenge the men on the Coors Light Freestyle Water-ski Pro Tour, which was about a month and a half away. I grabbed one of the jump ropes from Dave Dotter's jump skis and noticed a glaring difference between it and other jump ropes I had used before: it had a much bigger bridle opening than ever I'd seen. The bridle is the triangle formed when the ends of the rope emerge from the handle and are joined into one piece of rope, which is then hooked to the boat.

Before I hooked the rope to the quick-release safety mechanism, I spoke to Dave Dotter. "What is this crap?"

"They're from some new rope company," said Dave, shrugging. "If we say we like 'em, the company will give 'em to us for free."

By then Mark had nudged his way past and told the rider who had been spotting to get out of the boat because Mark himself is going to ride safety release. I can't remember the name of the rider whom Mark replaced, but I definitely remember that my boat driver was Donny Croft. Donny Croft was a hired boat driver with tons of experience, not just some guy skier I had begged for a favor. I said to Donny, "Take me 35 for my first jump, a heli, take me 35 for my second jump, a front-flip, and take me 36 for my third jump, a gainer." I glanced quickly at Mark to see if he'd say anything when I mentioned the gainer, but he just sat there holding the quick-release safety rope. I was getting super excited because Mark never rode for anyone; he was The Boss.

I took off the dock. Donny pulled me around for my first jump, and I landed a perfect helicopter. Then he pulled me around for another perfect landing of my front-flip. Finally he pulled me around for my first back-flip attempt, and maybe because my adrenaline was pumping extra hard because of the bigness of the moment, I popped off the top really high and over-rotated my back-flip, which I had never done before. In all my years of practicing, my crashing had always been because I under-rotated. This new "problem" meant that I went too far around and hit my butt on the water really hard and started to pitch forward, so I just let go of the rope handle. I could hear all the guys on the dock screaming for me, because they knew I had never gotten up that high or over-rotated and they were happy for me.

The boat pulled around to pick me up. I told Donny, "Same thing. Hit it!" On that next back-flip I tried to correct so I wouldn't go as high and over-rotate as much, but I still hit my butt on the water and started to pitch forward, though a little more slowly than the last time. I was bent at the knees and staring down at the triangle bridle and the water. Then I finally gave up on the landing and let go of the handle, and sunk into the water. I still got a few cheers of encouragement from the crowd on the dock, and even had time to look back at them as I slowly sank down into the water with my palms up and head tilted as if to say to them, "Bummer…I was so close!" I was psyched that everyone seemed to be with me at that moment. But I was shocked when the boat pulled around and I started to give my instruction to Donny and Mark interrupted me.

"Get tough on the landing, Blum!" My heart jumped. Did Mark just encourage me? He did, he did, I was sure I heard him right! I was so excited. I was determined to get tough on this landing. I would nail it. I would hold on to the rope handle come Hell or high water!

I said to Donny, "Last try. Hit it!" He pulled me up and around for the gainer setup, and I cut both wakes going 36 mph. I popped off the top of the ramp, threw my head back, came around, and corrected my over-rotation even a bit more than the other two attempts. But again I hit my butt on the water ever so slightly. I pitched forward, bent at the knees and staring down at the triangle rope bridle, but I was still determined to "get tough on the landing" so I was not letting go. I continued my slow roll forward, and my head and helmet slid into the triangle bridle. I was now being dragged through the water by the neck at 36 mph! My life started to flash before me, and everything seemed to happen in slow motion. I couldn't believe what was happening. I said to myself, "God, I'm a sinner!" and "This is how I am going to die." And I remember thinking, "The release is broken! He can't get me off- RELEASE!"

Then everything stopped.

My immediate reaction when I came up from the water was "*Get this f**king rope off my head*!" It had caught over my helmet, and the right side of the triangle of the bridle was under my chin. I unclipped my helmet from the back snaps, and threw it and the whole triangle bridle rope mess as far away from me as I could. It was like the devil to me.

Donny Croft zoomed back to me with the boat, and I started groping at the back of the boat to pull myself in. I was in shock and wanted out of the water. Normally I would never have tried to do that—it was not a normal reaction for me—but I wanted out of the water, away from the devil.

Mark pulled my hands off the side of the boat and said, "Are you hurt?"

As I started to answer, I could feel and hear weird noises coming from my neck and jaw. I mumbled as best I could, "Yes. My neck and my jaw!"

Mark guided me around to the back boat platform and told me to lay down on the back platform, but every time I started to move or try to lay down I could feel and hear those weird noises in my neck, and my head was starting to feel very heavy. I clasped my fingers together behind my neck and then clenched my elbows together as tightly as I could in front of me. The two men lifted me and placed me supine on the back platform of the boat. By the time we putted into shore there was a backboard stretcher ready on the beach. All the guy skiers had seen the fall and they knew it was bad. They knew we'd need the stretcher. They moved me from the back platform of the boat to the stretcher and then put me in the hallway.

The first aid nurse had already been called and was soon at my side. Skiers kept walking by giving me words of encouragement, but with looks that reflected their worry. Mark was talking to the nurse's aide (a male), giving him a recounting of what had happened, and he was writing it down.

Mark said, "On her third jump she under-rotated a gainer and the rope and bridle hit her in the face."

I started correcting him, mumbling. "No! It was my fifth jump, my third gainer try. I over-rotated, fell out the front, my head went into the handle!"

The nurse (a female) cut me off. "Try to be still," she said. "Don't try to talk. The ambulance will be here soon." She could see my jaw starting to swell on the right side, and could see friction burns on my neck. She and the aide put sandbags around my neck and taped my head, shoulders, and legs to the backboard stretcher. I remember feeling the piercing pain I felt right at the point where my head met the board and thinking that if I could just sit up I would be fine. I was also thinking, "*How long is this going to take to heal? I have to challenge the men in freestyle jumping in Orlando on April 19, 1989 and today is March 1.*"

I thought I might have to miss the first Pro Tour stop. But that was okay. I would make the next tour stop.

Wrong.

DDP-080501-8/5/62-GROSSE ISLE,MICH:Marine Capt.Tom Blum appears to be challenging the world's weight lifting record by holding up the helicopter that picked Commader Allan Shepard from his epic sub-orbital space flight.Blum is actually checking the mechanism that is used for recovering U.S. space capsules from the water,while Capt.E.O.Marquette holds the aircraft in a hover position.The two Marine pilots from New River,N.C.,performed the maneauver during a stop over at Grosse Isle Naval Air Station 8/5 while on a cross country flight. UPI TELEPHOTO jm

My dad under helicopter that picked up Alan Shepard from epic 1st sub-orbital space flight.

My "Top Gun" Dad Captain Ronald (Tom) Joseph Blum

My beautiful Mom Carol Ann Blum

Brad
Brent
Tamara
Shellie

Brent Joseph
Bradford Thomas
Tamara
Lynn
Shellie Ann

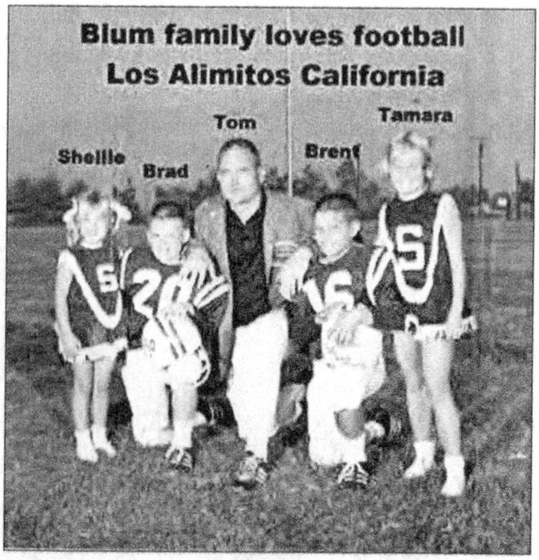
Blum family loves football
Los Alimitos California
Tom
Tamara
Shellie
Brad
Brent

Brad
Brent
Tamara
Shellie
49
47

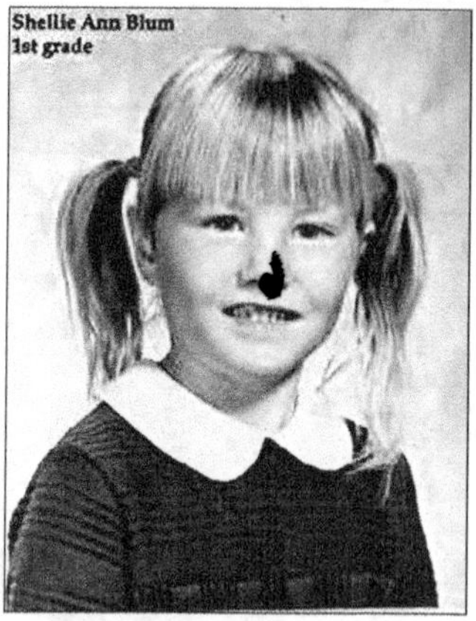
Shellie Ann Blum
1st grade

Lake of the Ozarks
6 yr. old Shellie

Lake of the Ozarks
Postcard
1976
Shellie
12 yr. old "Girl Wonder"
Knee skiing down 80 ft.
landing ramp.

Lake of the Ozarks
Shellie
barefooting as a
teenager

Lake of the Ozarks
Shellie jetskiing over jump ramp.
EVINRUDE
VIKING
Glastron Carlson
Coca-Cola

Lake of the Ozarks
Shellie peforming Helicopter

The 1982-83 Missouri Tigers
Shellie by Coach Rutherford
Front Row L-R: Joy White, Mary Bruggenstraas, Shellie Blum, Head Coach Joann Rutherford, Sarah Campbell, Polly Lueking, Lorraine Ferret. Second Row: Assistant Coach Peggy Zimmerman, Brenda Smith, Dee Dee Pirk, Trainer Eric McDonnell, Lisa Carrell, Graduate Assistant Freda Glover, Back Row: Kelly DeLong, Annette Schwander, Joni Davis, Debbie Walker, Melissa McFerrin

Shellie

Cypress Gardens
Started work on December 31st, 1986
Water Ski Capitol of the World
CYPRESS GARDENS
Shellie Blum

Cypress Gardens
4 tier human pyramid
Shellie

Jordan
King Hussein
Queen Noor
Shellie

Shellie
10 lbs lighter
after accident

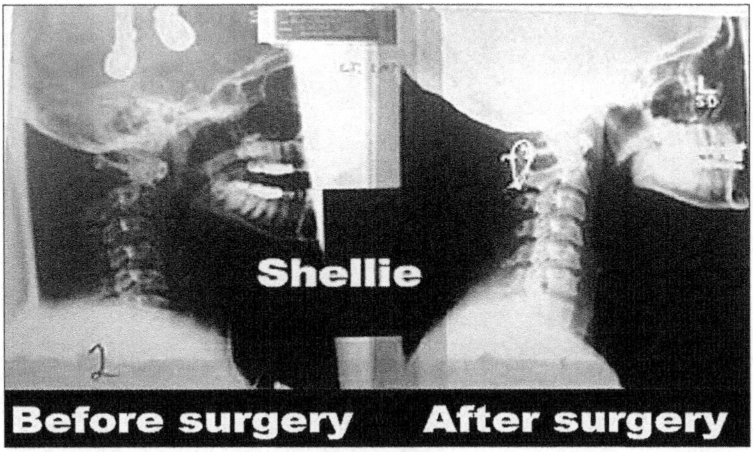
Shellie
Before surgery
After surgery

CHAPTER 8

Where's the Pick-Up Boat This Time?

The paramedics from the ambulance rolled a gurney into the hallway. On the count of three, they lifted me on, and I felt a piercing shock of pain. I moaned a bit. The pain seemed to intensify at every bump on the way out of Cypress Gardens, and I was starting to realize that this is not normal. The paramedics continued to talk to me all the way to the hospital. I told them that the pain is worse when the ambulance has to slow and stop, but it feels better when we start to pull away. After a while I couldn't talk anymore and dropped into a low monotone moan, mumbling Hail Marys over and over again. When we reached the hospital and the ambulance doors swung open, every tiny movement made me wince in horrifying pain, and my monotone moan would simultaneously pitch upward with every bump or turn. The floor liners, probably barely noticeable at most times, were like a rumble strip, and as each pair of wheels rolled over them they sent a shock to my neck. Every movement was like a knife stab.

"Is this the water-ski accident?" asked a nurse.

"Yeah. Her blood pressure is 124 over 80, her pulse 84, and she's in a lot of pain. Got her head caught in a ski rope handle, she says."

"Good job. We'll take it from here," she said. "Now first things first: we have to get some X-rays. It's your right jaw and neck. Don't worry, we're gonna take good care of you."

They wheeled me into the X-ray room and took the films. The X-ray technician stepped toward the hall to talk to the nurses who were standing outside the room. I don't think she knew I could see and hear her. I watched her describe what she'd seen with a motion: she put both fists together, and then snapped them down and apart. "Oh…my…God! I've never seen anything like it before," she whispered. "I know I'm not supposed to diagnose, but it's a miracle! That girl in there should be dead—and if not, at least paralyzed from the neck down. I mean no talking, no breathing for herself…. Her right mandible is cracked clear through, and there is a huge, and I mean very big break at cervical 1 and 2. That girl was hung!"

The others outside the X-ray room looked stunned and stared in at me where, for the first time since the accident, I was by myself. I lay there helpless and in unbearable pain, with tears streaming down my temples. It was only a matter of moments, but it felt like hours. Finally, I couldn't take it anymore. "Somebody help me. Somebody help me. Somebody help me! Help me…the pain!"

A nurse rushed in looked down at me, the shock of my injury still visible on her face. She gave me a shot and immediately the pain began to ease back a little, which was good considering that they had to start cutting my wetsuit off me. I was freezing, and my hair was still wet. The nurse covered me with blankets and wheeled me back toward the emergency room. There I was thrilled to see my mom waiting for us. Luckily, she had been in town visiting, and she had arrived at the hospital even before my ambulance had gotten there.

I kept running through the accident in my head, and the first thing I said to her was, "Mom, why didn't he release me?" She shook her head. Maybe she thought I meant the doctor. "Mark. Why didn't he release me?"

She grabbed my hand. "I don't know. Try not to think about that now."

Not long after that, the neurosurgeon came in carrying my X-rays. He slid them onto the light box on the wall and addressed my mother first. "Hello, Mrs. Blum. I'm Dr. Brackett," he said, shaking her hand gravely. "Take a look at these. Your daughter's a very lucky girl."

I was not feeling particularly lucky at the moment, but commenting seemed like too much work at that time. He looked down at me, which I took as a good sign. If he'd talked only to my mother I would have been even more worried.

"Hello, Shellie. I'm your doctor. You've sustained a very bad injury. You've broken your right jaw, and the top two cervical in your neck. The first thing I'd like to do is put you into traction." Dr. Brackett grabbed a shaving tool and started to shave the hair away at my temples. He wiped my skin with alcohol, then injected a long needle into my temple. While he screwed a metal tong into my head, I watched my mom out of the corner of my eye. She had been very brave up until then, but now she slowly slid down the wall she had been leaning against and started to cry.

This was more than I could bear. "It's okay, Mom. I'm going to be all right," I mumbled as best I could. "I promise. I'm going to be all right."

They wheeled me from the ER to the critical intensive care unit and moved me into a form-fitting Roto Rest® bed, a mechanical contraption that keeps you immobilized but at the same time makes it possible for your doctors and nurses to spin you into various positions. That way they can run their tests, keep you clean and tidy, and avoid nasty complications like pneumonia without having to lift you or move you all the time. It's about as much fun as I imagine it might be to go on one of those spinning carnival rides when you have the worst headache of your life, the stomach flu, and a panic attack all at the same time. Having no other choice, I just lay there at whatever angle the bed stopped while the hospital staff went about their routine. Systematically taking X-rays with a portable machine, poking the bottom of my feet to make sure I could still feel it, and asking me to squeeze their fingers. They added five pounds of weight to try to pull my neck and head back into the correct position, but even after 24 hours there was no improvement.

Two days after my accident, Dr. Brackett spoke to me and my family about my progress, or lack thereof. He had quite a crowd of eager listeners: my sister, Tamara, had flown in from Los Angeles, my second-oldest brother, Brent, from Dallas, and one of my aunts from Phoenix. Everyone wanted to be there to lend support.

"We added another five pounds to the traction we had hoped would pull Shellie's cervicals back into place… It's not working. We have her stable, but I have to warn you that the instability of her break at such a high level could result in the worst. I believe we need to operate, and quickly," he told my mother. "After a bone graft and fusion, if all goes well, another specialist will come in and perform surgery to correct her jaw."

The worst? That no longer meant just missing the first stop of the Coors Light Freestyle Water-ski Pro Tour. Or even the second. Dr. Brackett made it clear that without the surgery, it was very possible that the swelling in my neck could cut off flow through my carotid arteries and the pressure building on my spinal cord could cause paralysis or death. On the other hand, the surgery itself wasn't risk-free.

"I know this is a lot for you to think about and discuss," he said to me, "and I'm glad to see you have so much support, but please consider the dangers if we don't operate soon." He left us to discuss matters.

I was awake, but sometimes barely conscious, largely because of the pain meds. Even still, any movement made me moan. I even warned my family when I was going to try to swallow because I usually moaned and grimaced so much that it scared them. When the bed spun into a different position, changing the pressure on my spinal cord and neck, I remember fighting to remain conscious. I was afraid that if I fell asleep, I'd die. Perhaps someone else feared that, too, since earlier in the day I had been vaguely aware that there was a priest there talking to me about God. I was barely conscious for that, but after Dr. Brackett left I tried to stay focused. We needed to make a decision.

My mom went to Dr. Brackett's office. He turned down the volume on the little cassette player on his desk playing classical music and went back to staring intently at my X-rays, which were hanging up behind his desk.

"Dr. Brackett, I've discussed this with my family," my mom said. "We thought…we're thinking…well, perhaps a second opinion might help our decision."

Dr. Brackett wheeled his chair around angrily. "What do you mean, second opinion? I don't have to sell myself to you."

My mom was shocked, but came right back at him. "Excuse me, doctor, but I don't know you from Adam's off ox! That is my youngest child in there, and you're talking about a life or death operation. This is a small town. Now, either you give us a name of another doctor to talk to, or I'll have my daughter airlifted out of this place to Orlando."

Dr. Brackett quickly realized that he was dealing with a feisty momma bear, and changed his attitude. He didn't want to let this history-making surgery slip through his hands, so he answered calmly. "Now, let's just hold on a minute, Mrs. Blum. I don't want us to get off on the wrong foot. It's just that the potential of this operation could be very beneficial for your daughter, and to all of the medical community," he said. "I'll give you some names of competent neurosurgeons, even from Orlando, if you like, but they're all going to tell you the same thing: one, airlifting her out of here would certainly mean movement that could cause paralysis or death. And two, not doing anything could have the exact same result. I've never seen anything like this before." He shook his head, bemused. "Your daughter has so far survived a hangman's fracture, and she's not yet paralyzed. That, Mrs. Blum is nothing short of a miracle!" he reminded her. "I doubt any doctor came across this opportunity since the lynching days in the Old West."

My mom was not reassured. "Well, this isn't the Old West—we have telephones now. Shellie is my daughter, not an 'opportunity' for you. So the quicker you give me those names and numbers for those other doctors, the quicker I can get back to you with our decision."

Meanwhile, Tamara made some calls. Though she had an industrial engineering degree, she decided to change careers and was going to chiropractic school. She called some of her professors and contacts in Los Angeles. Armed with phone numbers from Dr. Brackett, she and my mom started calling neurosurgeons in Orlando. After everyone weighed in, we decided that the surgery did need to be done, that it needed to be done right away, and that it would be best not to move me, therefore it should be done in Winter Haven.

I was placed on a Stryker frame, similar to but simpler than the Roto Rest® bed. After nasotracheal intubation for anesthesia and respiratory support, I was turned prone for the operation. Dr. Brackett performed the cervical graft surgery. Beginning with an incision on the right side of my buttock to access the ilium (my hip bone) for the donor bone for the graft. He drilled and took shavings from my hip bone. The shavings would be packed around the fusion. He then made a five-inch incision from the middle of my head down to just below C4. He pulled the severely displaced top two cervical vertebrae together, packed the space with the hip shavings, and bound C1 and C2 together with wire. After he finished sewing up his incision, a second surgeon began working on the fracture to my right mandible.

"How do you think it went?" asked one of the nurses, as they returned me to ICU.

"We won't know anything, until she wakes up," Dr. Brackett told her. "But for now, she's still alive."

Thirty minutes after surgery, I opened my eyes to a crescendo. Mozart. One of the nurses saw me stir. "Welcome back. Do you think I could poke your feet with this needle? And can you squeeze Maggie's finger?"

I could feel the nurse poking the bottom of my foot. Then I squeezed the other nurse's finger as hard as I possibly could, like it was the devil! "You've got quite a grip there, girl. What are you, some kind of water-skier?" Maggie asked, smiling. All the nurses around me were grinning, happy that the difficult surgery had gone so well. Although there are patients in the world who have survived the so-called Hangman's fracture, very few of them had a case as severe as mine had been. And not only was I alive, but so far I showed no signs of paralysis or other problems. Ironically, since the surgery was recorded, it was yet another historic moment for me caught on video.

I tried to give the nurses a tiny grin, but my face was swollen and my gums were wired shut, so my smile was mostly bright silver metal. One nurse ran to tell the others, and the news quickly spread throughout the hospital that the Miracle Girl made it through surgery. My family and friends were celebrating, too. Brent cracked a joke: "Ahh, I knew she'd pull through. Brad and I didn't roll her up in hideaway beds when she was little for nothing!" This was his attempt at comic relief and it worked. Everyone was elated; I was still alive and not paralyzed.

My room became flooded with cards and flowers. And then my mom said she had a surprise for me. My friend Gayle entered the room.

"Hey girl, how're you feeling?"

I couldn't talk but slowly nodded my head as much as I could, and gave a small silver grin. My hair was shaved in the back, dirty and dark with all the blonde tips cut or shaved off.

"I am not supposed to be here," said Gayle. "We were instructed by Mark and Lynn not to talk with you because of possible lawsuits. But I decided to come any way." I was pretty drugged up, so a lot of what she was saying didn't make much sense, but the visit was short and sweet. She was the only person from my skiing life to come and visit during my weeklong stay at the hospital.

I was released just a week after the surgery. Not long after I started working at Cypress Gardens, I started buying a little singlewide mobile home. After the surgery it was there that I returned. The first day home I lay there on my bed, every little movement slow and very deliberate, wearing a big neck brace called a Philadelphia Collar. My mom was making me a chocolate shake when we heard a knock at the door. I heard my mom greet my visitor, Dave Dotter, and introduce him to the family.

"Come on in, Dave. Dave, this is Shellie's brother, Brent, and her sister, Tamara," she said. "This is her Aunt Connie."

Dave was carrying a ski rope handle with him. "I can't stay long. I'm not even supposed to be here, but I wanted to say hey to Shellie—and bring by this rope. It might come in handy someday. This is one of the new ropes sent by a new rope company for endorsement at Cypress Gardens. It's not the actual rope Shellie got hurt with, but it's exactly the same. The higher ups at the Gardens took Shellie's rope away right after her accident," he said. "I told them before she got hurt I thought the bridles were too big, but nothing was done about it until right after her accident. Then I was told to change the sizes of the rest so a helmet couldn't fit through the handle. We used them the rest of the day, but they got rid of them the next day."

Everyone looked at the rope in his hands as though it was the actual noose that had wrung my neck. "I happened to snatch this one before the rest disappeared," said Dave. "There are all kinds of rumors as to how Shellie's accident occurred. No one wants to admit she was basically hung, and that Mark was late on the release, but I saw the whole thing. I know what happened. If you ever need my help, let me know, but I guess I better…I have to go. Please don't tell anyone I was here, or where you got this rope."

My mom gave him a quick hug. "Thank you, Dave—for the rope, and for stopping by."

At my first checkup in Dr. Brackett's office, I found him again listening to classical music and looking at my X-rays, including the new ones from after the surgery, admiring his work. He wheeled around in his chair and said gruffly, "I don't talk to the media, and I don't talk to attorneys. What's this I hear about you suing everyone?"

My mom slowly sank down onto the couch in his office, shaking her head no. I was still standing in front of him and I had to yell just to talk because my jaws were wired shut. Try talking with your mouth clenched together and you will get the idea. "First of all, I've not claimed to be suing anyone. But secondly, the Cypress Gardens press release was wrong in saying that the handle hit my face, causing my injuries."

Dr. Brackett softened a little. "Well, yes, that's obviously wrong. I even documented the friction burn on your neck," he said. "Now, let's have a look at your stitches." He removed my Philadelphia Collar to view the back of my neck where I had a row of stitches very similar to the lacing on a football. "Excellent. Now then, let's take out those stitches on your hip." I slid my shorts down just far enough for him to pull out my stitches. My hip was still very tender, and each tug of the stitches made me wince. "Okay, we will see you in two weeks. Any questions?"

"Just one," I said through my teeth. "Can my mom drive me to the first Water-ski Pro Tour stop in Orlando on April 19, 1989?"

I think he may have smiled at that. "I guess I don't have a problem with that," he said. "Just…not too much excitement, right mom? And remember what I told you about those brackets and wires on her gum line." In fact, what he told her was that she needed to carry wire cutters at all times so that if I started feeling sick, she could cut the wires off my gums to keep me from suffocating on my own vomit. Yuck! My mom and I start heading towards the door. Dr. Brackett got up and opened the door for us, and I gave him a little hug. He seemed somewhat surprised by my show of affection, but I was just happy to be standing there.

My mom helped me to the car. She loaded me in to the passenger side and shut the door, but by the time she settled into the driver side, I was breathing quickly. We were headed to our second appointment of the day, the one with the jaw doctor, and I was already feeling worn out. When we got there, I was feeling wobbly and queasy, and fumbled my way into a chair. My mom rushed to the front desk. "My daughter's teeth are wired together, and she's feeling sick! Can you please take her right away?"

My mom started digging frantically through her purse for her wire cutters, sobbing hysterically when she couldn't lay her hands on them instantly. She asked the nurse who joined us, "Should we cut loose her wires? Her doctor said this might happen. Please, we can't let her suffocate on her own vomit!"

"Try to calm down, Mrs. Blum. You're not helping matters. We'll take her right in." The nurse took hold of my arm and helped me up from the reception chair, through the doors to the back office. My mom watched us go, a look of worry straining her face. The nurse guided me into a chair exactly like a dentist's chair. Leaning back, I started to feel better. "Are you feeling better now?" asked the nurse. I slowly nodded yes with my eyes, thinking how I should try to sit in a chair like this at home. The nights were the worst: no matter what position I tried, it was hard to get comfortable. And then once I finally fell asleep, my jaw would involuntarily try to open, and the shooting pain through the right side of my head would wake me up. I had ugly suffocating nightmares with lots of water all around—they were always about water, and drowning, and occasionally there would be blood mixed in. And I would wake up moaning.

But things were healing, if slowly. On April 19, my mom and I headed down the busy highway past downtown Orlando to Lake Ivanhoe. I was still wearing the collar, and found the flashes of cars in my peripheral vision unsettling. I felt nervous for the first time ever about being at a water-skiing event, much more so than when I was actually performing. We joined the crowds of people who had gathered at Lake Ivanhoe for the first Coors Light Water-ski Pro Tour stop of this season, but I felt like they weren't watching the water but me. Naturally, some of them were. Some people were staring, whispering, and I felt awkward.

The competition was just warming up and there was loud music playing. I started to roam around the ski product tents, knowing I had plenty of time before the final competition event of Freestyle Jumping would start. I was enjoying myself until I wandered into a tent and found myself staring down at a rope identical to the one that I had been using the day of my accident. I held the handle up to look at it, and started to flash back to that day—my head slipping into the noose, being dragged interminably through the water…and I had to steady myself on the table. A sales representative came up behind and startled me.

"Can I help you, miss?" I spun around—slowly, of course, which was how I was doing everything at that time—and was jarred from my flashback. But I couldn't answer, and not just because my mouth was still clamped shut. "That's our newest handle. It's the top of the line."

I dropped the rope and hurried away, putting my fist to my banging heart. I heard a loud announcement over the P.A. system. "All of you ski fanatics, if you're not somewhere that you can see the skiing site, you better get there now, because our final event of the day, the exciting event of freestyle jumping, is about to begin!" I found my mom and we sat and watched the whole thing. But during and after the event, it took everything I had not to cry. And after that I could not bear anymore. "Take me home," I said to my mom. "I've seen enough."

Eight weeks after the surgery I visited the jaw specialist and once again sat in the dentist-like chair. He pulled forcefully to remove the surgically implanted wires in my gum line and jaw. Finally, with him sweating profusely from his exertion and me whimpering in pain, he wipes his hands and smiles. "There. They're all off. Try to open your mouth." Before he can say anything more, I try to open my mouth, and a shock of pain shoots through both sides of my head. "No! Try it slowly, in gradual increments." I finally managed to work my mouth open for the first time in two months. It felt strange. He handed me a mirror. "Here. I bet you haven't seen your teeth in a long time." My top teeth looked damaged, and my bottom teeth were slanted inward. I tried to seem happy, but I was not. I was feeling very…broken.

As Spring wore on, I grew increasingly reclusive, staying home as much as possible except for visits to the doctors. In June I found myself again in Dr. Brackett's office. My hair had begun to grow back, but I was almost skeletal, having lost about 15 pounds from my 5'2" frame.

"Well, Shellie, I've been seeing you every two weeks for about four months," said Dr. Brackett. "I think this may be your last visit with me." He removed my Philadelphia Collar. "Now, for the moment we've all been waiting for…. I want you to try and rotate your head…slowly…left to right." He modeled the move for me. I tried to emulate his move and could barely move my head, let alone rotate it. "Come on, you can do better than that!" I tried again and managed a little more movement, but not much. "Okay, now up and down, like this." Again he showed me what he wanted, and when I tried I found that I could get a bit more range of motion in this direction. I was expecting to hear about the long road ahead of physical therapy and exercises, so I was shocked when he said, matter-of-factly, "Very good. I guess there's nothing left for me to do for you, so I'm releasing you from my care."

I was stunned. "That's it, you're done with me? What am I supposed to do now?"

And in the most condescending voice ever, he said, "Well, my advice to you, little lady, is to find a rich husband, and get a house in the country."

I was furious. "That's not what I meant. I mean, what are my limits? What should I do to rehabilitate myself?"

"Well, obviously, your water-skiing career is over," he said, smiling as though he had told a great joke. "And let's see no stunt work, no tumbling, no horseback riding, no motorcycle riding—basically nothing with high velocity danger. Your whole lifestyle must change. Oh, and you might want to consider getting some therapy. You know, a shrink. For dealing with your new life."

"My new...life?"

"Yes, it looks like you'll never again be able to rotate your head to full range like most humans. But considering what you have been through, you are a very lucky girl."

I was completely stunned at his callousness. Neither of us said anything for an uncomfortably long time. I fought back tears, but I managed not to cry, consoling myself by realizing that if nothing else was going right, it was at least the last time I would ever again have to see Dr. Frankenstein. Oops, I meant, Dr. Brackett, of course. He put me back together, and now he could write me up in his medical journals. I was grateful. After all, he had saved my life—but now he was done with me.

In fact, now that I was done with doctors (for the most part), it was time to really wallow in the mud. With lawyers.

My first worker's compensation attorney warned me that the insurance company for Cypress Gardens, ITT Hartford, was known in the worker's compensation world as being tough. He told me that the insurance company wanted me to give a deposition soon after the accident, and that they wanted to put me back to work right away. I was given a limited permanent disability, and Dr. Brackett reported that I was at MMI, or maximum medical improvement. All these legal terms were throwing me off, but when I heard they wanted to put me back to work, I freaked. I tried to explain to the first worker's compensation attorney that I didn't feel as though I had completely healed. I still had pain at the bone donor site on my hip, my right side of my jaw was tingly numb, but the worst was my neck, which was still very painful and gave me headaches every day that made me sick to my stomach.

That attorney was not particularly supportive. He reminded me that my treating physician had released me to work, although he prohibited me from doing what I was trained to do, of course, and rated me as MMI. "My advice to you is to settle this case, and get on with your life. You're young, you're attractive, and intelligent. I'm sure there's something you could do in the work field. What are you interested in?"

I couldn't believe what I was hearing. What was I supposed to do? "How about this?" I asked him. "I'm interested in being treated for what is hurting me now. Dr. Brackett did say something about therapy, a shrink. Couldn't I at least get that?" The first attorney told me that he would fill out the paperwork, and even recommended a doctor friend he thought I should see. But that in the meantime, he advised me, there was nothing really more he could do for me. He repeated his suggestion that I should really think about settlement and just get on with my life. As I left his office that first visit, we shook hands and he said, "My goodness, you have a cold hand."

I snorted. "I know. They've both been that way since the accident," I said. "It could be that something is wrong with my circulation. But hey, Dr. Brackett is done with me, right? Goodbye."

Shortly after that I tried to reach him by phone. I told his secretary I had been calling for four days in a row and that it was very important that I reach him, as I had not yet received my worker's compensation check. She gave me the usual line, that I should give it a few days, that checks can be late. A few days? I was bouncing checks now! But as I told the secretary, at least I was seeing his doctor friend, Dr. Fried, the shrink, and that I thought the sessions might be helping me cope.

Secretly I wasn't so convinced. At one of my visits, I showed Dr. Fried my X-rays. I had seen in his office a picture of him breaking a marathon tape, so I thought we had something in common; we were both athletes. I tried to show him in the X-rays the spot just under my brain stem where I had metal wire twisted up like a bread tie.

"But, of course, they've taken that out?" he asked.

I was shocked that he didn't understand what I'd just explained. "No, it's still in there. It will always be in there."

He looked at his watch, like he suddenly had somewhere to go although we had 15 minutes left in the session. I waited. Finally, he had no choice but to speak. "I understand all of your fears, Shellie," he said. "But you've been seeing me for about six months, and your worker's compensation attorney wants to know if you're ready to go back to work." He paused for a bit, then went on. "I'm going to tell him that you are.... How do you feel about that?"

"I've been telling you for those six months that I have constant pain, nightmares, feelings of guilt, depression, severe problems with the cold, and I keep losing weight," I said, trying not to sound as upset as I felt. "I've also opened up to you and told you my nature is not to show these problems. I'm constantly putting on a façade for everyone. I used to be a professional athlete; I put 13 years into my professional water-skiing career. I thought you could relate," I continued, pointing to the picture of him running, "but obviously you can't. But think about it. How would you feel if, from no fault of your own, someone told you that you had to find a new profession, and that you had to give up the thing you loved because doing it again could kill you?"

I paused to let that sink in for a minute. "I wish you would treat me like a professional or any other athlete who had lost his career. I can see now, that is not going to happen. I don't know if it's because

I'm 'just' a water-skier…or 'just' a girl. But you know what? It probably took you 13 years or more to become a professional doctor who's supposed to be trained to listen. But all this time I've been talking, you haven't heard anything. Have a great life, Mr. Fried." I made sure I called him Mr. Fried, because I wanted him to know I didn't respect him as a doctor. I picked up my X-rays and walked out, not stopping at the secretary's desk to make another appointment. She looked bewildered, as my huff out the door was not my usual quiet exit.

I immediately started checking the yellow pages for a new worker's compensation attorney. I called one and explained that I was unhappy with my present attorney because he hadn't returned my calls, that I hadn't received my worker's compensation check for over three weeks, and that my electricity had just been turned off. He suggested that I try to give the first attorney one more try, but that if I still wasn't happy, he thought he could help me. So I called my first attorney, and spoke with his secretary. I asked her straight out if she knew why I hadn't gotten my worker's compensation check, and she put me on hold. After I spent an annoyingly long time listening to bad music and doodling on my To Do list, she came back on the line. She informed me that since Dr. Brackett had listed me as MMI, I should be searching for a job. She at least had the grace to apologize for not telling me sooner. I politely told her to tell her boss that I no longer needed his services, and that my new worker's compensation attorney would be asking for my file. I hung up the phone and scratched *fire work comp atty* off my To Do list.

When I met with my new lawyer, he explained that ITT Hartford, the insurance worker's compensation carrier for Cypress Gardens, was using every tool they had to put pressure on me to settle, by sending my checks late, sending my checks unsigned, not sending the checks at all, and putting me on Job Search. I explained that Job Search sounded like more pressure than actually having a job would be, since it meant I was supposed to go out every day of the week and apply for two jobs a day. Wow! But at least this attorney was able to explain things better. I liked him, so I could then cross off *hire new work comp atty* from my list. He made it clear that the process was going to take time, and that the only way I would get my checks in the meantime to survive off would be to be listed as on Job Search.

I started going from place to place around town, asking companies if they were hiring. Most everyone wasn't, but I still had to have the companies sign my paperwork to prove I was looking. That was pretty easy. It was even easier, after I got my two Job Search signatures for the day, to just go on down the road with aching hip, jaw, and head, and stop off at the local bar. I started out dropping by the Office Pub or the Past Time Lounge for a draft beer over ice. Later in the day the draft beer over ice would turn into a rum and Coke® that would turn, later that night, into shots of tequila or, as I called them, shots of "To Kill Ya!" For a few hours of my day and night, I felt no pain.

One night at the local bar, I spotted my ski buddy, Dave Dotter. He noticed me and started to come over, only to have the guy skier with him grab his arm and whisper something emphatically into his ear. Dave stopped in his tracks, shrugged sympathetically, and turned away. My ski friends couldn't, or didn't want to, be seen talking to me. It was a lonely life, which may be why I started getting pretty good at playing pool. It was a competitive outlet for me, and I didn't have to move my head too much to play. But on more than one occasion I ended up fighting with some guy I was playing. Men don't much like women to beat them at billiards, and so many of them would play little tricks to try to get an unfair advantage on me. I would confront them, and that would lead to an argument that would escalate into a yelling match—which usually ended in me getting thrown out of the bar. There probably wasn't a bar in Winter Haven, Florida, in business back then that I hadn't been thrown out of at least once. I started to wonder about that old saying, "the apple doesn't fall far from the tree." Was I turning into my father?

My life settled into a gray routine: fulfill my job search quota, then drink the pain away and sleep in as long as possible. I didn't need an alarm clock, as more and more I was awakened by the phone and another bill collector explaining that their company had not received my payment. I tried explaining about the games the insurance company was playing with me, but none of them cared; they just wanted their money. The most worrisome one was the man who told me that this had happened too often, and the bank may be forced to foreclose on my home. I said what so many desperate people say, "I'll put the check in the mail today!" I hung up the phone and added another item to my To Do list, *get answering machine*. I knew that wouldn't make the problems go away, but at least I wouldn't be lying all the time. There was no way I could put a check in the mail. Hell, I could barely afford an answering machine.

It was only because I still had the threat of foreclosure still echoing in my head that I didn't even consider strangling my attorney later that day when he told me that Cypress Gardens was considering giving me a job, something menial that I could perform within Dr. Brackett's assessment of my disability limits. He warned me to be careful of what I did during the day. The insurance company would almost certainly try to catch me on videotape doing something I claimed I couldn't do with my disability—any sort of damaging material they could use if the case went to court. He did have some good news, at least: he found me a female psychologist who specialized in working with people with chronic pain.

I bought a basic answering machine and started screening my calls. Several days after I'd met with my attorney I heard his voice and snatched up the phone. "I'm here. What is it?" I was hoping the insurance company had decided to just do the right thing, but instead they had followed through on their latest threat to drive me crazy. "Please, no! Isn't there *anything* you can do?" I wailed. "I understand, but this is gonna kill me!" I slammed the phone down and it fell off the receiver. I opened the door of my singlewide mobile home and just started walking. My walk turned into a brisk stomp, until I finally ended up near a small lake about a half-mile from home. I sat staring at the lake, head in my hands, until I heard a man's voice yell, "Young lady, you're on private property!" I looked around and saw a man off in the distance standing next to a "For Sale" sign. I said nothing back and started walking again. I was exhausted—me, who used to run for fun!—and figured I might as well go back home while I still had one.

My attorney's call was what sent me the next day to a room broken up into many small cubicles: the P.R./media department at Cypress Gardens. There I met with Louise, the woman who had once gone with me on the media tour for Cypress Gardens. In my best fake playful voice I said, "I'm here to report for work, sir."

Louise turned around in her chair, and was shocked to see me. "Shellie! You look great!" Others in the department swiveled in their chairs or peeked up over the dividers. "Look who it is!" said Louise. "Doesn't she look great? So healthy!"

"Thanks, Louise," I said. "But I look a lot better than I feel." Reflexively I touched my neck, feeling self-conscious in my nice pleated shorts and short-sleeved blouse, and my black flats. This was the best I could do in the way of office attire; I had no other type of clothing, and no dresses or skirts. I never needed them before, and certainly couldn't afford them now. I doubted anyone would pressure me to dress the part, as I was pretty sure the whole "job" was a ruse on the part of the ITT Hartford Insurance Company, which had convinced Cypress Gardens to open a position in the P.R./Media Department that fell within my disability limits. I had once been a star performer for Cypress Gardens; now I was one of their lowest office assistants. My attorney called it, "sheltered employment." I called it pure torture.

Louise led me to an empty cubicle in the back corner of the room. There was a typewriter, desk, and a chair. Unfortunately, there was also a huge window that just *happened* to look out over the entire water-ski show circle. "Look, Shellie! You'll be able to watch the ski shows throughout your day."

I smiled, but inside I was crying, wondering if it could possibly get any worse. "What will I be doing?" I asked.

"Don't worry, sweetie," said Louise, patting me. "We'll find something to keep you busy." Great. My big job was "busy work." Sure enough, the next few days were filled with me stuffing hundreds of envelopes, trying to type letters (usually messing up and throwing the paper away), and trying to answer the phone and connect and transfer people without losing the calls altogether. I was left to myself. Most the other girls were much bigger than me, and seemed to enjoy the air-conditioned office, but I was always freezing cold. I needed to wear extra layers of clothing just to try and stay warm.

I sat at the lunch table by myself. One day I spotted a bunch of skiers coming toward the lunchroom, so I ducked out of sight to avoid them. When I thought it was safe, I came out from hiding only to bump right into Dave Dotter.

"Hey, Shellie! What are you doing here? You look great!"

"Thanks, Dave," I said. "You haven't heard? They put me to work in the P.R. department. Imagine me, a secretary." I rolled my eyes to show how little I enjoyed the "honor" of working there again. "But hey, it's a lot harder than people think, I give 'em a lot of credit."

"Brutal." He laughed. Then he leaned close and said, more quietly, "Hey, did you get that rope I brought by your house?"

I nodded. "Yeah, thanks."

"Well, I really think you should look into that rope situation," he said. "Some big wigs from the company have been asking around about it. I think they're scared. They know it was a piece of shit." There was an awkward silence between us.

I shrugged. I still found it hard to think about. I could see that he was anxious to move away from me. "Well, hey, I'm starved," he said. "And…uh…last I knew we weren't supposed to talk to you." He chuckled. Again, he spoke quietly. "Keep your chin up. Some of us are behind you." We gave a little wave to each other and walked in our separate ways.

I went back to my cubicle. Soon after, a ski show started, and I sat staring out the window. Adding to my pain was the fact that the background office music happened to be playing a Madonna song, "This Used To Be My Play ground." This was too much. I might have let a single teardrop fall, but I quickly brushed it away so no one would see. Finally, I went to Louise's office. The same song was still playing. Louise looked up from her computer and noticed me; she turned the volume down on her radio. Probably looking even more pathetic than usual, I said, "Louise, I'm not feeling so hot. In fact, I'm freezing. My neck is really bothering me, and I feel a migraine coming on. I'm going to check into the first aid department."

Louise said nothing. She just watched me walk away with a look of pity in her eyes. I spent the rest of the day, and many other days after that, laying in the first aid department staring at the ceiling in a dark room until five, when I could punch out and go home.

My second worker's comp attorney wanted to have a face-to-face meeting with me. He and the insurance adjuster for ITT Hartford had been talking, and he wanted me to understand that they really wanted to settle with me. Once again I tried to explain how much physical pain I still experienced, and the emotional stress that placed on me. In response he told me that I was young, bright, and pretty, and that he was sure there was a job out there for me—and that I should really think about settling soon because he was certain that a worker's compensation judge would see it that way, too.

I tried to picture him telling some guy who would never play football again that he should settle right away because a judge would see him as young, bright, and handsome, but resisted the urge to say how condescending I found his attitude. What I said instead was that I was confused, depressed, and extremely worried about my future if I still had to endure this much pain. "Please explain this to me. What happens if I settle right now for whatever they offer, but in a couple of years I'm still sidelined with all this pain, no one will hire me, and the money runs out?" I asked. "I can't just look at this as a way to get through next week or next month. I have to look at this settlement as not just the compensation for my 13-year skiing career so far but for all the years and all the money I won't earn from the pro tour because of what happened at Cypress Gardens."

There were a few things that really pissed me off about these workers' compensation attorneys. First, it was clear they did not think of me as an athlete who'd lost her livelihood, but as just a girl whining because she could no longer go to work in a bathing suit and would have to get a "real" job like everyone else. Second, they didn't seem to understand, or care, that even though I looked fully recovered on the outside, I was still a mess on the inside: drinking too much, chronic pain, paralyzing depression, nightmares, problems sleeping and eating. Of course, that last part the attorneys saw as an advantage. My looking thin and weak would add to the sympathy factor while they were negotiating the final amount, and a higher settlement would mean higher fees for them.

Finally, I couldn't argue anymore and said I had to go home and think about what they'd said. I was trying to look calm, but in the car I found myself shaking, gripping the steering wheel so tight I thought my knuckles would burst through the skin. Trying not to cry in frustration, I clenched my mouth closed as I started to pull out of the space. Suddenly something didn't feel right. I stopped the car and reached inside my mouth. When I removed my fingers, they were bloody. I stared down at what I was holding: a big chunk of my back tooth.

CHAPTER 9

Looking for Life Preservers

Part of my new routine was seeing Dr. Rowe, my new psychologist. One day while I drove to her office I noticed a gray four-door Aries K car following me. At first, I thought it was my imagination, but then the car caught up and pulled up alongside me. The passenger waved a badge and motioned for me to pull over, so I did. The Aries K parked in front of me, and a tall man wearing a white shirt and tie and dark slacks walked back to me. I was scared to death, wondering who he was and what he wanted, but I rolled down my window enough to listen to what he had to say. I guess it could have been worse. It turned out he was a repo man, and he'd come to repossess my car. I talked him into at least letting me go to my psychologist appointment.

Dr. Rowe was in her late forties, tall, with reddish brown hair. She motioned for me to follow her, and we talked a little as we walked to her office. By the time I was seated in the reclining chair, I had told her about the repo man situation. She sat in the big armchair across from me and asked if I was sleeping any better, and how I was feeling.

I shrugged, and told her that I felt a little better now that the psychiatrist she recommended put me on a daily dose of Elavil.

"And what have you been doing to keep busy?"

This was always the hard part. Therapy only works if you're honest, but sometimes you have to warm up with the easy things. "Um, I've been writing in my journal a lot, like you suggested. I've also been reading some books on philosophy," I said. That was all true. "And I've been getting into all of Anne Rice's novels." I hesitated.

"And?"

"She's so…I don't know…I think her vivid descriptions of the dark worlds have had a bad influence on me," I said.

"Causing dark thoughts? Or affecting your behavior?" Dr. Rowe was starting to get to know me pretty well. I think she probably knew what was coming next.

"I've been going out drinking at night way too much," I said. "Every day, at about the same time, I start to get a really wicked headache. I go out looking for my old ski friends, and start drinking. Then at some point in the evening I almost start to feel halfway normal."

She looked at me, waiting. She knew there was more. "I pay for it the next day. I also direct a lot of anger towards guys who hit on me. I try to politely refuse, and then they make some inference that the rumors they've heard must be true—that I'm gay. It's almost like they're trying to blackmail me into dating them. They don't get that I am just not interested in dating at all right now. And I'm still very protective of my injuries."

"You say they infer that you're gay. How do you know what they're thinking? Do they say something?"

I nodded. "They start with, 'Do you mind if I ask you a personal question?' I know right then what they're going to ask. Maybe because I'm always alone in there," I said. "And yeah, they do ask if I'm gay. So I've come up with my pat answer for their probing sexuality question: I'm not heterosexual, I'm not homosexual, I'm not bisexual. I don't sleep with men, I don't sleep with women, but I think about it. I'm bisensual."

I thought Dr. Rowe would ask me, too, but instead she surprised me. "You said that 'at some point in the evening, you start to feel halfway normal.' What did you mean by that?"

"Well, you know…I guess the alcohol kinda numbs the pain," I said. It seemed too easy, like a trick question. "Not only that, but I loosen up, and kinda show off. My problem is, I don't know how to be moderate. I have gotten myself into some pretty weird situations." I knew we'd be talking more about *that* next time.

"So you recognize that what you're doing isn't working. You've always been goal oriented, so maybe you should think about some new goals for yourself," said Dr. Rowe. "You enjoy reading, and writing in your journal. Have you thought about doing something more with writing? Maybe what you have is the outline for a movie or a book?"

For some reason, that clicked with me. I mean, everyone seems to think their own life would make a great book or movie, but my story actually had some real drama in it. I wasn't quite sure where the end was heading yet, but in the meantime Dr. Rowe's idea seemed like the right thing to do. I thought about my dad's violent death, my cleft palate issues, and my start as the 12-Year-Old Girl Wonder at the Lake of the Ozarks Water Show. I busied myself picturing who would play me in the movie when Dr. Rowe broke me out of my thoughts.

"I also think you should start coming in every Tuesday. There's a therapy group for severely depressed people, and I think you could benefit by hearing their stories and sharing yours," she said. "And instead of trying to drink away the pain, let's get you to a TMJ specialist—that's temporomandibular joint specialist—to see if we can't get some help for your jaw problem."

Dr. Rowe was also determined that I should see a physical therapist. She explained that with the recommendations from both her and Dr. Sarkar, the psychiatrist she had referred me to, the insurance carrier couldn't deny me those things because they were both necessary and directly related to my work accident. Wow! I was finally getting some of the help I needed. It reminded me of the way it had been trying to break into the all-male world of freestyle waterskiing: the men said they were all for it, but did little to help and were sometimes outright obstructive. The women, on the other hand, from Deena Brush-Mapple to Queen Noor, had been nothing but supportive and encouraging. It was the same here: with the female lawyer, therapist, and psychologist on my side, things were finally starting to turn around. It didn't seem fair, but it was no longer as surprising.

Dr. Rowe's last suggestion as I was leaving was to stay out of the bars and to keep writing. While she wrote down the information about the Tuesday group, I remembered something I meant to tell her earlier. "Um…I wanted to thank you and Dr. Sarkar for getting me out of having to work at Cypress Gardens," I said. "I felt like I was gonna die or kill myself if I hadn't gotten out of there!"

Later I got to read the transcript of what Dr. Rowe dictated when I left her office that morning:

> Our diagnoses for Miss Blum are Post-Traumatic Stress Disorder, Chronic Pain, and Major Depression, Single Episode. She has passive-aggressive personality traits, and anger is present. Her physical complaints are accident related. There have been signs of improvement, but she still feels significantly demoralized, disappointed, frustrated, and downhearted about the calamity that has befallen her. Continued counseling and therapy, as well as use of medications to help with depression, anxiety, and panic symptoms is necessary. Prior to her accident, Miss Blum was on the pathway toward great achievement. She suffered a tragic detour, and hopefully, will regain some of her verve, enthusiasm, spark and spirit. She continues to have a difficult mountain to climb. It will be a long time until this young woman finally finds some type of skill and is able to work herself into career involvement. She has a severe one hundred pound weight to carry around, and she has been significantly, emotionally traumatized by her accident; but it is hoped that she will work toward further rehabilitation. She should avoid the use of alcohol, which has been abused in the past. Stop.

While she was dictating her notes from the meeting, the repo men had waited patiently until after my appointment. Then they followed me home and took my car.

It was a Tuesday night. Four other patients and I sat with Dr. Rowe in a circle swapping stories. One girl told us that she had been waiting for authorization for an MRI, and that just before she had to go to court the insurance company cancelled—the second time that's happened to her. She started crying uncontrollably, and Dr. Rowe handed her a box of tissues. I soon learned that crying was a common occurrence in that depression group, which was made up entirely of patients with chronic pain issues. Dr. Rowe explained that the speaker had hurt her neck about a year ago lifting a heavy box at work, and that she too was stuck in the workers' compensation system, as were others in the group.

Another woman spoke. "There's a reason the insurance companies fight us like they do. I ought to know, because I've experienced both sides. I was an attorney for a worker's compensation insurance company," she said. "I made my living proving people weren't as hurt as they acted to be. The most extreme case I had was a man who claimed he had severely strained his back while on the job. He said he couldn't go back to work because of the pain, but then one of our investigators videoed him at night, dancing, and making money as a male stripper. I used to get so mad at people for trying to cheat the system, and it felt great when we caught them." She shook her head with a rueful smile. "But then I had a car accident on my way to a deposition—and I'm still having nightmares about it. I need this to be covered but, it…well, now I get even madder at the cheaters, because they're making it so hard for the people like us, the ones who really *need* the system."

I couldn't help looking around the circle and wondering if any of those people were sitting there now. I suddenly wanted to make sure the others knew I was not one of those cheaters. "My life sucks!" I said. "I go out about every night, drink, get into stupid arguments with stupid people, then wake up too depressed to get up out of bed, unless it means I'm gonna go out and get stupid again."

The others in the circle nodded as though they'd been there themselves. Encouraged, I went on. "I'm turning into a lazy vampiress. I try to be moderate, but that's not my nature," I said. "My work comp attorney is really pushing and pressuring me to settle. And sometimes I look at my life right now and I feel so guilty. I say to myself, 'Get off your butt! Get on with your life, and quit feeling sorry for yourself!' Then other days I'm in so much pain I wish I had died in my accident."

The woman who had spoken first had regained her composure. "I know how you feel," she said. "I also try to drink my pain away, but then I just get more depressed, it feels like a cement block is on my chest, and I can't get up in the morning."

"Shellie, we talked about you trying to stay out of bars," said Dr. Rowe quietly. "And setting goals. Have you done anything about finding a product liability lawyer to represent you for that defective rope that hung you?"

One of the other patients, a patent attorney, spoke up. "Shellie, I have a friend who specializes in product liability," she said. "After group, we can exchange numbers, okay?"

I could have hugged her, but I just smiled and said, "Yeah. Thanks, Stephanie."

Later, in the office of the product liability attorney she told me about, I wasn't so sure I should be grateful. "Stephanie told me all about your situation," he said. "We're...pretty close," He added with a leer. "Anyway, from what she told me, I think we can help."

I shrugged noncommittally.

"She told me you're unhappy with your worker's compensation attorney. We have an affiliate who specializes in work-comp cases. He's young and aggressive, and that sounds like what you need." Again there was a sexual innuendo to his tone. "His office is just down the road. If you want, we can go talk with him now. You can ride with me, so I can show off my new car. It's a Beamer, you know, the Ultimate."

The last thing I wanted to do was climb into a car with a sleazy egomaniac, but Stephanie said he was good at his job. And I despised my first two workers' compensation attorneys. We walked out to the parking lot. I felt even more uncomfortable when, as we walked toward his car, he said, "Here, come over to this side, and look at the control panel."

I walked around to the driver's side. He opened the car door and gestured for me to lean in to look. He was standing behind me. When

I leaned in, he put one hand on the window frame and the other hand on the car body, entrapping me. "You know the difference between an expensive new car and a girlfriend?" he asked. "They both cost a lot and you want to show them off. But you can't f**k a car."

It took all my effort not to wheel around, duck under his arms and run. I knew he'd be stunned standing there alone like an idiot. But just the wheeling around would give me a splitting headache that would land me in bed for days, so I turned around slowly and just kind of chuckled as though I was embarrassed and not totally creeped out.

I almost didn't go with him to meet the new workers' compensation attorney, but later I was glad I did. The new lawyer turned out to be a decent guy. I was impressed when the first thing he wanted to do was set up mediation to take care of some of my medical problems.

"We need to make the insurance company authorize your continued health needs, like physical therapy, TMJ doctor, your teeth work, you know that sort of thing," he said.

"I'm all for that!" I guess sometimes the third one really is the charm. I fired attorney number two and hired this young hotshot to represent me.

True to his word, the first thing he did was set up the mediation. When I got there, it was about 8 a.m. Four of us sat at the table: me, my attorney, the ITT Hartford attorney, and the mediator, who was a retired attorney. I was the only woman. They rarely spoke to me. I had to keep turning in my chair to follow them, swiveling as I watched three men volley words around like it was a three-way tennis championship game. They did not include me in the debate. By noon, I was getting really fidgety and achy. I kept rubbing my neck. The three men's words became a buzzing noise to me until suddenly I heard the word "settlement."

What? We weren't supposed to be there for that! So once again I started listening intently. The two lawyer men went back and forth across the mediator, and I was watching the tennis match again. They were no longer just talking about covering my current health costs but the whole thing, the final settlement, and they were already lobbing their way toward a middle figure. Abruptly, the men excused themselves and left the room, and I stood and stretched, trying to work the kinks out from sitting for four hours. When they came back in, it was evident that my new attorney had agreed tentatively, without asking me, to a settlement, and they were about to write up a stipulation to present. When I realized the magnitude of the decision—their decision, not mine—and understood that the figure they offered could potentially be what I had to live on for the rest of my life, and didn't even include future medical problems or bills, it was more than I could take. I choked back my tears. I stood up from the table. I flung the paper that had the settlement figure written on it, onto the table. I grabbed my purse from under the table and walked out of the room, leaving behind three very bewildered men.

That evening I didn't want to sit at home with my pain and my anger, so I made my way to a local nightclub called Norma Jean's. There I ran into my friends Jennifer Calleri and Gayle Millis. Jennifer is a world champion barefoot water-skier many times over. She'd been hired at Cypress Gardens just before I got hurt. She taught me how to back barefoot. The same year I learned back deepwater starts barefooting and backflips, the guy skiers jokingly nominated me for Most Improved Male Skier. But it was never to be: I never got my picture on the Cypress Gardens Hall of Fame wall—that wall I had cherished so much the first day, and every day I walked into work at the Water Ski Capital of the World.

I was glad Jennifer Calleri made the wall, because we had become good friends skiing together. But she was also part of the "A" team, and didn't have to fight to barefoot in the ski show as I had to fight to freestyle jump. She had women's barefoot competitions in which to prove herself, but there were no women's freestyle jump competitions, so all I had were the ski shows unless I could break into the men's pro tour. Though our situations were different in that way, Jennifer probably understood better than most what I had been up against trying to freestyle jump at Cypress Gardens.

The two of them were in good spirits, and they were filling me in on some of the latest gossip from the Gardens. It had been a little over two years since my accident and during that time the legal constraints meant that we hadn't been able to talk, so it was a bit awkward at first.

As usual, though, once we had a couple of drinks things got more comfortable. The waitress insisted on all of us showing our I.D.s, and after we stopped laughing about that Gayle told me the big news.

"Have you heard? Since Anheuser Busch bought the Gardens, they've been cleaning house. Bill Smith, Lynn Novakofski, and Mark Voisard have all been fired."

"Oh my God, you've got to be kidding me! Why was Mark fired?"

Gayle said, conspiratorially. "I heard it was something about falsifying documents."

"Ha! What comes around, goes around," I said. "But what about you guys? How are you doing?"

"I can honestly say I have my drinking and eating disorder under control. I am thinking about skiing at Marine World Africa, U.S.A.," said Gayle. "And you are never gonna believe this: I finally got my raise!" We toasted to that with another round of drinks. Then Jennifer told me that she had graduated with a business degree, and that she recently had her picture on the cover of *Water-ski Magazine*. Both Gayle and Jennifer were going to be part of a road show to Kuwait.

The talk was riveting—these were my people! My life! But I noticed that while I was listening to all their success stories, I was drinking more and faster than I should have. Finally, they stood up to go. Though I all but begged them to stay longer, they had somewhere else they had to be. I, on the other hand, had nowhere to go but an empty trailer. "Oh well, maybe we can get together again sometime soon," I said. "You know, we need to try and stay in better touch with each other."

They agreed, and asked if they could drop me off home. I said no thanks, that I just wanted to hang out a bit more by myself like I always did, and play a little pool.

"I'm getting pretty good at it, and it really pisses the guys off when I beat them."

Jennifer laughed. "You haven't changed a bit!"

She was wrong about that, but I guessed that on the outside I seemed very much the same. After they left, I checked out the rest of the bar and saw some other skiing buddies, Dave Dotter and Hank

Amos. One thing I hadn't told anyone, not even Dr. Rowe, was that I was growing even more serious lately about one of my big dreams, which was to start a family and be a mother. The problem, of course, was that I didn't really want to be around other people that much, let alone date them, which made that a little awkward. So I was only half kidding, really, when I started to tease Dave and Hank, pretending to size them up as potential sperm donors.

They laughed, though it really seemed to pique their interest in me, and I think they both overestimated their prospects for romance. I believe they thought I was kidding, and was just flirting with them; they didn't realize I was in many ways being sincere. But they both fit my notion of the ideal father figure, blonde and blue-eyed like my dad. That seemed to be the type of man that caught my eye.

His confidence bolstered, Dave asked me to dance. "Come on, Shell, you used to be such fun," he said. "One little dance won't hurt you." I just stared at him. He moved slowly back and forth to the music and then tilted his forehead against mine. He propped one hand on the wall to support himself and let his cheek brush quickly against mine. It was very sweet, and I think he was actually sincere, but I pulled back a little, not at all sure I was ready for anything. He tried to sneak in a quick kiss and I felt him massaging my right side, but then his hand slipped down to the top of my hip where the bone-donation site was still very tender. The pain made me jerk away from him. He read my reaction as simple rejection. I had hurt his feelings, which was not my intention at all.

"So it's true, what everyone says about you," he said. "You're a man hater. You like girls."

Sarcasm has always been my knee-jerk response when I'm upset. "Yeah, I like girls, don't you?" I said. "I like you, too, but if there was ever a chance of us getting together, that's gone now." I got up and stormed off. Dave started to follow me, a confused look on his face, but he stopped and went back to Hank. I kept going to the back area of the nightclub and slammed some quarters down on the pool table.

When it was finally my turn, I held the table for five racks. The same guys I had beaten in the first couple of games kept coming back to try to win back the table, but I beat them all. They were not pleased, so there were several disgruntled guys around the table rooting against me when a big black man who I had beaten earlier came back up for a second try.

He slapped down his quarters with a sneer. "Ain't no way in hell I'm gonna let a little white chick beat me twice. You're going down, little girl."

"Bet you a dollar," I said.

"Ha! You think you're that good?" he laughed, but it was not a friendly laugh.

"I *know* I'm that good." This would fall under the category of those "pretty weird situations" I had mentioned to Dr. Rowe: drink too much, then get up in the face of someone three times my size and ten times as hardass.

"You're on, little girl." All the guys around the table were listening intently, watching and hoping to see me get my ass kicked. Finally it came down to the last eight-ball shot. I took my shot at the eight ball and missed, but just barely missed, leaving the eight ball in the corner pocket at the breaking end of the table. My challenger realized he had no shot because his only other ball left, the five ball, was crammed up against the rail on the opposite end of the table. And unless he made a miracle shot, I'd be up again, and the eight ball was on the lip of the pocket ready for me to just tap it in. He calculated his odds, then angrily knocked the cue ball into the pocket with his hand. He started to walk away without looking at me, but then turned around and said defiantly, "Your shot, I scratched."

If he had scratched legitimately, I'd have to set the cue ball at the breaking end of the table and banked it back hard to knock the eight in. And I knew I could do that, because I'd made shots like that before. But he was trying to cheat, and that pissed me off. "Bullshit! You forfeited when you hit the cue ball in with your hand."

"No, I didn't, that was my shot," he said. "I scratched, so you have to bank the eight."

Fuming, I retrieved the cue ball from the end of the table. I held it up in front of the guy's face. "Okay," I said loudly to everyone nearby. "I have the cue ball, and I have control of this table. Who's next? And you"—I pointed using the hand holding the cue ball—"owe me a dollar."

The man shoved his face right up close to mine and hissed, "I'm not giving you shit. Shoot the shot, or give me the cue. Obviously, you don't know who the f**k I am."

"Obviously, I don't give a f**k who you are," I said, in the same angry tone. "And I'm not going to let you cheat me."

He pulled back and said, even louder, "F**k you, you little bitch. I'll kick your ass. Don't play with me. You don't know who I am, I play for the Cleveland Indians!."

"No! And you don't know who I am, and I could care less about baseball. But if you're gonna kick my ass," I said, moving closer and turning 180 degrees to stick my butt out at him, "get it over with. And do it now, tough guy. Beat up the 100-pound chick in front of everybody."

"You crazy little white bitch! You don't know who you're messing with!" he yelled. "I'll break your f**king neck."

That struck me as hilarious. Did he really think that was the worst thing that could happen to me? "Go ahead! It's already been done before, and I'm still here." I threw my hands out to the side, palms facing him.

By now, the yelling and commotion caused a crowd to gather in the back. Unfortunately, I was not unfamiliar at that bar, so when the bouncer came up behind me he just assumed that I was the one at fault. "Shellie, you causing shit again?"

"Not me—this guy is cheating."

"She's full of shit," the guy said. "I scratched, and she won't shoot the next shot."

Exasperated and probably just wishing he could go home, the bouncer said, "Shellie, you're always causing shit back here. I don't know what happened and I don't care. But either shoot the shot, or you're outta here."

I hate losing. And I hate losing to cheaters. Being forced to take the shot would have been like admitting I was wrong—that I was the one cheating. Finally, I'd had it. "I am not always causing shit. It's these guys who are always trying to cheat me," I said as calmly as I could considering how furious I was. "I'm not stupid; I know the rules. He hit the cue ball in *with his hand*." I looked at the others around the table to try to get some back up, but these were the same guys I had beaten over and over. They were not on my side. "C'mon, you guys saw it. Someone tell him what happened."

Nobody said a word. A couple of them snickered.

"F**k you, then," I said to the cheater. "And f**k you guys, too, for not standing up for me." Another bouncer came up from behind me and grabbed me from under my armpits. He held me suspended about two feet above everyone in the bar as he carried me out to the foyer. The whole time I was yelling and damning the club. "This place sucks! They take care of their cheaters! Don't try to get a fair deal here!" Then I noticed how high above everyone I was, and went for a laugh. "Hey, it's kinda cool up here!"

The bouncer had no sense of humor. He dumped me into a chair in the foyer of Norma Jean's and told me I couldn't come back for two weeks. I had run out of things to say. I just looked up at him, defeated, and with tears in my eyes. Just about that time, two black guys came walking up to me, we broke into a little chat. They asked what had happened, and I tried to explain the drama.

One of them said, "Let's go a couple blocks down to the next bar, Christy's Sundown." I thought, "Yea, Okay ". My night couldn't get any worse or could it? They said they were baseball players, which wasn't hard to believe, because the Cleveland Indians baseball team was here for Spring Training. I wasn't impressed, but I did think their car was cool. It was a two-seater Mercedes Benz convertible. The much taller of the two said, "Uh oh, there's no room for you", as he was saying that I dove into the back sliver of space between the front seats and the trim of the retractable rigid hard top roof, it kinda hurt, but I didn't let on, and yelled, "Safe!" They looked at me like I was a little crazy, but their grins also made me know they liked what they saw.

As we drove the short distance to the next bar, I sat up on the back rooftop ridge like a Homecoming Queen in a parade. I was cheesy smiling and doing that stiff robotic Queen wave, when all of a sudden there were police lights in the rear view mirrors. We pulled into the

Christy's parking lot, I sunk back down as far as I could in the sliver of space. The officer walked up to the car and asked to see the driver's ID and registration. He cautiously pulled it out of his wallet, and handed it to him. The officer looked at it, looked at the passenger, and stared me down too, then said. "Mr. Strawberry, your lady friend cannot be sitting up on the back of your car like that, she should be more careful". I spent the rest of the night with Darryl Strawberry, and his friends without knowing how famous and infamous he was, until I read in the paper sometime later about some of his other police and legal dealings. It had not been one of my better nights.

My mom was in town visiting, snowbirding to get away from the cold weather in Missouri for while. It made sense: after my car was repossessed, we both figured it would be good if we could share her car until I could afford another one. It was close to Christmas, and it's always good to have some kind of family around during the holidays. After my day at mediation and my night at Norma Jean's I slept late. I woke up feeling very sick from overindulging, and sore from having been carried like a trophy away from the pool table.

I sat at the table and stared down at my mug while I shamefacedly told my mom about the evening before. I also told her about the gossip and news I had heard about Cypress Gardens and all the changes since Anheuser-Busch took over, and how things were looking up for Gayle and Jennifer. But that reminded me how things were not looking up for me, and once I got started, I couldn't seem to stop.

"Mom, I'm a wreck," I said. "My car got repossessed. I don't have money for food. I don't have a tree. I don't feel Christmas; I can't even buy you a present. I'm almost 28 years old, my mom has to come take care of me, and…and I'm acting like a baby! I look like shit, I'm down and out, and these attorneys are circling around me for the kill, like sharks at a feeding frenzy."

My mom is the best. "Shellie, I don't care if you can't get me a present. And you know that if you'd let me I could probably scrounge up some money from family to get you by. But you won't, because you're stubborn."

"That's not the point. It's that I've always been independent. Ever since I started skiing—since I was 11!—I've never had to ask you or anyone for money, and I don't want to start now," I said. "I know you're being supportive, but I have to fight this thing on my own."

She nodded. Like I said, my mom's the best.

"I've been fighting this thing so long, though, and I'm just so caught up in my rage…I don't know what I'm fighting for anymore, or even if I should," I said. "Why can't I just give up? Why do I think I'm so special? Maybe everyone else is right, and I should just settle for something, anything."

I started to stand up to rinse my cup and went all woozy. "Whoa, I feel sick."

"How much did you drink last night?"

"Um…a lot, but that's not it. Something's not right—my heart is pounding a mile a minute." I start pacing back and forth, pressing the left side of my chest with my hand. My mom was getting worried.

"Should I call an ambulance?"

"No, no, I know what this is. This has happened before," I said. "Dr. Rowe calls it an anxiety attack. I feel like I'm gonna die, but she promised me that no one has ever died from an anxiety attack before. I just need to keep walking."

By then I was pacing frantically, sweating, fidgeting, closing and opening my eyes. "God, I hate this. Why does this have to happen? F**k, I hate this. Ohhhhhh, please stop!"

My mom had never seen me like that, and she was getting very worried. "Is there anything you can take?"

"I guess I could take my Elavil, but I'm supposed to take it before I go to bed," I said. "But yeah, maybe it would help calm me down. Can you get 'em? They're in my room by my bed." She brought me a pill and a glass of water, and I took them both from her. I swallowed the pill and kept pacing.

"Shellie, you're scaring me. How long does it take to work?"

"Sometimes it doesn't," I admitted. "Sometimes I'm up all night.

Maybe I should try to lay down. Will you stay with me?" We went into my room, and my mom sat on the edge of my bed. I was still pressing my heart, staring at the ceiling, and moaning the way I did at my hospital visits. I rubbed the bottoms of my feet against the mattress, up and down. "I'll be okay. You don't have to stay with me anymore. I just want to go to sleep. Wake me up when Christmas is over."

My mom laughed. "Well, that would be a mighty long nap. Are you feeling calmer? Are you sure you don't want me to stay with you longer?"

I didn't want to worry her anymore. "Nah, you can leave."

"I'll stay if you want."

"No, it's okay, really," I said. "I'm sorry to worry you. I feel stupid. I just want to sleep."

She told me she'd be right there in the kitchen if I needed anything, and after she left I continued to stare at the ceiling, moving my feet gently up and down on my mattress. I looked at the digital clock: 5:37 p.m.…7:17 p.m.…8:32 p.m.…I tried turning over, but I kept hearing the same things over and over in my head: Jennifer Calleri saying, "I got my picture on the cover of *Water-ski Magazine*!" Gayle Millis saying, "I finally got my raise!" The two of them saying, "We're going to Kuwait together!" My first attorney saying, "You should settle right away!" My second attorney saying, "You're young, you're pretty…find a job!" Dr. Brackett saying, "My advice to you little lady, is to find a rich husband and get a house in the country." My latest attorney that I left sitting at the mediation table looking bewildered saying, "$50,000 dollars is a very generous offer! You have to take it, Shellie!"

Finally, at 8:58 p.m., I looked at my pill bottle; the prescription said "one tablet before bedtime." Well, it was definitely bedtime. I popped another pill into my mouth and swallowed, willing the voices in my head to go to sleep, too. No such luck. The bouncer saying, "Shellie, you're always causing shit back here, shoot the shot, or you're outta here!" The cheater saying, "You crazy little white bitch, you don't know me! I'll break your f**king neck." Mark Voisard saying, "She's not as pretty and graceful as the other girl skiers."

I kept staring at the ceiling. At 10:45 p.m. I took another pill, but still the voices mocked me. Now I was going all the way back to my childhood, flashing back to my special education and speech therapy classes where I had to practice over and over, "Shellie sells seashells by the seashore"...my high school graduation and my sister grabbing the principal's pant leg. Now joining in the voices is me mumbling to myself, louder and louder. I got out of bed and stood up, sort of—I was half awake, but fully drugged up. I stumbled towards my mom's room at the other end of the singlewide and banged on her door, then pushed it open.

My mom jolted up in bed. "What in the hell?"

I fell onto my mom's bed, mumbling loudly, completely incoherent.

"Shellie Ann, what is wrong with you?" she asked. "What have you done?"

"Can't sleep, voices, can't sleep, can't do it." Then suddenly I jumped up from the bed and yelled at the top of my lungs, "Josh, where are you? When I find you I'm gonna wring your neck, and bop you on the head!"

My mom had told me later that my ramblings were from the Lake of the Ozarks ski show clown act, "Josh and Jenny ". Jenny is mad because she thinks Josh is cheating on her. Jenny jumps on Josh's back and he dumps her in the water for a laugh. But this was no laughing matter. My mom asked me, "Shellie, what are you doing? Wake up! You're not making sense! What are you doing?" Finally it dawned on her. "Did you take more pills? How many?"

I yelled out! "Only a few, I think. Josh, where are you?" I fell, tried to get back up, fell again.

My mom was frantic. "Jesus Christ, Shellie, what have you done?" She was trying to help me, trying to help me walk, but I was fighting her off and still yelling incomprehensibly.

"Just lemme sleep. Soooooooo tired." I fell down and went limp on the floor. When my mom couldn't rouse me, she called 911. Soon there was a fire truck, an ambulance, and a police car pulled up to the little singlewide in Sunny Acres Mobile Home Park. It caused a big scene, with lots of lights flashing and police radios squawking. The neighbors crowded closer to see and ask questions and my mom was crying, although she calmed down a bit when the paramedics explained that my vital signs were perfectly normal. She was on the phone with my psychiatrist, Dr. Sarkar, who was asking my mom how many pills I took.

My mom said three.

"You're sure? Shellie only took three Elavil at 150 milligrams over, maybe, a period of around five hours?" asks Dr. Sarkar.

"Yes, that seems to be what she's saying."

"And the paramedics say her vital signs are normal?"

"Yes, they say they are perfectly normal," said my mom.

"Well, then, Mrs. Blum," said Dr. Sarkar, her voice sounding very much relieved, "Shellie is in for a very long sleep, that's all. Just put her to bed, I'm sure she'll be fine."

"Thank you, Dr. Sarkar, and I'm sorry for bothering you so late on Christmas Eve…or no, I guess it's Christmas now," said my mom. "Merry Christmas."

Following the doctor's orders, my mom started to walk me toward my bedroom, but one of the police officers stopped her.

"Not so fast, Mrs. Blum," he said. "I'm afraid we're going to have to take your daughter to jail for attempted suicide."

"I never claimed she was trying to commit suicide," said my mom. "Believe me, if my daughter had wanted to kill herself, she'd be dead now. She doesn't do anything halfway!"

The other police officer chuckled, then tried to look serious as she glanced over at her male partner. She gave him a questioning shrug, and finally he relented. "Okay, the show is over. It's Christmas. Let's all go home."

The woman couldn't resist adding, "Merry Christmas to all—and to Shellie a good night."

The next time I was at group therapy there were two new people, one was a middle-aged woman and the other an elderly man. "Shellie, would you like to start the discussion off?" asked Dr. Rowe. "I heard you had quite a Christmas Eve."

Of course, Dr. Sarkar would have had to tell Dr. Rowe. I nodded.

"It was a pretty bad scene. I had an anxiety attack earlier in the day, and decided to take my Elavil early to try to calm down. Anyway, the pill didn't work so I took another, and then another, and by then I was completely out of it. I wanted to sleep, but I just couldn't."

"So what happened?" someone asked.

"My mom freaked, and I can barely remember, but there seemed to be a bunch of people around. All my neighbors were there for the commotion…I don't know, it was just a mess," I said. "Since then I've fired my most recent workers' comp attorney—number three—because he told me he didn't want to go before the judge with my case. And now I'll probably have to find another product liability attorney, because they work together. But he was creepy any way."

"Aren't you scared?" asked the new woman. "I mean, don't you feel vulnerable without an attorney representing you?"

"Not really," I said. "I was very hesitant when I was writing the letter, but once I sent it I felt relieved, like I was finally starting to take back some control of my life. I mean, I feel like I've hit rock bottom. I wasn't trying to kill myself—at least that's what I've been telling myself—I just wanted to disappear for a while."

There were murmurs from all around the group, as though everyone could relate. "Right now, everything sucks! I feel like my attorneys are bamboozling me, like they don't want to work for their money," I said. "And now that I've taken some time to think about it, I know that the only way to go is up. I need to get my shit together, and try to take better care of myself. No more partying all night, no more fighting in bars. I'm going to dive into my journal. I was a disciplined person before this happened to me, and I can get back there. My objective is to quit feeling sorry for myself, and to make a difference. I'm going all the way with this, whatever it may take, win or lose. I'm not giving up on principle. It's all I have left."

"Shellie, I have a worker's compensation attorney in mind for you," said Dr. Rowe. "Her name is Faith Horning-Keating. It's time you see her." The new patient spoke, too, giving me the name and number of the product liability firm that represented her. I took it gratefully.

Faith Horning-Keating would be my fourth worker's compensation attorney. An energetic woman in her early thirties, she oozed competence and confidence. I liked her immediately. Her husband ran the front office.

"Dr. Rowe explained some of the difficulties you've been having with previous attorneys," she began as she faced me across her desk. "First of all, I want you to know that I would never try to force a settlement on any of my clients. And I can relate to some of the problems you have had in the way of discrimination—there're plenty of it in the legal profession. It's definitely a good ol' boys club."

"It's been a tough couple of years, yeah," I said.

"I think I can help you. It's a very interesting case, and I can really get behind a case I believe in. I've gone up against the big boys at ITT Hartford and won. They don't like it, but they have to respect my ability." I had a momentary sense of déjà vu when she said, "The first thing we'll do is get your medicals authorized, and then take it from there." I was reassured 100% by her giving me information none of the other lawyers had bothered to mention. "Oh, and the insurance company may try to video you, so be careful. I'm not saying be a hermit, but keep it in mind."

So in this case, the third one was not the charm but the fourth. I finally had a fighter for an attorney. Faith Horning-Keating was taking my case, and I felt good about that. Funny: she also happened to be a woman.

Faith Horning-Keating was very, very good. Not long after our first meeting I found myself seated in a very large conference room surrounded by X-rays, a rope handle, a helmet, and my own water-ski video. Three men sat at the table while I told my story, describing exactly the way the accident happened. The men nodded in approval, and then finally Mr. Riley, the partner who would handle the bulk of my case, spoke up.

"If we decide to take your case, and it looks favorable that we will, you must understand the complications," he said. "Their number one defense is going to be what's called 'assumption of risk,' meaning that water-skiing is an inherently dangerous sport, and you knew this from the get-go."

I nodded and started to open my mouth but he held up his hand. "Another problem is proving that your head actually got caught in the oversized bridle as you have explained it—and proving that your supervisor pulled the safety release mechanism late. All of these issues will come into play in the event of a trial."

He'd explained more than my other three attorneys put together. "The more responsibility the rope handle company can place on others, the less they may have to pay should you receive a favorable judgment from a jury," said Riley. "Not only that, but you will have to pay a percentage of the reward to your worker's compensation lien. Putting all these problems aside, your case has merit. The opposition will want to depose you first to get your side of the story."

The deposition took place in a huge building in downtown Orlando. I met up with Riley on the 15th floor just outside the deposition office. The deposition would involve two days of being under oath, being videotaped, and being grilled by the rope company's attorney, James Powers. We would start early in the morning and wouldn't finish up until after five p.m. both days. The first day of deposition went fairly smoothly; we just went through my history. Powers was very thorough. The back and forth between us got tense at times, but for the most part, he was cordial. It wasn't until the next day that I found out that James Powers used to water-ski at Cypress Gardens. No wonder he seemed to know exactly what questions to ask me! During the second day of the videotaped deposition, we got further into how the accident actually happened. I got a little upset, to say the least, that the men didn't seem to believe that my head got caught inside the triangle of the water-ski rope handle?

At the end of the grueling two days, Riley explained that he wanted me to come to his office, and to bring all my material for discovery. I sat in the reception area of his law office with the notebooks that make up my journal. Becky, the receptionist, told me that she would be taking pictures of my head and shoulders so that Riley could have a bust made to better explain how the accident occurred. She collected my diary, journal, outline, and relevant correspondence, and then spent the next 30 minutes taking pictures of my head and shoulders, measuring everything.

When I returned to Riley's office two weeks later, I found him opening a big box. Styrofoam peanuts flew everywhere as he pulled out a large object: a life-size bust of me! He set it on the desk, then my water-skiing helmet on the head of the bust. When he draped the rope with the oversized rope handle over the helmet, it fit through easily. Now we had a clear, unmistakable visual to demonstrate for everyone to see how my head had gotten caught in the triangle of this oversized rope handle.

"Perfect," said Riley. "How do you think they are going to react when they see this staring at them when they walk in the mediation room?"

"Do you see how those foamy rubber things on the side helped draw my helmet into the triangle?" I said. "They are there to make the handle float, but see, because they twist around the sides of the rope like rollers, it helped my helmet slip right through."

"Yes, I see your point, and it's another strong reason the rope handle was defective," said Riley. "But let me make that observation, not you. We don't want the rope company saying you're some sort of expert on ropes. They would try to use that against us, you know? But our real Ace in the hole will be my simple question: If there was nothing wrong with the ropes, why did Cypress Gardens 'immediately' alter them?"

Riley started gathering up other material to take to the meeting. It was only then that I really took notice of all the work the law firm had done collecting props and evidence. There were two giant aerial pictures of the Cypress Gardens water-ski show site, giant blown up X-rays of my injuries, and sketches detailing my injuries and surgeries. All this was loaded into a truck, which we followed to the mediation site. We arrived first, and Riley set up all his displays, and he and I took our seats at one end of the table to wait.

The mediator walked in and looked around the room. "Quite a display you have there!" Soon after, James Powers, the insurance adjuster, and the president of the rope company walked into the room. They were laughing about something as they came in but stopped abruptly when they saw the display—especially the bust.

"Well, I'm not too sure about the likeness," joked Powers lamely, staring at the bust.

"It's not meant to be art. What's important is that the bust's features follow an exact measure of Shellie's head and shoulders," said Riley.

"Well, now, gentlemen…excuse me, *and* young lady," said the mediator. "Let's get started. This is court-ordered mediation, and I am the mediator. I am a retired attorney, so I've dealt with many cases. What we are going to try and accomplish here today is to resolve this lawsuit before it has to go to court. Either way, I get paid, so both sides should understand, I will be as unbiased as I can be." He looked around to make sure everyone understood. They did. Everyone shuffled slightly in their seats, preparing. I felt strangely calm.

The mediator continued. "I read submitted documents, so I'm familiar with both sides of the case. Perhaps, we should start with possible figures to resolve this." He turned to face Riley. "What do you and your client have in mind?"

"In light of this catastrophic accident, the loss of my client's future potential earnings, and pain and suffering, we are not comfortable giving a figure at this time," said Riley.

"I see. And Mr. Powers, where does your client stand as a starting point to resolve the case?"

"First of all, sir, let me start by explaining that we have a court order to throw the case completely out on a ruling for 'assumption of risk'—not to mention the fact that no deposition as of yet supports Miss Blum's theory that her head became entrapped in the ski handle bridle," said Powers. "Not only that, but there was conflict between Miss Blum and her supervisor, who apparently didn't pull the safety release mechanism in a timely manner. There is also the fact that Miss Blum was made aware of the rope's larger opening before her accident, and did not have a problem with it at the time."

I was no longer calm. I interrupted him without thinking, half-rising from my seat in anger. "That's a lie! I never saw that rope before the day of my accident, never before, not in my life," I said loudly. "Have you seen my X-rays, have you talked to the first aid nurse who…?"

Riley grabbed my arm, interrupting me. "Shellie, please wait," he said quietly to me. "Mr. Powers, we have a letter from a bio-mechanical engineering expert. The letter clearly states that the only way the accident could have happened is the way my client has purported from the beginning. Here are some sketches, and Shellie's X-rays to further support his findings." He slowly laid each item on the table and passed it solemnly toward Powers. While the others studied the letter and X-rays, Riley continued. "We also feel confident that the first aid nurse, the one who first attended to Shellie, will further support Shellie's explanation of the accident immediately after it happened. It's unlikely that Shellie's comments at that time were manipulative. We are certain her testimony at the time will ring truthful with a judge and jury, and fall within the scope of, and be validated by the 'excitable utterances' rulings." Riley paused to let his words sink in. "And last, but definitely not least, there is the surgeon who performed the surgery. His testimony, if needed, will support Miss Blum's theory of how the accident happened."

There was a pause, then the president of the rope company whispered to his attorney. "Would you please excuse us while we discuss these new issues?" said Powers.

Everyone except Riley and me left the room. Then the mediator returned and spoke to Riley. "You want to come with me to the other conference room, so we can further these negotiations?" Riley rose, nodding. He looked at me and reassured me that this was normal, that he'd be right back, and then he left the room, too.

I sat in the big conference room by myself, surrounded by a bust of my own head, X-rays of my neck and jaw, photographs of Cypress Gardens, and a ring of empty chairs. I stared out the window at downtown Orlando, breathing, trying to regain that calm I'd felt earlier. It was nearly an hour before Riley returned, alone, and sat next to me.

"The mediator wanted to discuss the other side's offer in private," he explained. "He thought it might upset you again—and quite frankly, it would have. Before I tell you how much, let me first say it's insulting, not only to you, but also to me."

I felt my heart sink. "And?"

"We of course are refusing their offer of $20,000. That wouldn't even cover my expenses thus far," he said. "But I can tell you that at least we've got their attention, and they are taking us seriously. Try to remain calm when they return."

The men filed in and took their seats. Powers spoke first. "After some discussions, we remain at our out-of-court settlement offer of $20,000," he said, in a take-it-or-leave-it tone. If Riley hadn't prepared me for the absurdly low figure, I probably would have said something…regrettable. Instead I stared back at him defiantly but did not speak. "Frankly," said Powers, collecting up his papers in preparation for leaving. "I'm curious to see how the judge will rule on the hearing based on 'assumption of risk.'"

My attorney stood and began collecting our papers. "Fine, we'll see you in court," he said. I was encouraged by his confident tone.

The elevator lobby was thick with tension. Riley and I stood aside from the others, talking, waiting for our own car so we didn't have to ride the elevator with them. On the way to the parking lot, he reassured me that things were going well, and proceeding as normal. He also warned me to be especially vigilant, as the investigators would be even more determined than before to catch me doing something incriminating on tape.

I barely left the house before the day of the hearing. That morning, while waiting in Riley's reception area, I was excited. My big day in court! Justice! I was imagining the scene when Riley called me into his office. He explained that James Powers had been calling all morning, and that in the most recent call he had said that they wanted to proffer a "good faith" offer to settle the case out of court.

"They've upped their offer from $20,000 to $200,000—which is great news," he said. "I really think we should think about taking it."

"But Riley, you've known all along that I'm uncomfortable about settling without knowing how much I have to pay back on my worker's comp lien—and no one can give me a bottom line," I said.

"Shellie, we have all worked really hard to get this far. I have to give a 'good faith' response back to them—they are expecting my call," he said. "Will you at least authorize me to give a 'good faith' response of $250,000, which is the total amount of their insurance policy?"

I didn't know what to say. It was more money than I'd ever had—but it might also be far less than I would need. "What would happen next then?"

"I don't think they will come up to that amount. But we have to give them a number back to show good faith," said Riley. "I know this seems rushed, but they are expecting a call back." Finally, I consented. He dialed the number. He didn't put the phone on speaker, so I could only hear his side of the conversation. "Mr. Riley for James Powers. No, she won't take it, but the total insurance policy—yes, the 250.... I see. Yes, I've tried. Very well; we'll be there in a few minutes." He hung up the phone and stared at me. I just looked down at my hands. He agitatedly started to gather materials for the trip to the courthouse. He didn't say anything for a minute or two, then repeated his position one more time. "I have to say this again. I think you're making a bad decision, not taking this offer," he said. "But if you won't change your mind, you can ride with me."

We rode to the courthouse in complete silence. He parked the car, and was carrying the bust, helmet, and rope handle toward the courthouse when we heard a shout. Powers and the rope company insurance adjuster caught up with us at the top of the steps.

"Riley, hold up a minute," said Powers. "I have been given authority to up the offer from 200 to 220 thousand dollars. What do you say?"

Everyone looked at me. I looked Powers in the eye. "I want to follow through with this," I said simply. "I want to hear what the judge will say."

Powers spoke directly to me, "Shellie, this is a lot of money. I know you want control of your life, but this is a bad decision," he said. "What if the judge throws the case out on this ruling? You'll have nothing."

I stared at him. I looked at the rope company insurance adjuster. I looked at Riley. Without another word, I headed toward the courthouse doors. After a stunned pause, the three men followed me. We passed through security, rode up in the elevator, and entered the courtroom without speaking another word.

While we waited for the judge to come out of chambers, the rope company insurance adjuster whispered to Powers, who in turn whispered to Riley, who whispered to me.

"Shellie, they've come all the way up to max out their insurance policy—$250,000," he said. "We have to take it. We got what we wanted."

I shook my head and stared straight ahead as the federal judge entered the courtroom and we all rose as directed. She took her seat at the bench and began to address the court.

"Good morning. You may be seated. Case number 92-224 Shellie Blum versus Straight-Line Water Sports, Inc. Can we have appearances?"

"Your Honor. Michael Riley for the plaintiff."

"James K. Powers on behalf of Straight- Line, the defendant."

"All right, we have approximately one hour for this hearing," said the judge. "The issue to be addressed is the expressed assumption of the risk."

"Your Honor," said Powers. "Before we begin.... There was on the table a demand for $250,000 to settle this case, which would cover the plaintiff taking care of liens and so forth. And I got authority, just as we're sitting here, to accept that $250,000 demand, and I think—"

The judge cut him off and looked to Riley. "Is there any reason to go forward other than it's an interesting legal question?" she asked.

"Your Honor, with all due respect, I find myself in a very awkward position," said Riley. "I conveyed to Attorney Powers a demand of $250,000 based on authority from my client, Shellie Blum. When the demand was accepted this morning, Ms. Blum indicated to me that she's not prepared to live with that. I need to ask her to go ahead and state whatever she wants to be on the record."

I was in shock. My attorney just asked for permission for me to address the court, which was not something for which I had prepared. I looked at Riley, panic written clearly on my face. He nodded, and I slowly stood up, shaking, so petrified I thought I might pass out from the stress.

I cleared my throat nervously. I closed my eyes for a second and tried to recall what it felt like to be on skis, doing what I loved. "Um...Your Honor. The only thing that I can think to say is that, um, this has been my whole life, and my whole career," I said. "I started skiing when I was 11, and it was a 13-year career. I was the only woman who could perform the tricks that I was performing—which meant a lot to me in potential income."

My voice shook. I had to stop for a minute, but then I was able to continue, more loudly and firmer. "There have been some misleading negotiations to settle and I feel like I… like I have been pressured. This is a decision that I just can't make at this point in time. And I don't know what else to say other than I'm very confused and baffled right now…and this was all shoved at me at the very last second."

"As I understand it, you gave authority to your attorney to make a settlement demand for $250,000, which was accepted before it was withdrawn," said the judge. "Is that correct?"

I nodded. "Yes, though even at the time I was uncomfortable with that. But Mr. Riley assured me that this was just how it is done, and that they would probably not come up to that figure."

"Did he exert any undue influence on you?"

"I'm not sure what you mean."

"He knows more about law than you do," said the judge. "You know more about water-skiing than he does. Okay?"

I was trying to feel confident, to feel that same fighting spirit I'd felt out on the steps, but it was hard. "I understand that, but I also know that I have a worker's compensation lien that is continually rising," I said. "They are still trying to decide if I am permanently totally disabled from working again. If that happens, I don't know how much the lien will be. I might lose all this to the lien."

Riley spoke up. "Your Honor, I don't want to walk away from here with Ms. Blum feeling that somehow I have betrayed her," he said. "I do feel uncomfortable about the way this is coming together without her having an opportunity to reflect on it."

"I don't see a factual reason here," said the judge.

"However, I'll give Ms. Blum five days to file a motion to set aside the settlement. But at this point, there's a binding settlement, and she's admitted on the record—although not under oath—that she gave you authority to do that. This hearing is adjourned."

The judge slammed her gavel down, closed the folder of papers in front of her, and walked out. I was upset and started to walk out, too. Riley rose to follow me but I turned and said curtly, pointing to the bust, helmet, and rope, "Aren't you going to get your stuff?"

He looked shaken. "Oh yeah, I'll—look, Shellie, I'm sorry this…"

I briskly threw my hand up to stop his words. He picked up the bust, helmet and rope and followed me. The others were gone. I walked to the elevator ahead of him, staying ahead of him until we got to his car. Riley tried to talk to me on the way back to his office.

"Shellie, I know you're upset," he said, when he parked in his office lot. "Why don't you come in so we can discuss things?"

"I don't want to talk. I don't want to think. I'm going home."

I hurried to my car, but I didn't go home. I was so upset, I stopped at the nearest pay phone to try and call Faith Horning-Keating. When I couldn't get through, I slammed down the phone and drove to her office. She was there, and I was ushered right into her office.

"Riley sold me out," I said. "He knew exactly what he was doing. He gets a bunch of money over half the settlement, the insurance gets a bunch back on the work comp lien, and I could end up with nothing or close to it. I have five days to do something!"

Faith gave me a worried look. "Sorry it went down like that," she said. "The judge gave you five days to file a motion to set aside the settlement? That doesn't give me much time."

"Will you help me? I mean, you'll help me write it?"

She smiled. "It's not what I specialize in, but I think I can put something together. What happened to you at the hearing just doesn't sound right," she said. "Sometimes, I'm almost ashamed when people ask me what I do for a living. But hey, there are a few of us that still believe in the law, and justice, and we keep our morals and ethics."

I felt better already.

"Listen," she said. "If I only have five days to write this thing up, I better get started right away. I'll send you a copy when I'm done."

"I'm so upset with Riley. If you could help me set aside this binding settlement, and feel it's too risky to take on the case yourself, I would just drop it," I said. "I mean, I need to be able pay the workers' comp lien somehow but…it's never been all about the money for me. It's been about telling the truth; it's been about exposing that rope handle. I truly believe it is defective. It hung me, and if it's out there, it can hang someone else."

I stood up to go and she started to walk me out. I turned back to face her. "Thank you so much for believing in me. I don't know what I would do if I didn't have you on my side," I said. "I mean that." I gave her a little hug, which surprised her, but she smiled.

I couldn't believe it. I actually asked someone outright for help. Maybe therapy was helping after all.

She tried. Faith wrote a motion to set aside the settlement and got it recorded just before the end of the fifth day, but the grounds just weren't strong enough. The motion was denied. A few days later, the mail carrier handed me a certified letter from Riley. I signed for it, and stepped back inside to read it. The more I read it, the more upset I grew. Then I called Faith. She had received the same letter.

"So what does it mean, exactly? I see. And I have to come up with three or four thousand dollars if I want to keep fighting this thing...so I guess this is the end of the line," I said. "No one will know the truth. The skiers and other people will just go on saying that the rope handle hit me in the face." I could feel myself starting to choke up. "Well, I don't have that kind of money, so it's over. At least...at least you put up a fight. I can't thank you enough."

After I hung up the phone I stared at the letter feeling totally defeated. I went to my room, pulled out my journal, and started writing. Within days my room was littered with books on how to write a screenplay and sell ideas to Hollywood, stacks of legal size yellow notepads, and 3-by-5 inch index cards all around me. I read, then wrote, and then read some more. I would not be silenced. I would tell my story in a screenplay.

CHAPTER 10

Heading for the (Hollywood) Hills

I became determined to write a screenplay and tell my story. Coincidentally, I heard through the water-skiing grapevine that "Banana George" Blair, an award-winning barefoot skier nicknamed for his trademark look of wearing bright yellow wetsuits, was going to be involved in a movie called *Captiva Island.* I wrote to him, asking if I could somehow be involved, perhaps as his personal assistant. He agreed at once, so I spent the next month driving back and forth from Lake Wales to *Captiva Island* to the movie set.

I wasn't his assistant so much as his personal slave. I drove him every where he needed to go in his big yellow Cadillac. I fetched him his bottled water, gave him shoulder massages, sanded the calluses on his feet, and even cut his toe nails—ugh. The cast and crew took to yelling out as he did, competing to do the best Banana George imitation, "Shellie, where's my water!"

One day we took George's big yellow Ski Nautique out into the ocean to film a barefoot skiing segment. I begged him to let me drive the boat out there since I would be the one doing the actual driving during the scene, but he insisted on getting us all out to the spot himself. He was like that. The director and cameraman were sitting with their backs to the bow of the boat in the shotgun seat. I was sitting in the back right seat just behind Banana George, facing forward. The camera equipment was attached in front of the windshield to the bow of the boat, rigged to a boom that protruded six or seven feet from the side of the middle of the boat.

From my vantage point, I could see that Banana George was heading too close to a big wooden pylon that marked the Intercoastal, so I yelled out, "George!" Banana George was extremely fit and sound for a man in his seventies, but even he still couldn't hear me over the roar of the boat engine. I leaned closer and yelled again, louder this time, "George! Look out!"

He was still heading too close to the pylon, apparently forgetting that we needed extra clearance because of the equipment on the side of the boat. Finally, I shrieked at the top of my lungs, "George!" I grabbed the side of the boat and was getting ready to jump overboard and duck when Banana George finally responded. At the last second he turned the boat just enough that we didn't hit the pylon squarely with the boom, although we did catch enough of it that the boom and camera equipment came crashing through the windshield, and the boat swung around 180 degrees. My yelling had at least alerted the cameraman and director, so when they saw me duck, they did, too. If not, they would have caught the full weight of the boom and the equipment in the backs of their heads.

We did not film that day. Banana George let me drive, or rather limp, the big yellow Nautique back to the dock. Everyone was rattled to the bone, including me. Later I saw the director sitting alone at the end of the pier staring off at the sunset. I could imagine what he was thinking: if I not yelled out my warning, he might well have lost his head that day, literally!

Near-death experiences will put anyone in a funk. I should know.

My *Captiva Island* movie experience wasn't all toenails and terror, though. For one thing, I got to meet Wilbert "Bill" Cobbs, and talk to him about his career in television and more than 120 movies. In fact, I spent the whole day of my 30th birthday on a yacht with him on the Intercoastal Waterway, talking about his roles—Charles, older brother of Medgar Evers, in Rob Reiner's *Ghosts of Mississippi*; Moses the Clock Man in the Coen Brothers' *The Hudsucker Proxy*; and jazz pianist Del Paxton in the Tom Hanks film *That Thing You Do*. But he told me that even though these were smaller roles, he was most proud of his performances in *The Color of Money* as Orvis, the crusty old billiard-parlor owner, and in his bit parts in *Five Corners*, *Silkwood*, and *The Bodyguard*. Modest about his own great talents, he spoke of what an honor it was to work with such a great actor and actresses as Paul Newman, Tom Cruise, Jodie Foster, Meryl Streep and Kevin Costner.

Meeting and spending time with Bill Cobbs was the most enjoy able part of the whole *Captiva Island* experience, and I soaked in as much movie and film history as I could. I did get to meet Banana George's co-star, Academy Award winner Ernest Borgnine. The one day he was there for filming, we were all sitting down to lunch set up by craft services. I was sitting alone, and Borgnine sat right across from me—probably because he, too, wanted to be left alone, and have as little to do with that project as possible. I could respect that. We nodded to each other when our eyes met. He said hello, and I said hi back, and that was that. That was good enough for me. I was as anxious to end my stint as unpaid gofer as soon as possible.

Actually, I had asked for payment. Specifically, all I had asked for in exchange for acting as personal assistant to Banana George was a film credit. When the movie finally came out in a local theater I went alone, and endured the whole painfully bad movie just to watch as every last credit had rolled up the screen. It wasn't there. Nothing, nada, zip. I had literally saved the life of the director and cameraman of the movie, but my name was never mentioned. Bummer. Why is it so hard for some people to keep their word?

My grandparents, who lived in Santa Ana, California, had split up. Although my grandfather was still sprightly, my grandmother was showing signs of Alzheimer's, and the most logical place for Nana was with my mom and me in Florida. So there we were, three generations of us living in my little singlewide mobile home. My grandfather sent a little money every month to help out, and the extra income helped. My mom had given up her house in Missouri since she was spending most of her time with me, some of the time with my sister, and the rest of her time with my brother Brent or my brother Brad. It was cozy, but we managed. Still, when my grandfather planned a month-long trip to London with his new gal pal from the Elks and offered me the opportunity me to house sit while he was gone, I jumped at the opportunity. Since his retirement community in Santa Ana was just 45 minutes by car away from Hollywood, I could sign up for a screenwriting conference and try to make whatever contacts I could while learning more about writing and selling a screenplay. I was still determined to tell my story—the truth of what really happened that day at Cypress Gardens.

Just before I was ready to drive out to California, I received a call from Faith telling me that a mediation date had been set for my worker's compensation lawsuit. The insurance company indicated that it really wanted to settle with me, and Faith explained that while there wasn't much negotiation room at our end, there was some. By that time I hadn't been in the work force for almost seven years, and she doubted that I could be hired for any type of job on an uninterrupted basis given my lingering medical problems. I would present a liability to any company that hired me. In her office just before we drove to the mediation, Faith said, "Don't worry. I'm not going to force you to take a settlement you're not happy with. If you settle your workers' comp, great—you can get on with your life. If you don't settle, fine—we'll fight to get you some kind of financial security. Either way, I'm not afraid to work for my money. By the way, how's that screenplay coming along?"

I laughed. "Well, it's been the only thing that has kept me halfway sane," I said. "I'm not at the point yet when I've met you, but it's getting closer. I only hope I can do you justice. A young, attractive, female attorney appropriately named Faith, who gave me faith when I needed it most."

"I only wish we'd met sooner, before you had all those other bad experiences with other attorneys."

"Well, you know Faith, they say everything happens for a reason," I said. "And I have come to figure that if there's no obvious reason, then it's my job to find one."

"If it makes you feel any better, I think you are doing and have done the right thing. Not everyone can tough out the system like you have. It's easy to just give in. Most people do."

At the mediation that day, I settled my workers' compensation lawsuit. I felt confident Faith had gotten everything she could for me. It is a state-regulated financial ratio; even the payment for her work is regulated. I had been collecting 66 and 2/3 thirds of my $8 an hour for almost six years. I had been hiding out like a hermit for fear of being filmed during the day, and going out and drinking at night like a maniac for long enough.

"I wish it was more," said Faith after mediation. "I know your skiing career would have been worth a lot more."

"It's so weird, I can't believe what I've been through all these years. It's like I've been in limbo," I said. "You look up the word insurance in the dictionary, and it's nothing like the definition in the real world. I worked hard all those years. I paid into a system, and when I really needed the money, the insurance company fought me tooth and nail. I guess they have to because of all the frauds."

"What are your plans for the future?"

I grinned happily. "Well, in the short term, I'm about to drive to Los Angeles and try to tell my story. Remember when I told you once about feeling guilty for holding out so long against the system? Later on, I remembered a quote from Golda Meir. She said something like, 'If I am not for myself, who will be for me? But if I am for myself only, what am I? If not now…when?' Faith, my when is *now*." She wished me luck, and we parted ways.

I packed up my little red Toyota and headed to my grandfather's house in Santa Ana. The screenwriting conference wasn't for another week, so I had plenty of time to get there. I had arranged to stay at the hotel hosting the conference for two days to increase my networking opportunities, and then I'd start the house-sitting gig. I kept in constant contact with my mom who was back home taking care of Nana. The affects of Nana's Alzheimer's were getting worse, and I was concerned for my mom caring for Nana all by herself. But it didn't stifle my excitement as I drove along singing with Sheryl Crow on the radio. I was anticipating the famous line "All I wanna do is have some fun until the sun comes up over Santa Monica Boulevard" because soon it would be my literal truth. I was going to Hollywood to sell my screenplay!

I settled in at my grandfather's place and prepared for my two-day screenwriter's conference. I called any of the agents who had showed a remote interest in the query letter I had been sending out for over a month, each one done the old-fashioned way on an ink cartridge typewriter. I probably typed and sent over 200 letters and envelopes this way and, like most writers, got back only the basic "thanks but no thanks" and "we don't look at unsolicited material" form letters in return, if that. A handful, though, had agreed to meet with me, and I scheduled those meetings for after the conference. I packed my little overnight bag and drove to the hotel with the attaché case that held my script and all my notes about who and where I was meeting agents.

As the second and final day of the conference wound down, I wandered down to the bar to soak in some of the Hollywood vibe. I was just starting my second rum and Coke when someone from the front desk came up and asked if I was Ms. Blum. I was thinking, *Aha! My Hollywood moment, when at last someone is about to tell me they want my screenplay. Maybe they even want me to star in the movie!*

I nodded. "Yes, I'm Shellie Blum."

"You received an urgent phone message from your mom in Florida. She said if you weren't in your room, we could probably find you here at the bar. She wants you to call her right away." Some Hollywood moment.

I went to my room and called home. My mom told me that she'd been sleeping in my room while I was gone, and when she went into Nana's room to check on her in the morning to see what she wanted to eat, she found that Nana had died peacefully in her sleep. "She seemed pale. And when I touched her, she was cold. She was gone."

I immediately asked if I should come back, but she said no, that Nana would have wanted me to stay put and follow my dream. My mom's two sisters were already in the air and on their way there. I went back down to the bar, and spent the rest of my evening choking up, debating whether to stay or drive back home right away. I blew off the last session of the conference. I kept telling myself that it was okay, that Nana was already gone and that a peaceful end for an Alzheimer's patient is really a blessing, but I felt guilty not being there for my mom. I was torn. I wanted to go home, but the next day I had two meetings scheduled with production people and agents. I didn't want to miss what might be my big chance. I stayed.

The first meeting, with Wanda Moore at the Gage Group, was scheduled for 3:00 o'clock. It was a decent-sized building with a pleasant reception area. A pretty, blonde, sharply dressed, up-and-coming development person came into the reception area and invited me into her office. We talked at length and she was very encouraging. She gave me some advice, although at the time it wasn't what I wanted to hear: she told me I should write my story as a book.

I thought, this woman is crazy. I just spent the last six years of my life devoted to my journal, which turned into my outline, which turned into my screenplay. I thought of joking to Wanda that I would just step outside for a moment and crap out a book, but fortunately I thought better of it. But seriously, I wasn't even a screenplay writer, and I was definitely not an author. I was just a girl with a story that sometimes seemed too unbelievable to be true. But it was true. Wanda explained to me that she was very interested in my story and thought maybe there was a chance to shop it around Hollywood, but she would have to run it by the higher ups, who, as it happened, weren't there that day. "Could you come back tomorrow and meet the boss?" she asked. "Most definitely!" I enthusiastically answered. We set up the appointment, and I left.

The next place I stopped off wasn't a personal appointment, just a whim. No one had agreed to meet with me. I stood outside the Egg Pictures building, Jodie Foster's production company, working up the courage to call and tell one of the two assistants I'd spoken with before that I just *happened* to be downstairs and wouldn't they just take a moment to please look at the script? I called, but I don't know if I reached Michelle Rosenblatt or Lisa Buono. I knew these names because they were the signatures of the "thanks but no thanks form letters I'd gotten back from my query letters. In any case, she politely refused—just as they had politely rejected my previous three query letters. But I just had to try. After all, how often would I just *happen* to be 3,000 miles away from home and in Hollywood?

So I worked up even more courage and went up into the building. I rode the elevator to Egg Pictures and approached the receptionist's desk. I asked if I could leave a video and/or a script or outline with her for someone to review when they had the chance. She called into the office and told someone inside that Shellie Blum was standing in the reception area. I chose to take it as a good sign that she seemed to think they would recognize my name, and figured they wouldn't be able to resist at least meeting this crazy water-skier stalker chick who wouldn't take no for an answer.

I was right, but not for the reasons I'd hoped. Someone, again probably either Lisa Buono or Michelle Rosenblatt, came out into the reception area in a huff. With forced politeness, she told me one last time that they did not accept unsolicited material, and that I would have to leave. Immediately. Without leaving anything behind. I apologized as meekly as I could, and turned to go. But I couldn't resist turning around one last time to look at the door behind which might be, at that very moment, one of greatest actresses of all time, Jodie Foster. So close! As I looked back, though, what I saw was not a glimpse of my idol but the somewhat comical scene of the assistant slash watchdog having locked herself out and having to ask to be buzzed back in. Being turned away of course made me sad, but that scene made me chuckle.

Of course, I was going about things all wrong, and I knew it. But when it came to getting my story told, for some reason I had tunnel vision. Just a month earlier I drove from my house in Florida three hours to Miami to drop a video and handwritten letter in Madonna's mailbox. And sometime before that I received a rejection from Madonna that at least had her autograph…um…I mean, signature on the green cardboard certified letter receipt. Sadly, that piece of memorabilia was one of the things that was to be stolen soon, or I would have framed it.

My next official visit was with an alleged agent. I say alleged because the setting seemed so sketchy. I walked up a flight of stairs in a not-so-great part of downtown Los Angeles, some sort of skid row. There was trash on the building's stairway, and the office itself was tiny. It was slightly bigger than a good-sized walk-in closet, and it felt claustrophobic because of all the stacks of papers, pictures, and miscellaneous junk. The much older man behind the only desk sat chatting away on the phone, smoking a cigarette. "Hold on a sec," he said into the phone, and paused for a moment so I could explain who I was and why I was there. "Oh yeah, right, you're the water-ski girl. I gotta guy comin' in who is gonna look at your script and give you some advice on it. Right now, though, I am on an important call, and…look at that, there he is."

He went back to his phone conversation while a guy in a Hawaiian shirt wedged himself into the tiny room and sat down. He introduced himself as a screenwriter/assistant agent in training. The agent had contacted him about working with me to improve my script. Once we got past the normal introductory chit chat, he asked to look at my script, so I retrieved it from my attaché case and handed it to him. He immediately started reading it, and marking it up.

After about ten minutes, he looked up from his work and said he was starving. "How 'bout we go out to eat and I can look this over some more while we have dinner?"

I was hungry, too—it was well after 5:00 o'clock—so I agreed. The guy had given me nothing but a laid-back kind of surfer dude vibe, so I was sure he was harmless. We left the agent behind and made our way down the messy stairs to the street, where the screenwriter shrugged apologetically. "Um, I don't have a car," he said. "It's okay I ride with you, right? I know this cool little Mexican place just down the road, and we could walk from here, but you got wheels, so?"

I wasn't thrilled, but again, I was pretty certain the guy was harmless. The minute we got into my car, he reached in his pocket and pulled out a joint. "You don't mind, do you?" At the same time he was asking me if I minded, he was already lighting up. He offered the joint to me, but I just shook my hand at it and said no thanks. I was still hoping that the guy was going to turn out to be legit, and a real agent who could help me, but my hopes were dwindling with each minute I spent with him. Still, I didn't see any harm in giving a guy a ride to a restaurant, especially when he knew the area and I didn't, and I was hungry.

At least he was right about the restaurant. It was close, and decent. We ordered nachos and by that time I was ready for a drink, so we added a pitcher of Margaritas, and our entrees. We ate, we talked, we laughed, and I was finally starting to feel confident that he was going to be a great connection when suddenly he looked at his wrist. Of course, he had no watch, either.

"What time is it?"

"About 7:30, why?"

"I gotta go—I gotta be somewhere!" He bolted from the booth and abruptly left without so much as leaving a card. I sat there, stunned, wondering what I should do. Then I figured that since I had a meal and a pitcher of Margaritas that I would be paying for any way, I might as well just eat and then figure out how to get back to my grandfather's place in Santa Ana. I still had half a pitcher of Margaritas left when, two women stopped at my table.

"Why are you sitting here all by yourself?" asked the first one, who was a beautiful very light skinned black woman, most likely bi-racial. I told her a little bit about the drama that had just unfolded, and they laughed. "How about me and my girlfriend help you finish your pitcher?"

Why not? "Yeah, I could use the company." The two attractive girls slid into the booth opposite me and we become quick friends. We were all similar in age. The bi-racial girl was a nurse, and her White girlfriend was studying to become one. Both were originally from Maine, and we had the exact same kind of cars: early 1980s MR2 Toyotas, although theirs was white with Maine plates, and mine was red with Oregon plates. My sister Tamara lived in Oregon at the time, and after my car in Florida had gotten repossessed, she had gotten the car I now drove from one of her chiropractic patients and I hadn't yet changed the tags. We started calling ourselves the Oregon-Maine girls, taking on Hollywood and loving it. Since I had blonde hair, the bi-racial girl had dark brown hair, and her girlfriend had red hair, we looked like *The Witches of Eastwick.* Three pretty girls with a Margarita buzz—we were getting noticed and we loved it.

The two of them had been in town for a while, so they knew some very cool places to go. When we finished up my food and the drinks, we decided to caravan to a place called The Palms to have some more fun. Apparently I was having a little *too* much fun on the dance floor, because the person who ran the place asked me to leave, which I found weird. Still, it was better than being carried out of a two-bit pool hall by a macho bouncer. I found the other two "witches," and when they heard I'd been asked to leave they decided to come along, so we headed to another place they liked, with me following their car.

It was late when we pulled up to the two-story building and parked both cars next to the curb across the street. I locked my purse in the trunk, leaving my attaché case and papers on the back seat, and pocketed only a small amount of cash, my I.D., and my keys. When I followed the witches into the main area of the second nightclub, it was like stepping into another world. The walls seemed to pulse with pounding music. There were at least three separate bar areas on the ground level, and several more on the second level, and people moved up and down and among them all, mixing and mingling. There were professional dancers in a designated area, and people tipped their favorites and cheered them on. I was dancing nearby when somehow I found myself pushed into the circle of the professional dancers; people cheered for me, too, and some even threw money my way. I just laughed and picked up the money and threw it back to them, then scurried back to the surrounding circle. I thought I had disappeared when I heard a voice boom out from P.A. systems, "Where's that little blonde chick? Where's our little sunshine?" I spotted the D.J./emcee, a large female impersonator with a red wig, scanning the crowd, crooning into the mic. The crowd nudged me back into the dancing area again. I tried to refuse, but I had nowhere to go, so I danced a little. I was just beginning to get comfortable when one of the professional dancers, a big black female impersonator, came up behind me and picked me up from the waist. He spun me until I ended up with my legs wrapped around him, grateful that I was wearing a nice pastel green slacks outfit so there was nothing revealing. The crowd went wild at the sight of this unique dichotomy of dirty dancing, but as soon as I could I freed myself, and again scurried to the sidelines. I started to wonder where my "witches" had gotten off to, so I pushed out of that area of the nightclub to try and find them.

As I made my way through the crowd, I was approached by a Hispanic man. He flashed his palm at me, revealing a couple of joints, and yelled something in Spanish. I could barely hear him over the music, but in any case I don't speak the language, so I tried to answer with what I did know, which was, "No habla Español!" I kept working my way through the crowd, muttering, "Sorry, sorry, just looking for my friends," but they were nowhere to be found. I was disappointed that I would have to leave without saying goodbye to my new friends, but I had a long drive ahead to Santa Ana, because I didn't have another night at the hotel where conference had been. It was a little after midnight when I walked to my car. I knew that the witches were still inside the club because their car was still parked right in front of mine.

As I reached out to put my keys in the door lock, I heard something a little over to my left, and thought for a moment that they must have seen me heading out and come to say goodbye after all. I turned my head that direction and suddenly felt a big blow to the side of my face and cheekbone. My first thought was that something must have flown off a car driving by or fallen off a building, but then I felt the second blow to the jaw, which knocked me back against my car. It finally dawned on me that I was being attacked and I deflected the third blow off to the side of my left temple. For the first time I got a look at my attacker—the Hispanic man from the club. He grabbed my wrists, which I had crossed up near my head to deflect the blows. My hair was intertwined in his hands.

When he started dragging me toward a nearby alley, I screamed at the top of my lungs. "Somebody help me! Somebody help me! Somebody help me! Every time I opened my mouth, bloody spit flew out. But I refused to buckle. I tried my favorite move from my scrappy days as a fairly successful schoolyard wrestler, and managed to outmaneuver the man. He kept trying to force me to the ground, but I wouldn't go down. I had survived his sucker punches, and I wasn't about to let him beat me out at wrestling. My adrenaline had kicked in and I was fighting back like a trapped wildcat. I knew I was fighting for my life.

Finally I was able to break free and I ran back into the club and collapsed on the floor. A circle of people gathered around me, *oohing* and *ahhing* over my bloody, swollen face. I put a tentative hand to my face, but all I could be sure of was that at least one front tooth had been knocked out. The faces around me came into focus, and among them I made out the concerned looked of my bi-racial and redheaded "witches". While they called 911, the black female impersonator stayed with me, holding my hand. "Oh girl, someone messed you up bad!" he said. "I am so, so sorry. We are right here for you. You hang on!" I did, until the paramedics put me in the ambulance, I started up with my all-too-familiar moaning and passed out.

When I awoke, a doctor was leaning over me. "You have a nasty gash inside your upper lip. We'll stitch that up right away—should take about ten stitches. And your front tooth has been knocked out," he said. "Now, here's the worst of it. We've taken X-rays, and your left jaw and cheekbone are crushed. They will need surgery." From the look on his face I could tell that the X-rays also told him that I had been through this before. He probably figured I was just another battered woman with a mean husband or pimp. If he only knew the truth! But what was the truth? Was I the world's unluckiest woman?

A broken jaw and cheekbone: I knew what that meant. I didn't know whether to be relieved or upset that my water-skiing accident had broken my right jaw, and now this was my left side. Ultimately, I decided it didn't matter, because no matter what it meant I would have to have my jaws wired shut again. The thought was more than I could bear. Until then I had moaned and whimpered but had not cried, but at the thought of being wired down again I finally let go. As I stared up at the ER ceiling, the tears streamed down my temples and into my ears.

Because of the time difference, it was after 3:00 a.m. when we reached my mom in Florida, but she was instantly awake and in decision-making mode. We decided that I wouldn't have surgery in Los Angeles, but that I would fly to my sister's house in Eugene, Oregon, and have my surgery done by one of her doctor friends who specialized in facial reconstruction. I spent the next day at the home of my sister's in-laws in the Valley, and caught a plane the next day for Eugene. When Tamara saw me get off the plane, she had tears in her eyes. It had been 48 hours since the attack, and my face had swollen considerably since the pictures that had been taken at the hospital right after the assault. I looked like the Elephant Man, and felt like him too.

Waiting seemed to have been the right idea, though. When I woke after the surgery, the surgeon said, "Don't try to talk. We had to put two metal plates in during surgery: two pieces along the break in your jaw, and we're considering putting one across your crushed cheekbone, but let's see how it heals, hopefully there's no deformity and it won't need it."

He traced the lines on my face so I'd know what he was talking about. "The metal shouldn't cause you any problems, and will remain in there for the rest of your life, unless we feel the need to remove it if your body doesn't react well to it," he said. "But considering what you've been through, I think you look pretty good." I nodded and smiled, showing off the wires on my gum line that would keep my jaws clamped down again, a couple of stitches hanging down from inside my lip, and the gap missing from my front tooth.

At my sister's house, I filled out California's Victim of a Violent Crime paperwork. Based on the police report, I knew that the crime took place just after midnight August 27, 1995, just outside at a nightclub called Catch One. Thank God, that night my assailant didn't "catch one," though it had not been for lack of trying. My car had been impounded for sitting on the street for so long, but my sister's in-laws finally picked it up. When we called and asked about my belongings, I discovered that my purse was still in the trunk where I put it under a tarp, but my attaché case and all my script material and other papers had been stolen out of the back seat. After all, the keys were probably still in the door during the fight, so the assailant would have had no trouble grabbing whatever he wanted. I had copies of almost everything, but I would not be framing my certified mail receipt from Madonna; her autograph…I mean, signature…was stolen, gone forever. Bummer.

When I finally returned home, I went to see Dr. Rowe. I still looked like hell. My face was badly bruised and swollen, the white of my left eye bright red, my teeth wired together, and my front tooth missing. Talking was very difficult.

"So you're angry," said Dr. Rowe. "Do you wish revenge on your attacker?"

I was fighting back tears while I tried to speak. Finally, I shook my head, no. "I've been angry for so long, it's worn me out," I said. "I feel pity for him. I wonder what his past was like, what his life is like, I mean, to have made him such a violent man." I paused and started thinking back to that night. What had I done to make this man so mad? Was he a serial killer/rapist come out of retirement, or maybe just starting out? Or was I dancing that night in the circle with his transvestite-transgendered lover? Was he seeking revenge on me for that? I'll never know.

Dr. Rowe waited for more. There is always "more" in therapy.

"And it's made me think about how my past has made me who I am today, and that I shouldn't have to apologize for that—for being a strong-willed aggressive girl. I fight to survive," I said with a shrug. "Revenge? I don't want revenge, but I AM angry. I should be allowed at least that and I guess I do want some kind of justification or reason for this to have happened to me. Even if I have to make up a reason for this to have happened to me, I will find the positive in this. I will see this through. Isn't that what life is all about? Seeing it through?"

This go-round with my teeth wired together didn't seem quite as bad. This time, instead of being limited to liquids like milk shakes, I was able to pull noodles and other soft things through the gap where my front tooth was missing, but I still lost a lot of weight. I grew even thinner, so I was always cold, always in pain, and always very depressed. And not having Nana with us made it worse. It's funny how some of the things that drive you nuts about people are often the things you kind of miss when they're gone. I would no longer hear Nana ask, "Did you hear Marilyn Monroe killed Clark Gable?"

Nana used to sit in what we called the Queen Bee chair reading the *Enquirer* my mom bought her. She kept that same *Enquirer* for a year, the one with the headline that claimed Marilyn Monroe killed Clark Gable. Every day it was all new to her, and every day she would tell us the same "news"—sometimes the same things five or ten minutes apart. We would just say back to her things like, "How horrible!" or "Tell us all about it, Nana." Toward the end of her life, we had to take all the knobs off the stove, because she would find straws and try to light them off the burners like a cigarette. Several times we found her in the car getting ready to drive "uptown." Sometimes I would get in my car and know she'd been there: the windshield wipers would be on, or the radio would be blasting. Every time I would put my hand on the doorknob to leave the trailer, she would quickly ask, "Hey, you going uptown? Could you grab me a pack of cigarettes?" Nana was from the Rosie the Riveter days. She sat in her Queen Bee chair, regal as ever, chain-smoking cigarettes until we had to make her stop—partly for health and money reasons, but also because we half-feared she might accidentally burn the place down.

I had to find something to keep me focused and not going to the bars. I was always fighting my depression and chronic pain, and the attack in Hollywood had made it all that much harder. On top of that I was now getting nothing but rejection letters back on my screenplay queries. But I am no quitter: I'd collected 114 rejection letters by then, but I wasn't about to give up. The letters were all very encouraging and yet discouraging at the same time. A few even asked for the screenplay, but shortly after that I would get the letter saying that the company was going to pass. And it was obvious why I didn't make it back to the agents that showed interest in meeting me in person: later that evening I was being viciously attacked.

At least I had a small chunk of money in the bank. The product liability attorney took over half of the settlement, and after I paid back my lien to the worker's compensation fund there wasn't a whole lot of money left, but I had enough and I would make the best of it. I loaned a pretty big sum of money to my sister, Tamara, to help her make a down payment on a house, and I loaned an equally large sum to my brother, Brent, as seed money to start a business. And I always tried to help my oldest brother, Brad, whenever he needed it. I paid off the mortgage on my singlewide mobile home, and started to look for property to move it. My lot rent at Sunny Acres had gone from $100 to $170 a month, and I could just not tolerate it, but even more, I wanted something I could call my own. I found some property not even a half-mile away—little pieces of parcel land from ½ an acre to ¾ of an acre—and decided I would not pay lot rent anymore. I bought a parcel of land in Waverly Loop, Lake Wales and moved my singlewide over there.

After I bought my piece of land, I started thinking about the kind of neighbors I might end up with, so I asked Carl Jackson, the orange grove owner who was selling the parcels of land, if I could start making payments on the parcels of land on either side of me. That way I would never have to have neighbors I didn't want. Carl Jackson was a savvy businessman, so he was reluctant to sell the other two parcels to me, but after much cajoling, I finally wore him down. I started looking in the paper for mobile homes for sale, and going to repo yards to try and find homes to put on my other two parcels of land. I finally found a nice singlewide for sale, bought it, and had it moved onto the parcel of land to my right. I lived at 255 Waverly Loop, and owned 265 and 218 to the left and right of me. This is not the easiest thing to do, as there was a lot of paperwork to be done: permits for septic systems, electric poles, driveways, and water wells, along with tons of other bureaucracies to go through, but those years after the accident strengthened my natural perseverance, and with some patience I got it done. And through the years, I have become proficient at it. Right now, if you needed a mobile home moved onto a piece of property and set up to go, I'm your man, er, uh, gal. I started renting out 265 Waverly Loop, and then later I started renting 218. Before I knew it, I had become a landlord.

Meanwhile, I was still waiting for Hollywood to call. The chronic pain was always with me, and my body had become a human barometer, so if I noticed myself feeling especially irritable for no reason, or my hip, ear, cheek, jaws, or neck throbbed even more than usual, I knew we had a change of weather coming. On really bad days, I still went out drinking, slipping back into my old routines of self-medicating with alcohol, for distraction I also started entering a lot of pool tournaments. A bar called ABC Liquors across from the local Wal-Mart had a cool giant circular bar that rotated. When I found out they held a pool tournament every Tuesday night, I started going. I won the first tournament I entered, and came back the next Tuesday. I won that tournament, too. When I came back for the third tournament, the bartender told me they cancelled the tournament. When I asked why, the bartender told me, "Nobody showed up. Guess the guys are tired of losing to ya."

It was still a fun place, and it was there that I bumped into an old ski buddy of mine, Mike Barnes, a Canadian champion snow skier who had crossed over and become a champion water-ski show jumper. Mike had what might just be the best—and *was* definitely the prettiest—back-flips in the world. Now that my lawsuits had been settled, he was no longer prohibited from talking to me. He and I sat at the bar, and eventually our conversation harkened back to my accident. When he started giving his explanation of what he thought he saw that day, though, my blood started to boil. I still don't recall him even having been there, but I let him talk. He tried to explain to me that he thought my right hand, the one holding the rope handle, went across my neck to the left side and that somehow I strangled myself by not letting go of the rope handle.

"Oh. My. God. You have to be f**king kidding me!" I said. "You think that I would be strong enough to hang onto a handle with my arm under my chin and be dragged through the water at 36 miles an hour so that I broke my jaw in half and my neck in two?" I shook my head. "Incredible. So, is that what people are saying?"

"Shellie, I'm just telling you what I think I saw that day," said Mike.

"Yeah, and Mark says the rope and handle hit me in the face. You are both wrong! It happened to me, don't you think I know what happened to me!" We were friends, but suddenly I found myself thinking that if I didn't get him out of my face, I was going to shove him—or worse, start crying. I had to leave. The court case might have been settled, but apparently the drama was far from over. Would the true story ever be told?

CHAPTER 11

Sticking the Landing

I bumped into Mike Barnes again at ABC Liquors the following week. I wasn't sure how it would go, but as it turned out, he apologized. He didn't change his story, he just let it drop, and we have never spoken of it again. We became good friends after that, and he became one of my new bar-hopping buddies. No blonde hair, but he was another blue-eyed guy I would occasionally bait with the idea I might let him be my sperm donor for my future kids. Like my guy friends in the past, he thought I was kidding, but I was not.

I found Mike's change of heart encouraging. One of the main reasons I had always been so eager to tell "my story" was that I wanted to make sure it never happened again. But in fact, that rope design was no longer even available on the market, and I strongly suspected that my case had been the reason for its removal and redesign. At least I had been successful in that part of my cause. Now I realized that what was driving my burning need to tell people how the accident happened was my realization that I felt wrongly accused of being some kind of faker or malingerer. Also, I felt certain there were people that thought I had just really messed up somehow, maybe even thought, "She shouldn't have been out there trying back flips anyway." Or worse, "She got what she deserved."

I had every right to be out there. I knew the true story of what happened. But many of the people I knew now and had known back when the accident happened also thought they knew what happened.

Some of them made up stories, sure—especially those who were afraid of being held responsible somehow. But most of the others just didn't really know what happened. I thought about how sure Mike was that I had strangled myself with my own arm, even though that was probably scientifically impossible given my physical size, the speed of the boat, the amount of drag, and the design of the rope. Sure, I was pretty strong back then, and as every beginner water-skier will tell you, when you're first starting out the urge to keep holding onto the rope rather than do the logical thing (let go) is surprisingly strong. But I was hardly a beginner: I'd been skiing professionally for thirteen years. And no matter how much I might have wanted to stick that landing, if I'd been able to just let go of a handle when everything went bad, I would have in a heartbeat!

But from far away on the dock, with the wake from the boat blocking the view, the people shouting in the boat, the other skiers would not have been able to tell what happened. Nobody had ever been hung by a ski rope before, so why would they think that had happened? All they would have seen would be me going down in a flume of water and not coming up until the safety release finally let go, or did the rope break? Whichever, the rope finally separated from the boat, and it stopped dragging me by my neck!

It was after talking with Mike that I really started to think about things in that way. I realized that even people who told a different story from mine weren't necessarily lying. They just saw a different "truth," or heard one from someone who was there. And these were my people—water-skiing people were my best friends. I wanted them to know, and believe, what I knew to be true: on my fifth jump, my third try at the back flip (gainer), I over-rotated, fell out the front, and because of a demonstrably bad bridle design, my head went into the handle...which might as well have been a noose.

So it was with equal parts anticipation and trepidation that I agreed to go to a birthday party for my friend Betty Bonifay at her house. Betty was one of the only water-ski friends who had stood by me through the years. When she knew how depressed I was, she would have me come over to her house and help with her ski lessons, or even just have me drive to the airport and pick up her ski lesson students, who came from all over the world. I guess she figured that anything that got me out of my house and out of the bars was good therapy, too.

Over the years she'd had other parties with water-skiing people, but she knew I wasn't always eager to mingle with the old crowd. Still, she kept at me. This time it was very low-key, her own birthday party. Her sons, Parks and Shane, whom I had known since they were toddlers, became champion wakeboarders, and they would be there. Wakeboarders had taken over a lot of the limelight from three-event competition skiing. I'm sure that if I hadn't had my accident, I would have made quite a splash in the wakeboarding world, too. Wakeboarders travel much slower than freestyle water-ski jumpers, and they jump off the boat wake rather than a six-foot jump ramp to produce their twist and turns. The best part was that girls had their own competitions.

Thinking about all the people from the old days who might be at the party, I was nervous. When I arrived, I started drinking right away, and eventually I relaxed a bit. As the night progressed, some of the skiers were mingling next door at the home of another water-skier who worked at Cypress Gardens. It was over there that one of the guys from the Gardens started hitting on me. I won't use his name. Let's call him Dick. It was late and we were both pretty drunk. We were feuding because he kept insisting that I had gotten a boob job, even though I explained that I hadn't, it was just that all the muscle around my breasts had deflated because I wasn't skiing anymore. Dick didn't believe me and kept telling me how good I looked, and how different I looked from when I skied at the Gardens. In my inebriated state, and given his probable incoherence, I interpreted it to mean that he didn't like me at Cypress Gardens when I was at the peak of my athleticism and strength, but now that I was skinny and weak, he thought I was hot! Not surprisingly, that didn't sit too well with me. It was only a matter of time before our conversation turned to the day of my accident, and I said something about Mark being slow on the safety-release of the rope.

Dick got right up in my face, his playful sexual overtones and friendly mood had gone dark and defensive. "I am not going to stand here and let you bad mouth my good friend, and the man, I think, who saved your life!"

I went into instant anger mode. "I was dragging back there! He was late on the pin," I spit back. "And you better get outta my face!"

Dick kept his face right up in my grill. "I saw it. The rope and handle hit you in the face!"

"You probably weren't even there that day. You're just repeating that tired old line of shit that they told you to say. Now get outta my face!" As I said the word "face" I gave him a little shove in the chest. Had we both been sober, that would probably have been the end of it. But he was unsteady on his feet, and he stumbled backward. Then he came back at me, and the next thing I knew we were in a brawl. I was trying to get away, but he kept coming at me. We were outside rolling around in the dirt and grass when I finally broke free and ran back into the house. I grabbed the frame of a white French door on the patio lanai and slammed it shut behind me, hoping to stop Dick from continuing his attack, but he kept coming. Finally, the owner of the house grabbed Dick from behind and pinned his elbows together. The owner was shouting, "Back off, back off. Get away from her!" I ran back to Betty Bonifay's house, got in my car, and left. The next day I got a phone call from the wife of the man who stopped the fight. She wanted to know if I was planning to pay for the damage to her patio French door. I asked in amazement, "What?" She said matter-of-factly, "Don't deny it, I know it was you because there were bloody fingerprints on it where you slammed it. And, you broke the window!" I told her I would get the money together to pay for the damage to her patio door.

After yet another fight about the truth of what happened that day I broke my neck and jaw at Cypress Gardens, all my tentative hopes that I could one day clear the air with all my friends evaporated in the steam of my anger. But I didn't let that get in my way of trying to move my life forward. Carl Jackson, the orange grove owner, started coming to me first with offers to buy his land. I mortgaged two more parcels and set up a mobile home on each of them. By then I had five pieces of property, four of which brought in a small but steady income. One day I was out walking and came upon the property on the lake where years before I ended up in my walking rage the day I found out that the workers' compensation carrier was forcing me back to work at Cypress Gardens. Unbelievably, the property was still for sale. I spoke to the owner—probably the same man who had yelled at me back then for trespassing on private property—and when he learned what I wanted it for, he told me not to buy it. It was too close to the lakefront and I would never be able to get a variance from the county to build there. Undaunted, I wrote down the number of the realtor, called, and made an offer. I made sure that the contract said that if I couldn't build on it, I could get my money back. My hope was that someday, when I paid the land off, I could get a variance and build a house there.

My mom was still living with me, but she was in the habit of taking trips every chance she got to visit the rest of the family. She could do that because one of my cousins worked for Frontier airlines out of the Denver hub, and was able to get my mom "companion passes" that allowed my mom to travel at a discount. Because she had done so much for me over the years, whenever my mom was gone on a trip I liked to surprise her with some new project when she returned. Not long after I bought the lakefront lot she was off on one of her jaunts and I decided while she was gone to surprise her by having the windows on her car tinted.

My good friend Betty Bonifay's husband, Pete, owned a window tinting business. Whenever a friend got a new car, he always tinted the car windows for a good price. I had scheduled the job on my mom's car for toward the end of the workday, and while I waited we got to talking about old times. The next thing I knew it was past 5:00 p.m. and I had a pool tournament I intended to enter. It would start at 6:00 p.m. at a different ABC Liquors, the one near Dundee, Florida. Since Pete and I often bumped into each other at the bars where we both played pool, I asked Pete if he wanted to go and play it with me. He wanted to, but he had somewhere else he had to be. He wished me luck, and as he handed me my mom's car keys he reminded me, as he always did, "Don't roll your windows down for 48 hours, or you'll mess up the tint."

I drove to the ABC Liquors on Highway 27. During the pool tournament, I ordered my usual starting drink of the evening, which was a draft beer over ice. Everyone always made fun of me for putting ice in my beer, but my theory was that with the ice it stayed cold, so I could drink slower and not get as drunk. That theory worked until I moved on later in the evenings to rum and Coke, or shots of tequila. There had been many nights when I would go out with about five bucks and come home with an additional six or seven from playing pool for a dollar a game. For that I have to give credit to my coach, Bob Forgiana.

Bob was the father of a world champion barefooter, and the best water-ski "show" barefooter I have ever seen, Robert Jr., also known as Punky Forgiana. Bob was the guy who had been trying out his camera and happened to catch my first-ever back-flip in practice, and then interviewed me afterwards. He liked to train, coach, and just plain motivate skiers from Cypress Gardens, and he was great at it; he had turned his son into a world champion. Bob owned a small concrete business, and was a hot-tempered Italian man but also my best friend. When my family of water-skiing friends from Cypress Gardens had ostracized me, he never had. Like Betty Bonifay, he kept my spirits up, dropping by my place after a concrete job to play poker or Mario Bros. on my Nintendo game. When I started getting well enough, I went out on jobs with him as his gofer; he paid me $6 an hour, which I would usually lose to him later playing poker. I didn't care about the money, and could have asked for more, I suppose, but I just "worked" for him to get out of the house and to be doing something. He always made sure I remembered to eat, too.

Many times after a concrete job we would stop off at a little pub called Friar Tucks, which was just around the corner from where Bob lived. We would get there around noon or so, and play pool until Bob had to get home to his wife for dinner at 6:00 o'clock. He paid for all the games, and we would wager a dollar a game, until it got closer to the time he had to leave. Then he'd up the wager to try to win back anything I had won that day, often betting \$5 or \$10 a game. And then he would pull out the big bet, the double or nothing bet, at the end.

It was because of Bob that I became a pretty damn good pool player. After a while, when he left at the end of the day he often owed me a bunch of money, but that really meant nothing because we would roll what we owed each other into the next day, or week, or month. Sometimes we had to quit early when we got thrown out of the place for yelling and screaming at each other when he would try to pull some shit on me: I learned from him how to spot all the ways people tried to cheat me. About that time I started smoking cigarettes, which I only did when I was out drinking, but that was pretty much every night. I thought about giving it up, but it was just too easy to bum them from Bob, because he was never without a cigarette. Bob smoked like green wood in a brush fire. I can still picture him sloshing around in that heavy-ass cement in his big white boots with a lit cigarette hanging out of his mouth.

I don't know how he did it—smoking like that and working so hard for so long—but he was a bear of a man, and very proud of it. He had jet-black hair, graying of course, and a black Italian mustache, the kindest sparkling blue eyes, and the biggest, best, most boisterous laugh. I always felt safe with Bob. No one would mess with me while I was with Bob; if they did, they might get a pair of cement shoes. He always beat me at poker, but he couldn't beat me at pool, and he hated it. Together we had a blast, cursing like sailors, playing poker like sailors, tossing darts like sailors, and screaming matches like well, like the devil. Terry LaMond, the owner of Friar Tucks, frequently had to yell at us from his kitchen to pipe down or he was going to throw us out.

Bob Forgiana was my most loyal and best friend, especially during that time in my life when I needed him most. It felt like I'd been punched in the face all over again when he told me that he had been diagnosed with advanced lung cancer. I knew he didn't have long to live, and while he fought the hard, brave fight, I did my best to be an ear for him: we had many deep, philosophical talks. I listened when he opened up about his life and deeds, good and bad, and often I had to hide my tears. My last visit with him in the hospital was on his birthday. I think he knew it was me, because when he heard my voice, he kind of perked up and tried to moan a bit. He seemed to be trying to say something to me, but he had just been given another hit of morphine, and I know all too well how that drug affects a person.

"Happy Birthday, Bob, it's Shellie," I said, loud enough to be sure he could hear me if he was really awake. "I'm here. Hey, listen the rest of your family just stepped out to get some lunch, so if you don't mind, I'll just hang out for a while with ya." He settled back down and quit trying to moan or talk, and I grabbed his hand and held it. When I heard his family coming back from lunch, I spoke to him again in a loud voice. "It's Shellie, Bob. Happy Birthday, Bob! I'll see ya later!" I let go of his hand. It was a few days later, while I was at Betty Bonifay's birthday party, that some skiers had asked me if I had heard that Bob Forgiana had passed away. No wonder I got in a fight later that night.

I thought of Bob every time I played pool, so he was in my thoughts as I beat every player at ABC Liquors during the pool tournament the evening after I had my mom's car windows tinted. At about 10:30 p.m. the bartender asked me if I was going to finish my second draft beer over ice, because she wanted to close down early. There were only a few people still there after the pool tournament, as it was a slow night. I befriended some guy who was spilling his guts to me about his marital problems, and the few of us left decided to go down the road to The Lantern, a little bar across from the Eagle Ridge Mall. I figured I'd go for a while, sing a few songs to celebrate my pool tournament win, and head home. I told the guy with marital problems he could follow me because he had never been to The Lantern, and we both hopped in our cars.

As we were getting closer to The Lantern, I slowed down going through a yellow light just before pulling into the parking lot, to let the guy following me know to turn right after the light if he got stuck waiting for the red. As I sat waiting for him, I thought I saw him walking up and I was about to hop out and talk to him, but it turned out to be state highway patrol trooper who had just pulled in right behind me. The trooper motioned for me to roll down my window, but I remembered what Pete Bonifay had told me, that I shouldn't roll the window down for 48 hours, so I opened the whole car door. The officer asked to see my license and registration, so I told him that I had to get them from out of my trunk, because I had put my purse back there during the tournament. The registration was there, too, because the glove box didn't work on my mom's car.

I produced the items he asked for, and then he asked me if I had been drinking. I was honest, and admitted that I had just been up the road at ABC Liquors, but said that I had not even finished my second drink, which was a draft beer over ice. I mentioned that if I seemed happy, it was because I had just won the pool tournament there, and that I hadn't lost a game. I don't think he believed me, but he did seem impressed by my USAA insurance card, which prompted our talk about my father having been in the military. I thought our friendly chitchat would lead to him warning to be careful while driving home. After all, my home was less than a half-mile away as the bird flies. I was wrong. Suddenly, he took me by the shoulders, whirled me around, and shoved me onto the hood of my mom's car. He pulled my wrists behind my back, snapped on a pair of cuffs, and told me I was under arrest for DUI, driving under the influence.

I was in shock the whole time he was guiding me into the back of the patrol car, and calling a tow truck to pick up the car. The thought of my mom's car being towed when I was so close to home, and all that waste of money and time getting it out of impound, made me break down. Of course, I was upset about being arrested for DUI, but I just knew that part would get worked out because he was wrong. It was a mistake. I wasn't under the influence, and I was sure at some point very soon I would be given the chance to prove it.

I knew my mom would have arrived back in town, so I asked if he would at least let me call her so she could come to get her car, but the trooper was having none of it. He took me to the substation, which was just around the corner no more than 400 yards away. He was parked there, next to the yellow light I had driven through slowly, and assumed that because I pulled into a bar parking lot in late evening, I was drunk. I worked myself into a pretty good snit over that before too long, and at the substation I asked if I could take one of my anti-anxiety pills. They allowed me to take a pill, but wouldn't let me take it with water for fear I was trying to dilute the alcohol in my system. The pill got caught in my throat, and I coughed it back up—not a stomach full of beer and drink kind of throw-up, but a small circle of spittle with a little pill in the middle.

They let me take another pill with a very tiny amount of water. I kept telling the officer who handed me the water to remember me. "Remember these eyes," I said sternly, doing that two finger peace-sign point into my eyes, then back to his eyes. "Because I will see you in court." I told him I would remember his name because it was Officer Waters, the one who finally gave me water so I could take my pill.

They had me take the Breathalyzer test, but when I blew into the machine, the state trooper accused me of not trying. A few minutes later, I blew again; again he said I wasn't trying. "Young lady if you don't try to blow, I am going to mark you down as a refusal for the Breathalyzer."

"I played trombone in high school, so I know how to blow," I said. "So either that machine is broken, or it just isn't giving you the results you want." I blew a third time. After a few minutes, the trooper came back and said he had written it down as a refusal. I spent the night in the Bartow jail until I was finally able to reach my mom, and she came and bailed me out. She knew I would have a surprise for her because she had been away on a trip, but I doubt she was expecting it to be the opportunity to bail her youngest child out of jail.

The state trooper who wrote up the police report got it all wrong. When the case finally went to court over a year had past. I was being cross-examined by the young prosecuting attorney, and I was able to refute a lot of what the police report said: he said he walked up to my car and I rolled down the window—which I didn't, because of the tinting; he said I got my I.D. and registration out of the glove box—which I didn't, because it was in the trunk; he said I was slurring my words and my voice was nasally—which, well, as I said on the stand, I was born with a cleft palate I always sounded like that. It became almost comical: line by line what he said fell apart in court. The report said my eyes were blood shot, and so I explained to the jury that I was bitten by a German Shepherd when I was about three, and it gave me a permanent red spot in my left eye, and a small tooth-mark scar on my right. I had to parade past the jury members one by one and look into their eyes for them to see.

The prosecuting attorney was a young guy named Matthew Kaylor, the son of the Honorable Judge Anne Kaylor. The judge who was hearing the case just happened to be good friends with Anne Kaylor. So though I knew the judge wasn't allowed to let personal biases affect his judgment, I couldn't help wondering whether he was rooting for the fair-haired, tall, good looking Matthew Kaylor to win. Heck, I was half-way rooting for him too, as I kept finding myself sizing him up as a possible father of my future kids.

"Well, Ms. Blum," said Kaylor. "You seem to have an answer for everything."

"Well, yes, because it's the truth," I said calmly. "And by the way, where are the test results for the three times I blew into the Breathalyzer?"

"I'm asking the questions here, Ms. Blum, not you."

But the real clincher came when the bartender from ABC Liquors swore under oath that I had had only two draft beers over ice over a period of about 4½ hours—not even finishing the second one—and that I had indeed won not only the pool tournament but every game of pool I played that night. It took the jury just 15 minutes to come back with a not guilty verdict.

The judge finally had a chance to weigh in, and my suspicions were all but confirmed. "Miss Blum, I just want to say for the record that I think you got off scot-free, and that it is an injustice." He was about to slam his gavel to close the proceedings when I spoke quickly to get my comments into the record.

"Your Honor, you are wrong," I said. "I have had to pay my attorney a considerable amount of money, and because the state trooper mistakenly said I refused the Breathalyzer I have not been able to drive for over a year, so this has been anything but scot-free." Scowling, the judge banged his gavel down, thanked the jury and dismissed them, and stalked away in a huff.

That night in the Bartow jail, and for all those months thereafter while I was unable to drive while awaiting trial, I had a lot to think about. And after that day in court I thought about things even harder. I knew that though I was legitimately not guilty of driving under the influence that particular night, there were many other nights when I had driven under the influence. I took this embarrassing episode as karma giving me a huge wake-up call, and I realized that I deserved whatever bullshit I had gone through during that year when I wasn't allowed to drive. I decided to make a few life changes. I quit smoking, and I quit drinking. I decided to concentrate on getting my body as healthy as possible within the limits of my past injuries, getting my house built, and researching the possibilities of trying to have children.

My sister came through for me in a big way by sending me a check to repay some of the money I had loaned her some years ago. There was a little sticky note attached to it: "Shellie, start your house."

Up the road from where I lived in the little town of Dundee, I found a builder who was a retired pastor. I figured that ought to be a testament to his fairness and honesty, and I knew he built affordable houses. I gave him a big down payment to start construction on my lakefront house. I had already navigated my way through the bureaucratic maze and managed to get the all-important variance that would allow me to build my house so close to the lake, and I was excited to finally have my house started. I picked out the house plans and waited for construction to begin. I waited, and waited, and waited. Finally, a year had passed and still nothing had happened except the builder had put up stakes and pink string to mark the foundation. Then I got a call saying I had to pay another $5,000 for fill dirt. Then it was another $3,000 for the well. Over and over things that should have been covered under the huge down payment I'd already given him kept popping up until finally I'd had it. I told him to give me my money back and I'd find someone else since he hadn't even started the work.

But the retired pastor turned building contractor would not give me my bundle of money back. It seemed I was destined to spend my life in courtrooms. I went before the Polk County Building Commissioners with a formal complaint. At the hearing, those gentlemen sitting up on the panel behind their little microphones listened to my side of the story, and then they listened to the builder's attorney. Finally, they explained that even though they didn't have authority to make the pastor give me back my money, they could suspend his contractor's license, and suggested that they were inclined to do so if he did not return my money. The contractor's attorney released my money to me within a week.

The new contractor I found, Roger Bairley, was a godsend—definitely the right man for the job at that particular point in time of my life. I say that because I had begun in earnest my efforts to get pregnant. My mom spent a large part of the time I hadn't been able to drive out in Oregon with my sister, who'd recently had a baby. So I had a lot of time to spend at home on the Internet. I gave up the idea of having a one-night stand with one of my ski buddies, as it just didn't make sense. How would I know if they were safe and disease-free? And how would we divide up the money our child would make for being a baby genius and curing cancer? So I had given up on finding Mr. Right, and even Mr. Almost. Instead I decided to take the bull by the horns, or rather the sperm by the nook.

The Internet gave me access to a vast wealth of knowledge at this point; all it required was time, which I had plenty of. I researched assisted insemination on the Internet, and decided to find a sperm bank and try to have a baby that way. I found a doctor in Orlando who said he could help me. He explained the procedure, which seemed rather simple. Once a month, when I was ovulating, I would go see him. I was already well aware of my cycles, because I had been charting my periods for the last six years. I had been sure at the age of 30 that I wanted to be a mom, and had been talking about and dreaming of it ever since. Sometimes when I was out and found myself flirting relentlessly with the men around me, chatting them up, a little thought bubble would appear in my head, and sometimes would spill out into the middle of whatever I was saying: "Oh my God, I must be ovulating!" The men would look at me with puzzled faces, and sometimes laugh, but I knew there was one reason, and one reason only, that I was putting up with their bullshit, and they were putting up with mine. I was ovulating!

My Orlando doctor told me I would need to find a sperm bank, and generally he liked for his patients to try assisted insemination six times before moving on to other methods of insemination or fertilization enhancement. I figured if I get to pick the donor, in deference to my dad I would go with a blonde-haired, blue-eyed male at least 6'2". Most of the sperm banks in the United States were pretty much tapped out in the way of donors of that description, so I tracked down a sperm bank at a medical school in Denmark that had no such shortage. I emailed the people at the sperm bank that I would need six vials, also called nooks or straws. The sperm, which was cryogenically frozen and stored in liquid nitrogen, would be shipped to me, still frozen, in special canisters. I told them I wanted a donor that was smart, good-looking and athletic—something along the lines of Thomas Enqvist, a popular Swedish tennis player—and was steered toward Donor 855. I ordered my six nooks of "the good stuff" to be sent to my doctor in Orlando and stored.

When my basal temperature told me I was ovulating, I went to the doctor's office. Using a syringe with no needle but affixed with a flexible tube on the end, he would inject the thawed sperm up into me. That was it! Each attempt cost $233 dollars. Not bad, I thought; kind of like a car payment. The sperm bank in Denmark hadn't yet set up a facility in the United States, but I was told that once they did, the price for "the good stuff" was going to triple. I had paid $495 to get my six vials all at once, only to discover that the doctor liked to use 2 vials for every attempt. Oops! Fortunately, there were still vials from

Donor 855, so I reserved a dozen more, wiring them US $815 dollars. I figured that would be enough for nine attempts, and if that didn't work, then in my mind that was the end of the road. I couldn't afford costly fertility treatments, and I definitely couldn't afford in vitro fertilization, which at the time cost anywhere from $8,000 to $15,000.

As it was there were some people in my family who were frowning on my decision to try and have a baby as a single mom, and probably frowned on it even more because of the way I had chosen to do it. I didn't even realize in the beginning that some people thought what I was doing was wrong until one day I went to my doctor's office to make my car payment…er…to pay for my procedure, and the receptionist had explained to me that my regular doctor was out of town. I said, "Oh no, I won't get to try this month?" The receptionist told me not to worry because the doctor had arranged for another doctor to fill in for him. But warned not to say anything about my situation, because this fill-in doctor "doesn't do singles." Wow! He would think of me as a criminal or something! But that didn't stop me from trying.

When I got to my eighth try, with one more to go before I would give up, I had figured it was a sign from God that I just wasn't supposed to be a mom. My own mom had gone to my sister's in Oregon for one of her extended stays. I thought I would wait until after she was gone to take the home test to see if I was pregnant, there was no sense in her flying depressed. Unlike some people in my family, my mom was all for it, and was riding the roller coaster with me. Ask anyone trying to get pregnant, and they will say the same about how it goes: up high and excited to test, and then back down low when it turns out you're not pregnant. So after my mom had gone, I went into my bathroom for the test, fully expecting to see nothing.

What? It wasn't just pink, it was dark maroon. Oh my God! I was pregnant!

I called my sister and my mom in Oregon, and they were so happy for me. In the middle of our conversation, I said, "I think there may be something wrong, because I feel so sick already."

My mom pulled her phone away from her ear, and yelled to my sister, "Oh, Tamara, you're never gonna believe it. Shellie is complaining about her morning sickness—isn't that great? She thinks there is something wrong—isn't that cute!"

I was trying to explain to my mom that I really, really thought there was something abnormal going on because it was still so soon after and I was already really, really sick, but she was just so caught up in the moment, she wasn't listening. After I hung up the phone, I went online and started researching why someone might have extreme morning sickness and there was always the possibility of twins. Could it be? The urine stick wasn't pink, it was maroon; and I was having what I was sure was abnormally bad morning-noon-and-night sickness. I kept my thoughts to myself for a while, though I started secretly thinking of two names for my babies. And I practiced what I would say to the doctor at the first sonogram when he would say to me, "Surprise! You're having twins." And that is exactly what he said.

I didn't say what I had practiced, but I thought it. "No, I'm not surprised." As I walked out of the parking garage in Orlando clutching my little sonogram picture showing two heartbeats, I was elated. I called my mom.

"You're never gonna believe it."

"What?"

"I'm going to have twins!"

"You're kidding?" she said. She was waiting for me to say Yes calmly, as I always did—it was a running joke between us.

"No!"

"You're kidding?" Again she waited for me to say the punch line, but I didn't. Then she said to me sternly, "Shellie Ann, this is not funny." There was a pause, and then she said, cautiously, then elated, "Are you really having twins?"

"I am! I am!" I started rambling on about the moment only to I realize I was talking to dead air. Stupid cell phones. I start to drive home, and had to stop more than once to be sick. I didn't care. I was having twins! I knew it!

My buddy Mike Barnes had been having trouble with his wife. They were separating, and maybe getting divorced, so I told him he could rent out one of my places until things had been resolved. He moved in just down the road from me in Waverly Loop. One clear September morning I got an early call from him. "Shellie, turn on your TV. I heard on the radio that a plane hit a tower in New York."

He walked up to my place with his roommate, John, and the three of us watched the news of the 9/11 attacks unfold together. They didn't have a TV hooked-up yet, so they stayed at my place all morning and afternoon watching, but after a while, I couldn't handle anymore. I went in my room, shut the door, shut the blinds, and lay curled up in a ball, saying "Our Fathers" for the rest of the day. I was six months pregnant and I wanted to give as much positive energy to those twins as I could. I spent much of my time praying that my twins would be healthy, and trying to give as much of myself as I could to those babies.

I thought about them all the time. I knew that having twins was a high-risk pregnancy, especially for someone with my medical problems and my age. But I just kept telling myself, my injuries were mostly from the neck up and I was going to push all my positive energy to down below. I could do this. And all the time I was building two new little lives inside of me, my contractor, Roger Bairley, was building my house. I probably drove him crazy, constantly telling him that he needed to change this, and he needed to change that, but he was so patient with me, and I couldn't be more grateful. He was another blonde-haired, blue-eyed man in my life.

In early December, my mom returned from Oregon. She and my sister-in-law helped me get the nursery ready in my newly built house. I was getting closer to my due date of December 18, and thinking that it could be any day because twins so often come early and are smaller, right? My twins, however, did not read the book on coming early or being small. A week before my due date I was pleading with my doctor to do something because I felt so huge and looked like something from the *X-Files*. I mean, it just didn't seem possible that a person could be stretched that way: I gained no other weight but in my stomach area. I have pictures of myself wearing a two-piece bathing suit, and from the back I looked perfectly normal. But if I turned around, the sight of me would scare people.

I was told at one of the sonograms that Baby A was most likely a boy, and would come first, and that Baby B was probably a girl, although they were less sure about that. Again my babies took after their mom, and were defiantly stubborn. In the last two weeks before the due date, Baby B said, "Oh, no you don't; I am going out first."—either that, or Baby A said, "ladies first." Apparently they were both very flexible already, as there could hardly have been enough space in there to change their minds, let alone their positions, but sure enough, they managed to swap places. My due date came and went. Then two more days past. Finally my doctor decided to start inducing labor, and hooked me up to an IV of Pitocin.

After a few hours, they wheeled me into the delivery room. My mom was with me. When I was finally dilated enough to start pushing, boy did I. This was not a small baby, and I am not a big woman, so after a few third-degree tears—one of the nurses said, "Let me put it this way, there is no fourth degree"—the doctor performed an episiotomy. Finally, the first baby, Baby B, came out and sure enough, she was a girl. The doctor put her immediately up onto my chest so I could see her, and she was squalling and bawling from the get-go. But I wasn't done yet. There was still Baby A.

Baby A seemed to have changed his mind. I was pushing just as hard for the second baby, but he wouldn't come. Maybe he was pouting because his sister had popped out first, I don't know. Anyway, the doctor tried to ease him out with tongs, then tried some kind of suction contraption thingy, finally he said, "Put her on the other table." He meant the surgery table. I knew this meant they would do a Cesarean section. When they slid Baby A out of the C-section incision, they whisked him away immediately to another room instead of laying him on my chest as they had my little girl. I was panicking.

My mom, who had been standing just over my left shoulder, asked, "Is it a boy?"

And the doctor said, "It was a boy."

I thought, *He said "was"! I lost my little boy! He didn't make it!* Tears started streaming down my temples, but then I choked back my tears and actually sang in my head, "You and Me against the World." I would be thankful. I had my little girl, and I would be strong for her. It would be her and me against the world.

My mom saw my tears, and I knew she had picked up on the fact that there was something wrong with me. She asked, "Did you hear him?" I thought she meant the doctor, and prepared myself to hear her tell me that my little boy didn't make it. I swear she must have read my mind, though, because she understood at once what I was thinking. "No, Shellie, do you hear HIM?" She pointed toward the room they had whisked my little boy into, and I can hear him. He's crying! OH MY GOD! He is alive and crying! Talk about a roller coaster.

My little girl, Josie Lynn Lois Blum was born at 12:13 a.m. on December 21, 2001. She was 19½ inches long and weighed 7 pounds. Dashiel Alden Blum was born 46 grueling minutes later the same day, 12:59 a.m., and was 20 inches long and weighed 7 pounds 3 ounces. As I said, the twins decided to be different, and be neither early nor small. When I finally saw my boy, he looked like he had been in a boxing ring, with bruises all over his head from the efforts to remove him before the C-section. To this day I can gauge how badly he is hurt or upset by how sharply those blotches come out; if I can really see them, it's for real.

Josie Lynn Lois was so named because I loved the Steely Dan song on the *Aja* album, "When Josie Comes Home"; it was the pre-show music at the Lake of the Ozarks Water Ski Show summer after summer when I was growing up. The second part of her name is because my sister's name is Tamara Lynn. Josie Lynn's middle name is Lois, which was my Nana's middle name. My sister named her daughter Bailey Ann. My name is Shellie Ann. My mom's name is Carol Ann, and my sister's mother-in-law's name is Anne. So I just had to give my sister her propers. Dashiel Alden was so named because when I was pregnant I was into biographies, and loved Dashiell Hammett's work. My grandfather's middle name was Alden.

I'm not sure if I just look like the kind of person who is easy to swindle, or if I'm too trusting, or if my experiences have just made me quick to fight back, but before my house was completely finished I ended up in court yet again. It had nothing to do with my contractor Roger Bairley. He's wonderful. But in February I hosted a Super bowl/family reunion party, and my pool contractor was refusing to finish my pool. I had even invited him to the party. Everyone was admiring the new house, the new twins, and the pool, but the pump and hot tub were not working. We put water in the pool, and I even think my brother-in-law our pal Al went for a brief swim, but the water was not flowing and the hot tub did not work. When I asked the pool contractor about it, he pulled me aside and told me he would need another $3,000 to make it right.

"My hair is not really that blonde," I joked. But then I told him in all seriousness that I didn't understand the extra cost when it was all part of the original contract, and I was not going to let him gouge me for another three grand. Soon after, I was served the papers that started foreclosure on my home; the pool contractor had put a mechanic's lien on my new house. I found a prominent attorney in Lakeland to take my case, explained the situation, and gave him a sizable retainer to help me fight this crooked pool contractor. To make a long story short, the attorney turned out to be as bad as the contractor, and kept pushing me to settle, all the while billing me for about twice what the pool guy wanted. We parted ways, and when I refused to pay him, either, he also put a lien on my house. I filed motions and tried to defend myself until I finally found Claire Margaret Groover, an attorney who felt so bad for my situation that she drove all the way down from Orlando, an hour away, to ask a judge to give me more time to find an attorney. Then Claire referred me to James Markel, my attorney/knight in shining armor.

James Markel was nearing the end of his career, and had an aura about him that made me think of F. Lee Bailey. He was out to right any wrongs he could—including the problems I had with the attorney who quit on me and the crooked pool contractor. He referred me to Michelle Beane Kane, an attorney who specialized in construction law, and she eventually took the crooked pool contractor case and won an award that ended up being three times the amount of the judgment; in Florida, if a building contractor isn't licensed you can get treble the damages. Once again, it seemed that if I really wanted to be taken seriously in the world of legal maneuverings, I had to look to the women: it took a female attorney and a female judge to right the pool lien wrong. In the end, "Sir Markel" and I lost the case against my attorney who quit on me. Mr. Markel even argued my case at the appellate level, but in the end the attorney who quit got his inflated fee. Still, God bless Mr. Markel for fighting the good fight, and for doing it out of the goodness of his heart, pro bono. There are still good and decent attorneys out there, but they are few and far between—especially, it seemed, among men.

By 2004, when the twins were not quite three years old, we were finally feeling all settled into our beautiful, finished waterfront home. Then on August 13, Friday the 13th as a matter of fact, Hurricane Charlie dropped by for a visit and tried to blow us off our foundations. The eye of the storm crossed over our house. My mom and I were hiding in my closet with the twins, trying to appear calm so we wouldn't scare the children, but we were scared. After one particularly ferocious noise my mom asked me quietly, "Did we lose the roof?"

"Don't know...and don't wanna look yet!" It didn't feel safe to even peer out my closet door. The pressure in my ears was like the pressure you feel in a plane, and it just wouldn't go away. We cowered in the closet for about two hours while all around us we heard horrendous crashing and shredding noises, so we feared the worst as we finally crept out when it was over. At it turned out, we realized that our home had actually held up pretty well—thank you again, Roger Bairley!—but we had lost our 100-year-oak. Seeing it uprooted brought tears to my eyes because we had sprinkled Nana's ashes on the roots and in our little lake.

When we went to check on my five mobile homes, four of the five were totally destroyed. Only one was still livable. No one was in them, so no one got hurt. I would have to start all over putting new homes on the parcels of land, which would be no easy task. I got a small business disaster loan from FEMA, and eventually I got all of the homes back together again, and even started working toward purchasing two more pieces of property. Once those pieces were paid off, I put two more homes on them. It was sort of like rebuilding my life, I decided: it took time, and a lot of baby steps, but if I was patient and persistent I could manage to continue moving forward. After rebuilding in the wake of Hurricane Charlie, I felt pretty good about life. I had my beautiful twins, my mom, my own house on the lake, and seven income properties. Things were going pretty well.

About that time my friend Gayle Millis started calling me collect from somewhere in San Diego. She had skied at Marine World Africa U.S.A. years before, and even borrowed my jump skis to learn how to jump when she skied somewhere in Malaysia, but now she was once again struggling with her weight and drinking. She'd call late at night, drunk and incoherent, saying she thought she should walk out in traffic. I spent hours talking to her, and thought she was doing better, too. I spoke often with the woman running the halfway house where Gayle was living, hating the fact that I was so far away and felt so helpless. I was still caught up in wondering what, if anything, I could do to help her.

Then one of my old ski buddies from the Lake of the Ozarks and Marine Africa USA, Cherie Duffus, called. She told me that Gayle had indeed walked out into rush hour traffic, stepping out onto the six-lane highway by the halfway house in San Diego, and been killed. This hit me really hard, and stayed with me for weeks. Not long after that I got a strange call from someone looking for John Serocrat. That was Mike Barnes's roommate. John had a drinking problem, but one I could relate to: he was self-medicating because he was in chronic pain. When I heard the message I thought it was a wrong number, but it turned out the caller was actually looking for people who had known John…so they could come to his memorial. He had hung himself in a tree just up the road from his trailer. Then I heard that the crooked pool contractor had been found dead in his house, and I heard later that he, too, had killed himself. *All those poor souls,* I thought, *and there but for the grace of God, go I.*

CHAPTER 12

Mending Bridges

I found myself thinking once again about how I had gotten to where I was in my life. Part of me thought if not for my twins, if it were not for my babies, there were times when I too might have been right where Gayle, John, and the pool guy ended up. Part of me also knew that I was not one to give up easily. I'd made it through many years of trials, tests, and intense emotional and physical pain. In fact, there were only two things that I hadn't yet managed to do that I knew I had to do. One, I had to tell my story. And two, I had to come to some sort of peace with the whole thing and just let it go.

I received a call from Betty Bonifay telling me about a cocktail party that was being held at Mark Voisard's house in honor of Lynn Novakofski, who was about to be inducted into the Water-ski Hall of Fame. Betty said she would go, but only if I would go with her. Me? Go to the house of Mark Voisard, the man I still blamed for making my injuries even worse by being too slow on the safety release? Could I really do that?

Somehow, I knew that I had to try.

I had gone with Betty Bonifay years before to an induction ceremony at the Water-ski Hall of Fame for my good friend Jennifer Calleri, for her accomplishments as a World Champion Barefooter. This wouldn't be the actual ceremony, just a cocktail party the night before the actual ceremony, so I would be able to leave at any time. I thought of earlier such events, and my scraps with my old water-skiing buddies over their versions of "the truth," remembering myself wrestling with "Dick" until our friend pried us apart. Could I make it through the evening without getting into a tussle? I was older now, and through with therapy. I was a mom, even! Surely, I could manage to get through one evening with people?

When Betty and I arrived, I at first stayed mostly to myself. I managed a little bit of idle chit-chat with some of my closer friends from Cypress Gardens, the ones who made their way over to me, but for the most part I didn't initiate anything. I sat by myself, alone. Then someone set up a big chair for Lynn Novakofski to sit on in the middle of the room, and people started volunteering to walk up behind his chair and make little observations or share a memory they had of Lynn. Some people were quite funny, and roasted him royally, which he accepted with good grace. The chair I was sitting in most of the night happened to be just to the right of the chair they set up for Lynn. Finally, when quite a few people had spoken their piece and it was clear that this part of the evening was winding down, I stood up. I stepped closer to but not directly behind Lynn's chair, and I could hear a hush fall over the room. People seemed stunned that I was going to say something, or maybe they were worried about what I would say. Maybe they thought I would pick a fight and ruin Lynn's big night, but that has never been my style.

I looked around the room. So many people I knew and had not seen in so very, very long! I hadn't prepared anything before I stood up, but I just cleared my throat and started talking. "I just wanted to thank Lynn for always making me go into the weight room to lift weights." I said. "I hated it! I always thought I was plenty big enough, but as my doctors told me later, if it had not been for my strength, I would not have made it through my accident." The room was very quiet. "So, thank you, Lynn, for making me a stronger person." I moved closer to him and gave him a little sideways hug. He seemed kind of shocked, and didn't really hug me back. The whole room stayed silent for what seemed an interminable amount of time. But then I made my way back to my seat and the next speaker got up, and the awkwardness passed.

Later that evening, I found myself face to face with Mark Voisard. *This is it!* I thought. *Time to make my peace.*

And we did. I don't remember what we said, or who said what, but by the end of the conversation it was as though we were two guys who had duked it out in the alley and now we had shaken hands and everything was all forgotten. Could it really have been that easy? It was strange: although I don't think either of us said as much out loud, we were both finally over what had happened at Cypress Gardens all those years ago, and we both moved beyond it. That night I understood that no matter what happened, my instincts on that day were right on: when Mark said, "Get tough on the landing, Blum!" he really was on my side and hoping for me to succeed. He was encouraging me, not challenging me. Could he have pulled the safety release earlier? Maybe. Could I have let go sooner? Maybe. But it was all in the past, and like I came to believe, things happen for a reason. I gave Mark a hug that night, and it was a genuine sharing of goodwill. He knew it, and I knew it.

Sadly, not long before the party was scheduled, Cypress Gardens, the historical landmark that had been a fixture for so long in Central Florida, was sold. It was reincarnated as LegoLand. There was a message there for me, I thought. If Cypress Gardens could morph beyond itself and turn into something brand new, surely we skiers could also learn to move beyond Cypress Gardens.

I felt as though I was almost able to cross off one of my two big remaining goals. I had almost, but not quite, made peace with the whole episode. I still had the feeling that many people thought that my injuries from the accident at Cypress Gardens had not been as serious as I had made them out to be, and that my dragging out of the settlement and workers' compensation process was some sort of elaborate play acting, or even a ploy to get sympathy and attention. Telling my story would help that, of course, but in the meantime there were still people somewhat close to me who just didn't know how badly I had been hurt.

Anyone who heard the story about what happened to me on my trip to Oregon for my niece's bat mitzvah, however, would understand. The actual ceremony took place at the temple on August 27, 2011. Although I didn't understand much of what was said since it was in Hebrew, it was very moving and positive. My mom, the twins, and I had flown out for it and the celebratory party to follow, for which my sister had rented a local swim park.

At the swim park, everyone was having a great time. My brother Brent had been showing off, jumping and diving off everything. My sister Tamara did a running back-flip off the lower diving board. I rated my brother's attempts off the high dive ("Six! You didn't keep your legs together! Eight! Much better, but your toes weren't pointed!") and watched my nine-year-old twins jump off the high dive and do cannonballs. Just about everyone under 60 went down the giant water slide—except me. I'd been sitting off on the sideline in the grass with my now-elderly mom and few other adults, wishing I could do even half of what I used to do without thinking. Water was my element! I was most at home there…or had been. Now I was watching everyone else have all the fun.

All day Brent had kept coming up and saying, "Come on, Shellie, go get your suit on!" My kids wanted me to swim with them. Finally, it got to me. I just couldn't take it anymore. I went to the locker room and changed into my two-piece bathing suit, which was pretty close to my pre-twin size. I had a little extra skin around my middle, but despite having looked like the Goodyear blimp for a while, I came out of it with no stretch marks. So when I came out into the sunlight from the locker room, I felt a little bit like my old self. It was…exciting. I couldn't wait to get into the water.

I went by myself quietly to the lower diving board and stood at the edge and dove. The water felt cold whisking by me, but it was fun and exhilarating. Then I climbed the ladder out of the pool, walked back onto the low diving board, walked out to the edge and turned around, put my toes on the edge, and pushed off to do a back-flip. I didn't do a running back-flip like my sister, but I wasn't performing. No one was watching me. I was just having fun in the water.

Josie Lynn came running up. "Mommy, Mommy, you're out here! You're swimming!" She couldn't believe I was swimming, because I rarely get into our pool to swim at home in Florida, unless it is a hot, hot summer day, or unless the hot tub is what we call "Momma hot," which is *really* hot! But my kids were both like me: they could swim before they walked or talked.

Even though it was the peak of summer, we were in Oregon, not Florida, so soon I started to feel cold. The air was dryer, and there was a little breeze. Josie Lynn and I got into the hot tub, and I was floating around with Josie in my arms, singing some silly little song, when I heard Brent yelling from the bottom of the high dive.

"Shellie! Come show us how it's done!" The hot tub had warmed me up, and I did want to get back in the pool, but I wasn't so sure the high dive was a good idea. Brent yelled again. "Come on, Shellie! Show us how it's done." Other people heard him goading me, and they were grinning at his antics. He was partway up the platform, yelling over the side to me. "Shellie, come dive! Show the twins your legacy!"

I heard "dive...twins...legacy," I heard my brother daring me, and my mind was made up. I got out of the hot tub and walked toward the high-dive platform, eyeing it as I approached. It wasn't an official high dive—it was only 15 feet high; it said so right on the side. Brent stood at the top and held my place in line while I climbed the ladder. I walked out to the edge of the cement platform, which had a metal railing that went all the way around except for the opening over the water. I walked to the left edge of the platform grabbed the metal bar on the top so that I could lean over to look at the water. I have done this throughout my life, mostly when I was young and diving off the Lake of the Ozarks cliffs: I concentrate on the surface of the water until I am able to focus it in so that it looks closer to me.

While I was doing this, the lifeguard directing traffic at the top said jokingly, "You're not gonna be able to go if you won't let go of the bar." I thought, *This guy is kidding me; he thinks I'm scared!* I shook my head at him and made a face that clearly said *Duh!* Then turned my back to him, let go of the bar, and let my body start to fall forward slowly into the dive. It felt like old times…until I hit the water.

I didn't feel my hands hit the water, but I did feel them flying past my head under the water. My arms were forced in a horrible pinwheel motion backwards like they might snap off. At the same time I felt an electrifying shock in both my shoulders. I bobbed up out of the water in agony, thinking, "Oh my God, not again…this is *bad*!" I clutched the top of my bathing suit with both hands to keep my arms pressed to my chest as best I could and used my legs only to swim to the side of the pool right beside the lifeguard's chair. Josie Lynn was right there, and she could see the pain on my face.

"Mommy, are you okay?"

I answered her as calmly as I could. "No, I'm not. Go get Aunt Tamara, please?"

As Josie Lynn ran for my sister, Brent called down from the top of the platform. "Shellie, are you okay?"

I shook my head no. "I'm hurt!"

He dove off the platform and swam up behind me to where I was holding onto the edge of the little step-down that goes all the way around the pool. I was gripping it with just my fingertips, with my chest pressed right up to the ledge. "Is it bad?" he whispered.

"It's bad, Brent."

"Hospital bad?"

"911 bad!" We started toward the shallow end with me facing forward and kicking lightly and him supporting me down low on my back. When we got to the floating lane dividers, he started to lift me up over them but I said no, we needed to go under them. We both held our breath and I went under, still holding my hands at my chest and my brother right behind me supporting my lower back. By the time we could actually feel the bottom of the pool with our feet in the shallow end, my sister had jumped in, too, and was on my left side helping to support me. She was asking me all kinds of questions, and relaying information to people at the edge of the pool, telling them that someone needed to call 911 right away.

I slowly, gingerly walked out of the pool using the steps at the shallow end, with Brent and Tamara still supporting me on either side. They walked me into a room near the swim park office and I sat on a folding chair to wait for the ambulance. I leaned a little bit forward because I found that for some reason that eased the pain somewhat, and soon we were joined by others from the party: an ER doctor, a general practitioner, and two other people from the medical field, all of them asking questions.

"Where does it hurt?" asked one doctor.

"My shoulders down to my elbows."

"She probably got a little zinger."

Tamara shook her head. "No, I think it's more than that," she said. "My sister has a high tolerance for pain, and she is saying it's bad, so it's bad!"

My mom hovered near the door, with Josie Lynn at her side holding onto my mom around the waist. They both looked so worried and scared for me, so in my calmest voice I said what by then was almost a habit I'd had to say it so many times before: "Don't worry, mom. I'm gonna be all right." And I added, for my daughter's benefit, "It's okay, Josie Lynn. Momma will be fine. I will be okay."

One of the doctors said, "I think she may have pinched a nerve."

Another one said, "She might have damaged her rotator cuff, or maybe dislocated her joint." The ideas went back and forth as we waited for the ambulance. Finally my sister asked me.

"Shellie, what do you think?"

"I think I broke both my arms, and the right one is worse." Just then the paramedics arrived, and right away they wanted to get me onto a backboard. When I stood up, the pain was excruciating since the adrenaline protecting me from the pain had worn off while I sat. It was when they held the board up against me, strapped me on, and then started to lean it back to the ground that I finally started to yelp.

I heard my mom in the background. "What if it's her neck again?"

I admit that I was worried about that, too, and was much more scared than I wanted to let on. And my arms were causing me unbearable, excruciating pain once they laid me down, I begged them to stand me back up but of course, they couldn't. They put me on the rolling gurney and into the back of the ambulance, and as I had so many times before, I dropped into my familiar moaning. I asked the paramedic to give me something for the pain and he put an IV in my hand and gave me something, but it only dulled things. It was déjà vu: moaning in the ambulance, arriving at the hospital and feeling every little jolt and jiggle like an electric shock, and people rushing me off to X-ray with concern on the their faces.

Finally, the ER doctor came in with the X-rays and announced that I had indeed broken both shoulders in a three-part fracture, and the right one was worse. He was certain that it would require surgery.

"But…you can fix me? I can be fixed, and it's not my neck?"

"Well, I can't fix you," said the ER doctor. "But an orthopedic specialist would probably be in early the next morning to do the surgery."

Brent had stayed by my side throughout, and even rode in front of the ambulance to the hospital. After I was finally good and drugged up, he noticed I was rubbing my feet up and down on the mattress. "Are you uncomfortable, do you need more drugs?"

I was still hurting, but I didn't want any more drugs, because they would knock me out, and I wanted to know what was going on. I was doing what I always do when I am in extreme pain. While moaning, I was rubbing the bottom of my feet on the mattress, in alternating directions making sure neither foot touched each while sliding past the other. I told Brent he should go back to the party. His eyes welled up several times. "It will be okay. It's not your fault!" I said. "And in a weird way, if something like this was going to happen, I'm glad it happened to me. I'm the best person to handle this. I mean, what if this was you or Tamara—how would you guys work? It's best it happened to me."

Brent pleaded with me to ask for more pain medication, but I knew I was at the limit. In my mind I wanted to tell him, "*You're not helping me being worried about how you feel seeing me like this. If you can't stand seeing me in pain, then leave.*" But instead I said, "Have fun Brent, go back to the party." Then, he asked, "How bad is it, the pain?" I told him, "It's nearly unbearable, but I know there will be an end. Until then, I have to just keep on keeping on." Finally, he said his goodbyes and went back to the party.

Evidently the rest of the day went off without a hitch, and hardly anyone even knew that I had been hurt, which was exactly what I'd hoped. I didn't want to ruin my niece's big day and awesome party. From the swim park, everyone had gone back to Tamara and Al's house, where my pal Al and his band, The Fret Boys, played late into the night. At some point, Tamara got tired of answering questions about me, so she finally stood up on a cooler and announced to the whole party, "My sister, Shellie, did in fact break both her arms. She is having surgery on her right arm tomorrow morning. But she is okay, and will pull through—like she always does."

The next morning the orthopedic surgeon explained that while he wanted to do surgery on both my arms, it was common protocol to do just one first, and the other one later. In this case he would be operating on my right arm, both because it had suffered the most damage and because it was my dominant arm. He told me that I should be prepared to have surgery on the left arm in the future. The whole time he was talking to me, he was shaking his head.

"In all my years of doing this, I have never seen anything like this—both arms, two sets of three-part fractures, just from a dive," he said. "You didn't even hit the bottom—the *water* caused this. It just seems so impossible." They did a bone density test to see if that was a factor, but found that I actually had higher bone density than was average for my age. "It's just so unbelievable. But don't you worry. After the anesthesiologist does a block on that right side, you'll be numbed up for 24 to 36 hours, and we'll put that right shoulder and arm back together."

Then the anesthesiologist had me look at a screen and tell him when I no longer felt him poking a needle into the right side of my neck. Ugh—not soon enough! Then they put me all the way under, and performed the surgery, inserting a titanium plate in my shoulder and arm that looked like the head of a guitar, but with about 10 screws through it. I would have to carry a copy of my X-ray to get through airport security from now on, as I would forever more be setting off their detectors.

After I woke up from the surgery, my main concern was how quickly I could travel. All I could think of was getting home to the twins. They had come to see me right after the surgery, but only briefly on their way to Portland with my mom; they would spend the night there and catch an early morning flight home on Monday. The doctor said that depending how tough a broad I was, I could fly right away if I really wanted to, but that he had scheduled an appointment to see him a week from the upcoming Wednesday. He wanted to keep me in the hospital until that first Wednesday, but I talked them into letting me leave on Tuesday. I stayed at my sister's until I had made arrangements with my cousin, the Frontier flight attendant, to meet her in Denver that Sunday, exactly a week from the surgery date. I would blow off my Wednesday appointment and see someone in Florida instead. After all, the doctor said that if I was a tough broad I could fly as soon as I wanted—and I was definitely that. I just wanted to get home. I stayed one night at my cousin's place in Denver and then flew to Orlando Monday morning carrying a copy of the X-rays of my two broken arms through security to explain why I was setting off the airport scanners. It was a nightmare, and the pain was nearly unbearable, but I did it.

I was so happy to see the twins and my mom at Orlando International. During the week we'd been separated—the first time I had been away from my children—they had had a couple of meltdowns. I showed the twins the cool scanned copy of my X-ray I had been carrying through all the airport security. Dashiel said, "It looks like my Bionicle" the Lego toy action hero figure his Uncle Brent had given him last Christmas. I thought to myself, it did look bionic, but I figured it would go along with the rest of the metal hardware that doctors had used to put me back together over the years.

Dashiel, who was usually my little comedian, was hit particularly hard by all of it, once we joked about the bionic x-rays it relieved a lot of his fears.

My own fears did not fade so easily. The orthopedic surgeon all but said that these breaks would not have happened just from my dive into the water if I had not broken my neck so severely all these years before. Clearly it had left me vulnerable in more ways than even I had known. I had survived, again, but I still struggled to make sense of it all. Why had this happened to me? Then I got a text from my sister, whose answer to that question made sense to me: "Maybe this happened to prove to you that you don't have to prove yourself anymore."

She's right, I thought. *Maybe God wants me to look around and appreciate all of my blessings.* And after that, everything did seem clearer, brighter somehow. Of course, every new motion regained was a minor miracle. Being able to eat lifting my own fork was pure joy. Being able to wash my own hair was a milestone. Finally getting more than one hour of sleep at a time was a gift.

My recuperation was difficult, and even typing this made my arms burn with pain. But I found a new inspiration to write: that is the day my neighbor called my house from the Elks Lodge to ask me for my autograph, and to let me know I was a star. They were all watching me on TV. You see Hollywood finally did call but not for my screenplay. It was the Judge Alex show. I had tenants who were suing me in small claims, and they just had to have their day in court. Believe me, I know the feeling. I tried everything I could to avoid the trip back out to Hollywood, "my last visit there didn't work out so well," but in the end I let myself be talked into appearing on the show.

After building a career of 16 years in rental properties, doing my best to treat my tenants fairly and feeling pretty good and confident about knowing my stuff, once again I had a male authority figure holding me back and silencing me. When I saw the edited down TV version, it.wasn't near as bad as what really happened, in fact the little YouTube video the show put out, makes it appear as though we won, we didn't. And suffice it to say even though I didn't get my face bashed in, I did feel ambushed and bullied. Hopefully, Judge Alex would be the last man to yell at me to "Sit Down!" and shut up. But really, *that* whole story is for another time, another chapter. Who knows, maybe another book?

In a way though, I should thank Judge Alex for re-igniting my passion for the truth to be told. That and my brother Brent had encouraged me to write a short story exposé a year ago when it happened, as a way to cathartically move on from the unpleasant TV episode. So I did, and it worked. Thank you Judge Alex for helping me try to set to another world record first because one week after the courtroom segment was aired on Friday the 13th, 2012. I started typing this, and 25 days later I had over 88,000 words, maybe not that impressive to the speed typists or real professional authors, after all I am just an ex-water skiing chick who has rental properties, but remember, this is just a little over 4 months after breaking both of my arms.

Why did I sit at all hours of the night and day typing with burning, aching arms? Well, because I still had to fulfill that other major goal before I could really be at peace with my past and move forward. I had to tell my story. I did my simple arm exercises, weaned myself off the pain narcotic oxycodone, and kept working at this book. All the while, fighting back tears of pain and emotion. I would see this through. Someday, somehow, it will be published. It will be read. My story will be out there.

So for all of you looking for that "Aha!" moment, here it is... I know, I know, the critics might say "It came too fast!" or "It took too long!" or even "I wasn't satisfied with the ending." But that's how life is; it's messy. Some lives are more messy than others and I've come to think that everyone's life is one big "Aha" moment full of ups and downs. But we all have them. And if any of you are going through one of your downs, hopefully my story has given you a break, a little escape, a little breather. Sometimes, that's all a person needs, just a little support or connection with one another. Imagine if someone could bottle that up. Sharing my story with you is my bottle. If it has floated into your hands with my message inside and has made the smallest impact on you, "Good! We're even! I used the thought of sharing my story with you in my deepest darkest downs to help get me through. And now, in return, if even in the smallest of ways, I hope you use me for all your journeys back up.

And maybe, just maybe, even if there is just one person out there wondering what happened to that little 12-year-old Waterski Girl Wonder, don't wonder anymore. I've been through a lot, but I'm all right and doing just fine. I've learned to live with my pain. I don't water-ski anymore. I don't think I'll be high diving again, either. And perhaps, I should add roller-skating to the not-to-do list as well. Because recently, I broke my wrist skating. Resulting in, yet again, another surgery that added more metal to my growing array of jewelry I wear on the inside of my body.

However, regardless of my limitations, I will always, always be in or near the water. It's where I belong. I've been a stubborn, headstrong proponent for the underdogs all my life, and apparently I attract accidents like ponds attract ducks. Some people will say I am a troublemaker. If that means that I stick up for myself and the people I love, well then yes, I am. If my dad were alive, I think he would be proud of his troublemaker daughter.

And I realized something not long ago when I was talking with my mom. She's had to pick me up, bail me out, and call 911 more than once, but she still says I am "the best mistake she ever made." If I am a tough broad able to make my way in this shark-infested world, it's because of her. I have learned from the best. It was because of her that my need to have children was so obsessive, so strong. What I came to realize through them and from her was that I have two crucial elements shaping my life, not just one: water and *family*. My mom has always been there for me. She has been both anchor and rudder, keeping me from rushing out of control and helping to guide me up to and beyond Cypress Gardens. And so, just as my children say to me, I say to her, "Thank you, Mommy." I'm right where I want and need to be, and I can end this chapter of my story and turn the page with a blessed life that has taught me to keep on keeping on.

AFTERWORD

He Ain't Heavy, He's My Brother

Four days after I sent the first draft of this book to a proofreader, my second-oldest brother, Brent Joseph Blum, went missing on February 19th, 2012. His wife called my mom the day after, and said he was gone, along with his Harley Davidson, his I.D., and his debit card. When my mom came into my room to tell me, her voice made me know it was bad. Yet for four days, we held out hope that he would be found okay.

He was not. A utility worker working near Mesa, Arizona, found Brent's bike in a canal and called the police. The first responders found my brother's body underwater in the canal. He'd suffered blunt force trauma to his neck, a broken neck and found in water. Whoa! What a torturous coincidence. They told us he had died instantly. While that may be medically true, emotionally my brother suffered for a long, lonely, depressive time. His wife of 13 years had cheated on him earlier in their marriage, even filed divorced papers, but he was trying to make it work. On his last birthday, while we celebrated at my house—without his wife, by the way—he swore to me with tears in his eyes he would not agree to a divorce. "Til death do us part, Shellie, and I mean it," he said. "If anything happens to me, I want you to make sure Mom and Brad are taken care of. I really don't think we're gonna make it, and I won't go through it with her again. I'll just take off on my bike and never come back, I'll run myself into a wall!"

I couldn't fathom what my brother was saying to me. I still didn't want to understand it after they found him dead in the water. But when I got a copy of his autopsy, what he'd told me was confirmed for me: my brother had committed suicide, and told me his plan to do so less than two months earlier.

I tried to see that his final wishes were met, but his widow manipulated her grief—or was it her guilt?—as a shield to avoid all our questions and to ignore us. It could have, and should have, been so different. We wanted so desperately to grieve with her, to work it all out, but she was having none of that. She chose instead to avoid us, and to travel the world in the months right after his death. She sold his business, and received a huge life insurance policy. We estimated she was sitting on nearly a million dollars in cash, and yet before she took a trip with her church to Fiji, she let a bunch of her friends have a fundraiser to raise money for her and her trip. We received an email inviting us to go to the fundraiser or, if we preferred, to just send money in an envelope for her cause.

All that time, we were sitting on the knowledge that Brent had told my mom that he had put his business and life insurance policies in my mom's name. This happened during the period when Brent and his wife had been separated, early in their marriage, after she had an affair. I also remembered clearly my brother's very last words to me, spoken as he and my mom were heading out the door to the airport to return home from that last birthday visit. We'd talked about a lot of things that last night, among them the idea of him moving closer to us.

"Brent, were you really serious about buying my neighbors house? Did you really talk with him about it?"

"I'm working on my exit strategy, Shellie, but yes, I talked with him about it, please. I'm serious, I want to come here." he said, his eyes flashing instantly with tears. "Dead serious!" He stepped out of my bedroom doorframe, out of my sight. Those were the last words I heard my brother speak.

In the beginning, after Brent's death the only way his widow allowed us to communicate with her was through texting, and only when she contacted us first. We complied, giving her space to grieve. Six months after his death, she texted me that she was ready to go through Brent's things. I replied that my mom would fly out there; I don't think she expected this. My mom made arrangements to fly to Arizona so they could go through my brother's personal things with his widow. This would be the first time my mom had seen her since the search for my missing brother and then his Memorial Service, which I had been unable to attend. I couldn't even wash my own hair yet; I was still dealing with my two broken arms.

I prepared my mom with an acronym: AWW. I knew it would be a very intense time for my mom and she might not be able to think straight—and in fact my mom said the whole time she was with Brent's wife she felt that if she pushed too hard for answers, she would be asked to leave. AWW was a reminder to ask about three things. The A was to ask whether she had made up her mind about whether to let us have some of Brent's ashes. The first W was a reminder to ask if there was anything in writing, like a will. (My mom said that when she asked this question, Brent's wife folded her arms and shot her a look that said, "Are you really going to go there?") The final W was for the most important question, especially for my mom: *Why?* Why did this happen? Why did my brother, her son, go out into the desert, leaving his house with the screen door shut but the front door open, his computer on, and his DVR running? Why did he leave in an apparent hurry to drink himself into a self-induced coma and run his bike in a straight-line acceleration into a pedestrian bridge over a canal?

My brother's widow didn't offer to pick my mom up at the airport, so my mom had to rent a car. She also didn't offer to let her stay at my brother's house, so my mom had to get a hotel room. When Brent was alive, things were very different: my mom had been welcomed there many times, and had even stayed there alone, and house-sat for their dogs. This time, when my mom went to the front door, she rang the doorbell over and over, but no one answered. She was just about to drive away when my brother's wife finally answered the door.

My mom said spending that time with Brent's wife was one of the most torturous things she had ever done. I still can't believe my mom had the strength to go there, but it was the right thing to do. She asked her AWW questions, but got no answers. She added a few questions of her own, too, like "Did you see the autopsy?"

"I shredded mine!" Brent's widow snapped back fiercely. "Those things aren't always right, and I haven't shared that with anyone." When my mom shared that exchange with me later, I couldn't help wondering what other documents she may have shredded. But I had my copy of his autopsy and I knew that because he was in the canal water for 4 days, he would have been bloated. His body weight description of being an obese man of 244 pounds would have seemed inaccurate to his normal walking around weight of 180 pounds. Brent would have never let himself get that overweight. I also knew that his blood alcohol level of .33 and vitreous eye fluid being at .23 meant that the alcohol was consumed so fast it didn't have time to saturate in his eyes. Something so horrible happened that made him go out in the desert, drink himself into a self-induced coma, and run himself into a bridge. I was also beginning to realize his wife was never going to tell us what happened.

Now, there may be people who think my mom's motives were selfish ones. But as she said to me, "What mother out there wouldn't want to know why? I have a right to know!" He was her son. I cannot believe how poorly Brent's widow treated my mom, and there was no reason for it.

When they stood together in my brother's closet, there wasn't much to go through. A small pile of his clothes lay on the floor, but most of my brother's things had already been picked over. My mom grabbed a few things for my sister (some T- shirts her husband could wear), and brought home two bathing suits for us.

After my brother's widow treated my mom so horribly, we didn't know how else to get answers. I hired an attorney to try and get answers, and to fulfill Brent's last wishes. We asked his wife to set up a trust for my mom and my disabled oldest brother, Brad. He had a serious traumatic brain injury (TBI) and never quite fully assimilated into society. He was Brent's dark secret, because as much as I loved my brother Brent, he was very concerned with his image. Brad, our brother with the TBI injury was Brent's Black Sheep of the family, so much so, in the 13 years Brent was married, his widow never once met our oldest other brother. Brent cut Brad off, and in the end when Brent was contemplating big philosophical questions, contemplating taking his own life, he wanted to make things right with Brad.

I know this, because on his last birthday, he confessed all these regrets to me, and it's unfathomable to me that Brent didn't discuss trying to help his brother with his wife. But as the probate case moved along it was clear to us, my brother's widow was refusing what he told me he wanted, mainly to help his older brother who would always have a hard time helping himself. She was going to dig her heels in and refuse to work with us. She would hide behind her attorney and new money. She would give no answers about my brother's probate estate or the event that led to his suicide.

My sister, Tamara, became so frustrated in wanting answers, she requested and received the City of Mesa, Arizona, Police Department's missing person's report and the Maricopa County Sheriff's office report on the recovery of our brother's body. Among many misrepresentations given to the police about our brother by his widow, one stood out more than any of the others. The one fact we would never have known about without searching for our own answers: Before leaving on his motorcycle on that fateful day, Brent took off his wedding ring and left it behind.

My brother's widow's misrepresentations and obfuscations continued. She convinced her attorney that I was lying about the loans I had made to him. Even though I provided the promissory note for $20,000, notarized and signed by Brent, that was the seed money I invested in his business; court documents verify that she told her attorney it had been paid off 10 years ago. Then, she reversed that claim and swore under oath in an affidavit, there hadn't ever been one payment made back towards my (imaginary) loan, and that there was never a business for the loan I made to my brother. Even her attorney, in court documents, was labeling me an extortionist. Ugh!

I wouldn't be able to prove Brent hadn't paid off the loan I gave him for her engagement ring, I had nothing in writing. And the loan for travel and their move back to Dallas after living rent-free in one of my rentals for over a year—I couldn't prove that either. She could probably prove he paid back the loan I made to him just recently to cover some taxes. But she would never be able to prove he paid any of the $20,000 I loaned for his business, because she quite possibly didn't even know about it! That investment was made before they were married. Brent always told me it was like money in the bank, and it was written up so that if he sold his business it would be paid off with 5% interest. Throughout the years, it was kind of him to always bring it up when we talked or he visited so I didn't have to feel awkward reminding him of it.

Brent's widow's attorney said the statute of limitations on the promissory note was expired, and threatened in writing to sue me if I tried to collect on it. ("In the event your client attempts to pursue such claims, we will request the court's award of attorneys fee, costs and such other sanctions as may be appropriate as such action would be frivolous, without substantial justification and taken solely for harassment of my client.")

Evidently, my brother's widow had convinced her attorneys that we were greedy monsters after my brother's money. Or perhaps it was just a coincidence that shortly after I filed to be my brother's personal representative of his estate, she unfriended me on Facebook, along with the rest of Brent's blood relatives. One by one most of the people who were her friends, not Brent's, unfriended us, too. It hurt us deeply, but that's okay. I saved in a screenshot the last words my brother spoke to me on Facebook. I had finally gotten brave enough to post my waterskiing highlights video on Facebook Jan. 19th 2012. I was getting anxious when I hadn't heard anything from Brent. I started writing my book, and sent him the first few pages. Now, I wondered what he thought of my video. Finally, Brent posted a couple a days later at 8:43 p.m. on Jan. 21, 2012 "You're someone very special, we're all lucky to have someone like Shellie in our lives…love you Shellie." Less than a month later, he was missing.

It was apparent Brent's widow was not going to work with us to get the answers we wanted. For us, it was never about money, but about trying to do what Brent wanted. As it was, I borrowed money for the retainer to hire an attorney to follow his wishes. So every month, my $50 payment is my friendly little reminder of my love for my brother and proof to myself that I tried to do what he asked me to do, and what he wanted me to do. It is one of the hardest choices I have ever had to make in my life, to walk away from this, but I have no choice. The strain is too much for my 76-year-old mom. That being said, if my mom finds the strength to continue on in our fight for answers, I will too. I have forgiven my brother, and will spend the rest of my life trying to forgive his wife. After all, she finally did give us some of Brent's ashes…and a couple of pairs of his swimming trunks.

When my attorney wrote the letter explaining I would withdraw my Petition for Appointment to be my brother's personal representative of his estate if she would set up a trust for my mom and my oldest disabled brother, he also pointed out how upsetting it was to us to know from her Facebook posts that she was off vacationing in Mexico, Montana, California, Dallas, New York, and Fiji rather than discussing matters with us. Her attorney replied, "My client's travels are irrelevant to this matter and to whether or not she is grieving, and I request such comments from your client be kept to herself." My gut reaction was, "What? Her attorney is the thought police, telling me what I can and cannot say! Another authority figure trying to silence me."

Guess what? It didn't work. Her attorney's scare tactic to silence me made my resolve to tell the truth, to tell my side of the story, even stronger. I have been tormented over whether or not to share this part of my story, my brother's suicide. I kept trying to figure out what my brother would want, what would Brent say. Would he want the world to think he had just messed up on his Harley, or was there more to *his* story?

Finally, after tons of contemplation, I started putting together the bread crumbs my brother had left. I think back to all the times he teared up on me, he was a sensitive man. Not too long ago on one of his visits, we were lying in my bed and he was telling me the story about being in a car wreck when he was 17 and his nose ended up with a pretty good gash in it. The parents of the kid that wrecked the car gave my brother 200 dollars for the stitches he had to get, but Brent was confessing his dreams of being a model, and how he probably would never be able to do that afterwards, he was mad, he told me with a choking, cracking voice, "No one fought for me Shellie, Mom was too busy working, and so no one fought for me." Another time, he teared up when he was talking about trying to have kids, he said, "I don't think it's gonna' happen for us." His tears were of regret he would not be able to have kids of his own.

On his last visit, on his last birthday he spent at my house without his wife, he shared some of the troubles he and his wife were having with not having kids. I'm sure it was a very contentious subject. I told him there are so many ways to have children nowadays, that if he really wanted to, they could find a way, I also said that there was always adoption, but I was pretty sure his regret would be that no blood line from the Blum boys would be carried on.

Later that same evening, I remember him sitting on my beach at the edge of my little lake. We had a bonfire going in the pit. It was just him and me, it was close to midnight, and one second past midnight, he would be a year older. He was belting out the Zac Brown Band lyrics on his mp3 player, "I got my toes in the water, ass in the sand, not a worry in the world, a cold beer in my hand, Life is good today, Life is good today," of course, I understood exactly why he was singing all this because at that moment it was all true, then he got to the chorus, and he sang out even more enthusiastically, "Adios and vaya con Dios, Going home now to stay, The senoritas don't care-o there's no dinero, Yeah, I got no money to stay," his eyes welled up again, but he was smiling. He was so excited at the end, he couldn't wait to explain to me what the words meant, "Do you get it, Shellie, do you get what Adios and vaya con Dios means? It means, Goodbye and Go with God", he was so alive and animated. He was smiling, but somehow I knew he was crying on the inside. He had his beer in one hand,

and a cigar in the other, he tilted his head back and stared up at the night sky with its gazillion stars. He was thinking big thoughts. It felt big then, but I didn't realize at the time, just how big. He was gone two months later.

It was Brent who planted a seed of confidence that I could write a story, and that seed blossomed into this book. Brent got to read the first few pages—and now I hope he can know the rest of the story through everyone else's eyes.

I dedicate this book to my brother Brent. Thank you for helping to make me so tough. You have prepared me well to get through this beautiful thing called life. I will miss you and always love you, Brent. The roller coaster is going up! Hang loose.

Your little sister,
Love especially,
Shellie

CPSIA information can be obtained at www.ICGtesting.com
Printed in the USA
LVOW03*1152241015

459301LV00005BA/5/P